# AFRICAN AMERICAN HISTORY AND CULTURE

*edited by*
**GRAHAM RUSSELL HODGES**
COLGATE UNIVERSITY

# PROPHETS OF RAGE

## THE BLACK FREEDOM STRUGGLE IN SAN FRANCISCO, 1945-1969

DANIEL CROWE

GARLAND PUBLISHING, INC.
A MEMBER OF THE TAYLOR & FRANCIS GROUP
NEW YORK & LONDON/2000

Published in 2000 by
Garland Publishing, Inc.
A member of the Taylor & Francis Group
29 West 35th Street
New York, NY 10001

10  9  8  7  6  5  4  3  2

*Library of Congress Cataloging-in-Publication Data*
Crowe, Daniel E.
    Prophets of rage : the Black freedom struggle in San
Francisco, 1945-1969 / Daniel E. Crowe
        p. cm.—(Studies in African American history and
culture)
    Includes bibliographical references (p.) and index
    ISBN 0-8153-3766-3 (alk. paper)
    1. Afro-Americans—Civil rights—California—San
Francisco Bay Area—History—20th century. 2. Civil rights
movements—California—San Francisco Bay Area—History—
20th century. 3. San Francisco Bay Area (Calif.)—Race relations. I. Title. II. Series.

F860.S39 N428 2000
305.896'073079461—dc21
                                                00-022424

Printed on acid-free, 250 year-life paper
Manufactured in the United States of America

*For Leslee*

# CONTENTS

# ACKNOWLEDGMENTS

This project would not have reached its present form without the generous assistance of many people. Profs. Craig Buettinger, John Garrigus, and S. Walker Blanton guided my vision when I began this work an undergraduate thesis at Jacksonville University. The manuscript has changed tremendously since then, and for that I thank the faculty and graduate students of the University of Kentucky for their criticism and support. Profs. Gerald Smith, David Hamilton, Daniel Smith, Mary Anglin, and Scott Hunt deserve particular mention for reading the volume and offering advice and encouragement. My advisor, Prof. Fon L. Gordon, was instrumental in helping me craft this history of Bay Area African Americans, and without her, my efforts might never have come to fruition. I owe a special debt of gratitude to my editors at Garland Publishing, Richard Koss and Prof. Graham Russell Hodges, for accepting my work and helping to place my book in their "Studies in African American History and Culture" series. Many archivists and librarians also provided invaluable aid during the completion of this manuscript, including Linda Seelke and the staff of the Lyndon Baines Johnson Presidential Library, Walter Hill of the National Archives in College Park, Maryland, Bonnie Hardwick and the staff of the Bancroft Library of the University of California, Berkeley, Susan Sherwood of San Francisco State University's Labor Archives and Research Center, Amy Holloway of the San Francisco African American Historical and Cultural Society's Research Library and Archives, the staff of the Pacifica Radio Archive in North Hollywood, California, the staff of the John Fitzgerald Kennedy Presidential Library, Willa

K. Baum and the staff of the Regional Oral History Office of the Bancroft Library, and Danice Nutter and the Interlibrary Loan staff of the University of Kentucky's William T. Young Library.

Other friends and colleagues have offered their support while I was crafting this manuscript. Prof. Charles E. Jones of Georgia State University shared his knowledge and his extensive research on the Black Panther Party. Prof. William Issel of San Francisco State University gets a hearty thanks for treating me to a tour of the Bay Area and an excellent lasagna dinner during one of my research jaunts. Albert Broussard, Quintard Taylor, Ula Y. Taylor, Kevin Leonard, Wanda Hendricks, Ronald Coleman, Gerald Horne, Matthew C. Whitaker, Angela D. LeBlanc-Ernest, Stuart McElderry, Uche Egemonye, Jeff Matthews, Dan and Lelanya Kearns, Bart Jarmusch, and Deborah Blackwell have earned my gratitude and respect for their warmth and assistance.

Finally, my family has provided both spiritual and financial sustenance during the long process of writing this book. I owe my parents and my in-laws a debt that I can never repay. My wife, Leslee Gilbert, sustained me with her love and confidence, and I credit her with giving me the strength to finish this work.

Any errors in fact or interpretation are mine alone.

# ILLUSTRATIONS

# Prophets of Rage

The Black Freedom Struggle
in San Francisco 1945–1969

# Origins

The roots of the Black Revolution that shook the San Francisco Bay Area to its foundations during the 1960s stretched far back into the region's past. The long history of conflict and discord between the white majorities and black minorities of Berkeley, Oakland, Richmond, and San Francisco, thinly veiled by the cities' liberal reputations, led to a dramatic explosion of black rage in the Age of Aquarius. Although many of the African American radicals spawned from the ghettos of the Bay Area would eventually gain national and even international fame, the origins and nature of modern Bay Area black radicalism, especially that of the Black Panther Party, can best be understood by examining the social, economic, political, and cultural environments present in northern California's urban centers since the Second World War. During the 1940s, southern black migrants flooded into the San Francisco Bay Area in search of lucrative employment in the burgeoning war industries. The promise of upward economic mobility for thousands of African Americans proved chimerical, however, and the black newcomers faced an ever-hardening system of employment discrimination, residential segregation, unequal education, and police brutality. Conditions worsened for African Americans during the next two decades and growing discontent among working-class and low-income blacks over economic, political, and social injustices erupted in the 1960s. Abandoning the nonviolent and integrationist tactics of mainstream leaders like Martin Luther King, Jr., African Americans from urban ghettos in the West preached revolution and redistribution of wealth and power. The move toward Black Power marked a distinctive shift away from the modern Civil Rights Movement, and the radicalization of many African Americans changed the nature of black protest, the rhythms of everyday life, and the course of federal welfare policy.

The massive influx of African American migrants into the Bay Area during the war years upset the racial status quo that the established white majority and tiny black minority had carefully crafted and maintained for more than a century. Prior to 1940, less than 15,000 African Americans called the Bay Area home. By 1950, however, the black population of Oakland alone had jumped from 8,462 to 47,610; a decade later, blacks in San Francisco and Oakland numbered in excess of 237,000. Due to their small sizes, black communities in the Bay Area were relatively autonomous before the Second World War, although white residents kept African Americans at the bottom of the social and economic hierarchy. After the arrival of the wartime migrants, however, race relations in the Bay Area deteriorated, and a pattern of discrimination and segregation common to the rest of the nation took hold. Despite the tenacity of white racism, however, African American migrants left an indelible impression upon the Bay Area. The newcomers helped to draw a new cultural landscape in northern California, and their patterns of speech, dress, religion, cuisine, and music forever altered life for blacks and whites alike. The migrants and their children would also form the vanguard of racial protest and black nationalism in the Bay Area, and established residents grappled with the shock waves of black migration for decades.[1]

The realignment of racial boundaries strained relations between whites and blacks, and the postwar crises of black unemployment, inadequate housing, segregated schools, and police brutality produced in the Bay Area a virtual race war that culminated in the Black Revolution of the 1960s. Although African Americans did benefit from wartime prosperity, the 1950s saw a rapid decline in the social and economic standing of many black migrant families. As in other parts of the United States, black workers were often the "last hired, first fired" segment of the industrial working class. Barred from many postwar unions and replaced by returning white GIs, many black workers quickly joined the ranks of the chronically underemployed and unemployed segment of urban America. In addition to their employment woes, African Americans also faced an unnaturally limited housing market. Segregated in the abandoned industrial cores in San Francisco and the East Bay, blacks had little access to the new lily-white suburban developments that sprouted like weeds along the region's coastline. Those African Americans who were not fortunate enough to purchase homes in the limited market available to them remained in segregated public housing projects until urban renewal officials ordered that the units be leveled to make way for high-rent, high-rise apartment buildings. Residential segregation throughout the Bay Area led to the *de facto* segregation of the cities' neighborhood-based public school systems. Since blacks were confined to a small number of census tracts, many schools had majority African American student bodies, even though blacks did not make up more than half of the total population of Berkeley, Oakland, Richmond, or San Francisco. White parents rejected black calls for school integration throughout the 1950s, and civil rights groups filed numerous lawsuits against Bay Area city governments to end segregation. Finally, black community-police relations soured in the tense postwar environment, and they continued to spiral downward throughout the 1950s and 1960s. The four Bay Area cities' nearly all-white police forces drew frequent criticism from African Americans, and allegations of police brutality skyrocketed during the postwar era. By the early 1960s, tensions between white and black residents had reached the boiling point, and many African Americans felt that their California dream had turned into a nightmarish reality.

In the face of white racism, moderate African American leaders agitated for reform. Black community organizations, mutual aid societies, and churches provided for the majority of the social service needs of Bay Area African Americans. Since many blacks found white social workers to be condescending or unresponsive, African Americans relied on their own community centers and mutual aid organizations. The Bayview Community Center and the Booker T. Washington Center, for example, created youth programs, sports leagues, dance classes, arts and crafts courses, job-training seminars, and drug and alcohol workshops for the black youth of San Francisco. African American churches provided for the spiritual needs of their black parishioners, and they supported and sponsored many Bay Area civil rights initiatives throughout the 1950s and 1960s. The National Association for the Advancement of Colored People (NAACP) had strong branches in San Francisco and the East Bay, and it often led the fight against employment discrimination and residential and educational segregation. The NAACP was the strongest civil rights organization in the Bay Area during the 1950s and early 1960s, and its leaders, in cooperation with other moderate groups like the Council for Civic Unity, won important victories in the fight against racism, including the passage of a statewide Fair Employment Practices Act in 1959. The Congress of Racial Equality (CORE), after several false starts in the 1940s and 1950s, finally became a significant factor in the Bay Area's Black Freedom Struggle during the early 1960s. Eschewing the moderate stances of the NAACP and other black leaders, CORE embraced the nonviolent direct-action tactics that were in vogue in the southern Civil Rights Movement. CORE's shop-ins, sit-ins, picket lines, and marches brought the issue of civil rights to the front pages of the cities' white newspapers and into mainstream public discourse. By 1965, many members of CORE radicalized and called for more dramatic protests to hasten the fall of discrimination and segregation in the Bay Area. Following the pattern in the national organization, Bay Area chapters of CORE turned to black nationalism and embraced the emerging philosophy of Black Power.[2]

Despite the attempts of moderate African American leaders to push for civil rights and black equality in the postwar era, a new generation of militants came to the fore in the 1960s. Emerging from the direct-action protests of the Congress of Racial Equality and the Community Action Programs of the War on Poverty, this new radical leadership agitated for black self-determination and trumpeted black pride and self-sufficiency. As poverty rates among African Americans continued to rise, community activists turned to more radical and dramatic civil rights tactics. Gaining access to the large sums of money dispensed by the federal War on Poverty, the radicals broadened the scope of the Bay Area's Black Freedom Struggle to include economic justice as well as civil rights. The militant leaders of many of the government-funded Community Action

Programs involved low-income African Americans in the planning and implementation of their freedom projects, and the mobilization of the poor dramatically altered the course of black protest in the Bay Area. Conflicts between moderate and radical leaders tore apart the civil rights consensus in northern California, and as Washington bureaucrats struggled to regain control of their poverty programs, African American leaders frantically sought to right the listing ship of black protest.

From this maelstrom sprang the Black Panther Party, led by two ghetto toughs whose families had fled Dixie for the promised land of California during the Second World War. The Black Panther Party for Self-Defense, formed in the back office of an Oakland anti-poverty center in the fall of 1966, drew the bulk of its membership from the masses of the Bay Area's young unemployed and low-income African Americans. Fed up with the long history of discrimination and segregation that circumscribed black life in northern California since the 1940s, the Black Panthers called for immediate reforms and revolutionary changes in Bay Area society. The Black Panther Party's Ten Point Platform and Program included a long list of grievances and demands that addressed the employment, housing, educational, and security needs of Bay Area African Americans. Emerging at a time of increasing civil unrest, the Black Panthers first gained notoriety, however, for their armed patrols of Oakland, which the Panthers claimed were necessary to curb police brutality against the black population. Although this tactic did gain the Panthers many adherents from the legions of young blacks in the Bay Area, it ultimately cost the party dearly, as rising tensions with law enforcement agencies ended in bloody shoot-outs and the frequent incarceration of the Panther leadership. The party was able to increase its base of support among Bay Area blacks with the introduction of the Community Survival Programs in 1969, which Panther leaders created by drawing inspiration from their days as anti-poverty activists during the War on Poverty. Despite their more moderate attempts at revolutionary reform, however, the Black Panther Party unraveled under the strain of outside law enforcement oppression and internal divisions created by the party's institutional culture. Although their efforts to build a national and international revolutionary movement ultimately failed, these prophets of rage would transform African American protest, change the character of domestic policy, and redefine the meaning of blackness in America.

Building upon the historiography of the black urban experience during the Great Migration of the First World War, this work explores the racial climate of the modern American West and the internal dynamics of African American communities that grew dramatically in that region at mid-century. This history of the Bay Area's Black Revolution continues the story of the development of African American communities in the urban West that has recently flowered under the leadership of Albert S. Broussard, Gretchen Lemke-Santangelo, Shirley Ann Moore, Quintard Taylor, and others. Events in the San Francisco Bay Area during the late 1950s and 1960s have been relatively unexplored, however, and this study seeks to deepen our understanding of the tumultuous days that preceded the upheaval of the 1960s. A clearer picture of the recent past will also shed light on the history of the Black Panther Party, which remains hotly debated by a host of former party members, historians, journalists, and other critics. Finally, *Prophets of Rage* also contributes to the contentious discussion over the origins and nature of America's modern "underclass," and it develops further the connections between community activism, social and economic change, and local and national politics.

For years, scholars have studied the exodus of African Americans from the South to the urban North and West in search of greater freedom, improved employment opportunities, and better race relations. Despite northerners' feelings of regional superiority, African Americans often found that Yankees only hid their racism behind a thin veil of civility and that their struggles for racial equality would require more than a change of address. During the Great Migration of World War I, African Americans left the South for northern cities like Chicago, New York, Cleveland, Pittsburgh, and Milwaukee, but they often found that their entrance into the industrial working class was blocked by racial barriers and limited by prejudice. Through community organizations, black churches, and civil rights groups, however, African Americans worked to improve their lives and build strong communities in the North. Another great migration of blacks to the North and the West came during the Second World War. Historians have been slower to develop studies of African American life during this period, but recent attention has focused more on the urban West than on the long-studied communities of the East and Midwest. African American migrants bound for the San Francisco Bay Area faced many of the same challenges that awaited blacks who left the South for Chicago, Detroit, Los Angeles, New York, and other major urban centers north and west of the Mason-Dixon line. Despite the liberal stereotypes associated with northern California, the San Francisco Bay Area proved a most inhospitable place for the southern black migrants, and race relations in the Golden Gate cities fell squarely into the pattern so common among other large urban areas in the North and West.[3]

This book builds upon the findings of the literature on black migration in the United States and is informed by the recent renaissance in African American urban history. The new scholarship pays particular attention to the lives of the black migrants themselves, rather than to the structural formation of institutionalized ghettos in large inner cities. The historiography has developed several new themes, and important among them are a renewed interest in black agency and everyday resistance to white oppression, a study of the divisions within the black community, a focus upon everyday life and culture, an attempt to redefine the periodization of black urban life, an analysis of black women's experiences, and an examination of grass-roots organizations and civil rights movements. This study attempts to answer many of the important questions about black life in the San Francisco Bay Area that the new African American urban historiography has raised. In doing so, it places the history of African American communities in northern California into the context of discoveries that other historians are making about urban black America.[4]

In its investigation of the postwar history of San Francisco and the East Bay, this volume also contributes to our understanding of the origins of the Black Panther Party in the mid-1960s. Although numerous other historians, journalists, and former members of the party have chronicled the Panthers' history during the late 1960s and the 1970s, relatively few critics have probed the origins of the Black Revolution that spawned the party. Several historians have connected the Black Panthers with earlier black nationalist movements, in particular with the efforts of Marcus Garvey to organize African Americans in the early twentieth century, and although some of their arguments are compelling, the historical record suggests that connections with prewar black nationalism had only a minor effect upon the development of the Bay Area's Black Revolution of the 1960s. Likewise, the recent suggestion by several authors that black protest during the 1960s grew out of left-wing labor and political movements during the Great Depression and the 1940s does not hold for the development of the Black Panther Party. Other writers have argued that the Panthers drew their inspiration from the southern Civil Rights Movement, the student radicalism at the University of California, Berkeley, the general social and political instability of the Sixties, and the liberation of black Africa after the Second World War. A careful reading of the party's Ten Point Platform and Program, however, reveals that the Panthers' main grievances were for long-standing problems that had haunted Bay Area black communities since the Second World War. A better understanding of these crises will illuminate the nature of the party itself, its challenge to white America, and its ultimate success or failure in bringing about the revolutionary changes that the Panthers sought.[5]

Finally, *Prophets of Rage* adds to the debate over the history of the federal welfare state and the growth of the urban "underclass." Numerous scholars and critics have analyzed the origins of the War on Poverty, the rise of the welfare state, and the development of an "urban crisis" in modern America. By examining the San Francisco Bay Area's failed attempt at eradicating poverty, this study reveals how federal programs were received at the local level and how local conditions affected the course of federal policy making. The conclusions offered here refute some notions about the origins of the War on Poverty and support some of the conclusions by other scholars on the effectiveness of the reforms offered by Washington's poverty warriors during the 1960s. The case of the San Francisco Bay Area reminds us that the history of welfare reform in America is an incredibly complex one; a story with great variation at the local level, where residents played a key role in shaping the poverty programs and ensuring their successes or hastening their failures. The attempts to end poverty wrought many changes that the authors of the 1964 Economic Opportunity Act and local welfare agents never intended, and the legacies of the 1960s War on Poverty promise greater challenges for future generations' attempts to reform welfare and bring everyone to America's table of plenty.[6]

The history of San Francisco Bay Area African American communities in the postwar era was often a bitter one. Faced with the great social turmoil created by the Second World War and the obstacles to equality erected by white residents, African Americans struggled for decades to improve their station and solidify their communities. As in any history, these efforts met with some successes and some failures. Although many African American leaders and ordinary citizens hoped that conditions would continue to improve after peace with the Axis powers, blacks saw their wartime gains in employment and social freedom quickly evaporate as GIs returned home and white residents sought to return Bay Area society back to the days before Pearl Harbor. Race relations worsened and black frustrations grew during the Ike Age, and as the second generation of black migrants came of age in the early 1960s, a new social movement was afoot that would challenge the basic tenets of what it meant to be an "American." African American militants pushed the Bay Area's race war to the front pages of newspapers across the country, and as J. Edgar Hoover called for their heads, the black radicals urged their people to rise up in revolution. As the wave of violence crested in the final years of the decade, the San Francisco Bay Area trembled at the roar of a great black panther.

# Notes

1.    United States Department of Commerce, *Sixteenth Census of the United States: 1940; Population*, Vol. II, Part 3 (Washington, D. C.: United States Government Printing Office, 1943), 636; United States Department of Commerce, *A Report of the Seventeenth Decennial Census of the United States, Census*

*of Population*: 1950, Vol. II, Part 5 (Washington, D. C.: United States Government Printing Office, 1952), 57, 206.

2.   For the national history of CORE, see August Meier and Elliott Rudwick, CORE: *A Study of the Civil Rights Movement, 1942–1968* (Urbana: University of Illinois Press, 1973). For a similar account of the radicalization of the Student Nonviolent Coordinating Committee, see Clayborne Carson, *In Struggle: SNCC and the Black Awakening of the 1960s* (Cambridge: Harvard University Press, 1981).

3.   For representative studies of the Great Migration, see, Peter Gottlieb, *Making Their Own Way: Southern Blacks' Migration to Pittsburgh, 1916–1930* (Urbana: University of Illinois Press, 1987); James Grossman, *Land of Hope: Chicago, Black Southerners, and the Great Migration* (Chicago: University of Chicago Press, 1989); Kenneth Kusmer, *A Ghetto Takes Shape: Black Cleveland, 1870–1930* (Urbana: University of Illinois Press, 1976); Carole Marks, *Farewell—We're Good and Gone: The Great Black Migration* (Bloomington: Indiana University Press, 1989); Gilbert Osofsky, *Harlem: The Making of a Ghetto; Negro New York, 1890–1930* (New York: Harper and Row, 1966); Allan H. Spear, *Black Chicago: The Making of a Negro Ghetto, 1890–1920* (Chicago: University of Chicago Press, 1967); Joe William Trotter, Jr., *Black Milwaukee: The Making of an Industrial Proletariat, 1915–45* (Urbana: University of Illinois Press, 1985); Joe William Trotter, Jr., ed., *The Great Migration in Historical Perspective: New Dimensions of Race, Class, and Gender* (Bloomington: Indiana University Press, 1991). Three such studies of the North are Arnold R. Hirsch, *Making the Second Ghetto: Race and Housing in Chicago, 1940–1960* (New York: Cambridge University Press, 1983); and Nicholas Lemann, *The Promised Land: The Great Black Migration and How It Changed America* (New York: Alfred A. Knopf, 1991), both of which examine Chicago; and Thomas J. Sugrue, *The Origins of the Urban Crisis: Race and Inequality in Postwar Detroit* (Princeton: Princeton University Press, 1996). The more numerous studies of the urban West include Katherine Archibald, *Wartime Shipyard: A Study in Social Disunity* (Berkeley: University of California Press, 1947); Albert S. Broussard, *Black San Francisco: The Struggle for Racial Equality in the West, 1900–1954* (Lawrence: University Press of Kansas, 1993); Douglas Henry Daniels, *Pioneer Urbanites: A Social and Cultural History of Black San Francisco* (Philadelphia: Temple University Press, 1980); Gerald Horne, *Fire This Time: The Watts Uprising and the 1960s* (Charlottesville: The University of Virginia Press, 1995); Marilynn S. Johnson, *The Second Gold Rush: Oakland and the East Bay in World War II* (Berkeley: University of California Press, 1993); Gretchen

Lemke-Santangelo, *Abiding Courage: African American Migrant Women and the East Bay Community* (Chapel Hill: University of North Carolina Press, 1996); Kevin A. Leonard, "Years of Hope, Days of Fear: The Impact of World War II on Race Relations in Los Angeles" (Ph.D. diss., University of California, Davis, 1992); Shirley Ann Moore, "The Black Community in Richmond, California, 1910–1963" (Ph.D. diss., University of California, Berkeley, 1989); Quintard Taylor, *The Forging of a Black Community: Seattle's Central District from 1870 through the Civil Rights Era* (Seattle: University of Washington Press, 1994); and Quintard Taylor, *In Search of the Racial Frontier: African Americans in the American West, 1528–1990* (New York: W. W. Norton and Company, 1998).

4.   See, especially, the special double issue of *The Journal of Urban History* 21 (March and May 1995), for a discussion of the new directions of African American urban history. Many of the recent works cited in note 3 above are excellent examples of this new scholarship on blacks in America's cities.

5.   General histories of the party include, Terry Canon, *All Power to the People: The Story of the Black Panther Party* (San Francisco: Peoples Press, 1970); Charles W. Hopkins, "The Deradicalization of the Black Panther Party, 1967–1973" (Ph.D. diss., University of North Carolina, Chapel Hill, 1978); Reginald Major, *The Panther Is a Black Cat* (New York: William Morrow & Company, Inc., 1971); Gene Marine, *The Black Panthers* (New York: New American Library, 1969); and Hugh Pearson, *The Shadow of the Panther: Huey Newton and the Price of Black Power in America* (Reading, MA: Addison-Wesley Publishing Co., 1994). Studies of the Panthers' conflicts with police include, Ward Churchill and Jim Vander Wall, *Agents of Repression: The FBI's Secret War Against the Black Panther Party and the American Indian Movement* (Boston: South End Press, 1988); Commission of Inquiry into the Black Panthers and the Police, *Search and Destroy: A Report* (New York: Metropolitan Applied Research Center, 1973); Paul Chevigny, *Cops and Rebels: A Study in Provocation* (New York: Pantheon Books, 1972); and Kenneth O'Reilly, *"Racial Matters": The FBI's Secret File on Black America, 1960–1972* (New York: Free Press, 1989). Autobiographies and participant narratives of Panther members include, Elaine Brown, *A Taste of Power: A Black Woman's Story* (New York: Pantheon Books, 1992); Angela Davis, *Angela Davis: An Autobiography* (New York: Random House, 1974); David Hilliard and Lewis Cole, *This Side of Glory: The Autobiography of David Hilliard and the Story of the Black Panther Party* (Boston: Little, Brown and Company, 1993); Huey P. Newton, *Revolutionary Suicide* (New York: Harcourt Brace Jovanovich, Inc.,

1973); Bobby Seale, *A Lonely Rage: The Autobiography of Bobby Seale* (New York: Times Books, 1978); Bobby Seale, *Seize the Time: The Story of the Black Panther Party and Huey P. Newton* (New York: Random House, 1968); and Assata Shakur, *Assata: An Autobiography* (London: Zed Books, 1987). Two studies that link the Panthers with earlier black nationalists are Theodore Vincent, *Black Power and the Garvey Movement* (Berkeley: Ramparts Press, 1970); and Christopher Lasch, *The Agony of the American Left* (New York: Alfred A. Knopf, 1969), esp. 127 passim. For authors who argue that 1960s radicalism grew from earlier labor activism, see, for example, Michael K. Honey, *Southern Labor and Black Civil Rights: Organizing Memphis Workers* (Urbana: University of Illinois Press, 1993); and Robin D. G. Kelley, *Race Rebels: Culture, Politics, and the Black Working Class* (New York: Free Press, 1994). Gerald Horne argues along similar lines in his study of Los Angeles's Watts Riot of 1965. Horne suggests that the destruction of an interracial working-class movement during the 1930s left a void in the history of black protest that African American radicals filled in the 1960s. See Horne, *Fire This Time.* For authors who posit that the Panthers emerged from the instability of the 1960s, see, Hopkins, "The Deradicalization of the Black Panther Party," 34; W. J. Rorabaugh, *Berkeley at War: The 1960s* (New York: Oxford University Press, 1989), 76–86; Pearson, *The Shadow of the Panther*, 68–94 passim; and Jennifer B. Smith, *An International History of the Black Panther Party* (New York: Garland Publishing, 1999), 22–24.

6.    Some of the studies that were most helpful for this project include, Irving Bernstein, *Guns or Butter: The Presidency of Lyndon Johnson* (New York: Oxford University Press, 1996); Gareth Davies, *From Opportunity to Entitlement: The Transformation and Decline of Great Society Liberalism* (Lawrence: University Press of Kansas, 1996); Michael B. Katz, ed., *The "Underclass" Debate: Views from History* (Princeton: Princeton University Press, 1993); Lemann, *The Promised Land*; Peter Marris and Martin Rein, *Dilemmas of Social Reform: Poverty and Community Action in the United States*, 2nd. ed. (Chicago: Aldine Publishing Co., 1973); Allen J. Matusow, *The Unraveling of America: A History of Liberalism in the 1960s* (New York: Harper and Row, 1984); Lawrence M. Mead, *Beyond Entitlement: The Social Obligations of Citizenship* (New York: Free Press, 1986); James T. Patterson, *America's Struggle against Poverty, 1900–1980* (Cambridge: Harvard University Press, 1981); Jill Quadagno, *The Color of Welfare: How Racism Undermined the War on Poverty* (New York: Oxford University Press, 1994); Sugrue, *The Origins of the Urban Crisis*; William Julius Wilson, *The Truly Disadvantaged: The Inner City, The Underclass, and Public Policy*

(Chicago: University of Chicago Press, 1987); and William Julius Wilson, *When Work Disappears: The World of the New Urban Poor* (New York: Alfred A. Knopf, 1996).

# CHAPTER 1

# Migration

San Francisco is a city shrouded in whiteness. One of the most striking features about the San Francisco Bay Area is the fog. A dull, white blanket of mist often covers the peninsula and hovers over the mainland cities of Oakland, Berkeley, and Richmond. A silent guardian, the fog hides the cities' flaws and denies the probing eye a vision of the truth that lies beneath. This fog also reaches back into the past where it shrouds a history of conflict and discord. A half-century ago, several hundred thousand wartime migrants streamed into the Bay Area and fundamentally transformed its political economy and society. Established residents feared and misunderstood the tide of newcomers, whose foreign cultures, alien dialects, uncouth behavior, and racial diversity shocked the Bay Area natives and ultimately led to the segmentation of a society that had prided itself on its fairness and openness. After the Second World War, when the natives realized that many of the migrants had decided to settle permanently in the Bay Area, the fear and mistrust evolved into hatred. For the African American migrants, the chorus of denunciation grew loudest, and a pattern of discrimination and segregation hardened into official policy and sprouted from the hearts of many of the long-time white residents. The end of the war against fascism and totalitarianism abroad would see the beginning of a race war in the Bay Area. The fog rolled in and out, but a cloud of ignorance and intolerance remained.[1]

## LIFE BEFORE THE MIGRANTS

Prior to the 1940s, African Americans in the San Francisco Bay Area inhabited an ambiguous place in the rather fluid racial hierarchy that existed in cities like San Francisco, Oakland, Berkeley, and Richmond. This fluidity was a result not of the good will of the white majority but was rather a reflection of the small numbers of blacks who were widely dispersed among the general population. African Americans accounted for only three percent of the total population of Oakland in 1940, and that city had by far the largest number of black residents in northern California, at 8,462. In San Francisco, the prewar population numbered less than 5,000, and in Richmond, there were only 270 black residents by 1940. Their small numbers meant that African Americans posed little threat to the racial hegemony of the white majority, and although discrimination and segregation did exist throughout the Bay Area, the boundary lines that separated the races were much softer in the prewar era than they would be after the influx of numerous African Americans from the Old Southwest during the war years.[2]

Established white residents prided themselves on the openness and fairness of their society. The liberal mythology that San Franciscans had created about their fair city was widely known throughout the West and the rest of the United States. To judge from the historical record, however, the area's reputation for fraternity was overrated. According to one scholar, "despite the small size of San Francisco's black population between 1900 and 1940 and the nominal economic competition between black and white workers, most whites perceived blacks as an inferior racial caste and restricted their progress socially, politically, and economically." Although long-time white residents would later claim that southern whites brought racism to the Bay Area when they migrated there in large numbers during the "Dust Bowl" crisis of the 1930s and the war years, the roots of racism had been firmly planted in northern California soil for more than a century. Established white residents even attempted to hide their culpability in the Bay Area's growing residential segregation during the 1940s and 1950s by accusing southern white migrants of refusing to have black neighbors or by arguing that black migrants themselves were responsible for their housing plight because they chose to form their own groups and rejected the idea of integration.  Reflecting on her youth in the Western Addition during the 1940s, the poet Maya Angelou noted that "San Franciscans would have sworn on the Golden Gate Bridge that racism was missing from the heart of their air-conditioned city. But they would have been sadly mistaken."[3]

Despite the reality of discrimination in the Bay Area, however, the hard edge of racism was somewhat dulled by the absence of a large, concentrated population of African Americans.  Residential segregation between blacks and whites, for example, was much less formal before 1940 than it would be during the 1950s and 1960s. According to the famous black scholar Charles S. Johnson, "no rigidly segregated Negro community existed in the city" of San Francisco before the 1940s, and African Americans were relatively free to intermingle with other racial and ethnic groups.  Blacks, whites, Chinese, Irish, West Indians, Germans, Mexicans, and Italians all lived together with no sharp lines of separation dividing them.  Although African Americans were often excluded from the most prestigious neighborhoods, real estate markets throughout the Bay Area were much more open than any found in the Jim Crow South.  After the war, however, public housing bureaucrats and white landlords pushed black residents of the Bay Area into concentrated ghettos, and real estate agents and bankers prevented African Americans from purchasing homes or renting apartments in the expanding and desirable suburbs on the outskirts of San Francisco and Oakland.[4]

Although the housing market was relatively open for most blacks, the job market remained closed.  For the first half of the twentieth century, African Americans in the Bay Area occupied a tenuous position near the bottom of the economic ladder. According to one established black resident, "prior to the second World War [sic] there were very few Negroes working in many crafts and industries."  Concentrated in the service sector of the economy, black men and women worked as domestic servants, porters, musicians, and janitors, and although there were some opportunities in industrial and manufacturing jobs for black men, few if any African Americans ever worked as foremen or supervisors.  In 1900, nearly eighty percent of black women in San Francisco worked as domestic servants, and by 1930, the number had increased to nearly ninety percent.  Half of the black men employed in San Francisco worked as domestic servants at the turn of the century, and three decades later, almost six out of ten black men did so.  According to Edward Alley, a long-time black resident of San Francisco, before the arrival of a large number of industrial, working-class blacks during the Second World War, "we only had one class.  You know, we were all the same."  Another "old-timer," Willie Brooks, agreed: "Blacks only had jobs as bootblacks, doormen and,...janitors...that was about it.  There weren't any...job opportunities....  There wasn't anything...there were a few, a damn few...five, six, seven maybe that worked in the office...that had office jobs.  They didn't pay a damn thing."[5]

This lack of economic opportunity helped to reinforce the other, mostly informal, policies that separated the races in the Bay Area. It also fostered a rough consensus among many African Americans and encouraged cooperation across tenuous "class" lines.  The economic and social distances between the black working class and the black middle class were much shorter before 1940 than they would become in the next two decades.  Due to their small population, blacks in the Bay Area worked together to fight discriminatory and racist laws and customs, and they often ignored conventional social barriers in order to gain the strength of consensus and united action.  According to Willie Brooks, "when they turned out to an affair, Black pimps and the whores and everybody went to it.... You had people from all walks of life was there....  Hell, if you didn't take...everybody that was in every category, you had nobody there, you know, because there weren't that many Blacks in San Francisco at that time."  Locked out of the finest neighborhoods and trapped at the base of the economic pyramid, African Americans in the Bay Area relied on their own community organizations and a carefully crafted racial code of behavior to navigate the dangerous social waters of San Francisco Bay.  From the first gold rush of 1849 to the "second gold rush" of 1941, African Americans in the Bay Area subsumed notions of class and status under the banner of racial solidarity and strove to define a secure place for themselves in society.[6]

The general consensus among African Americans in the Bay Area would unravel, however, with the arrival of massive numbers of black southerners seeking war-industry jobs in the 1940s. Established residents feared and resented the hordes of migrants who pushed their way into the Bay Area, strained existing patterns of race relations, and upset the economic, political, and social status quo. The carefully crafted web of social networks and understandings that black residents of the Bay Area had fashioned snapped under the weight of thousands of new African Americans. According to historian Shirley Ann Moore, "black newcomers initially met a chilly reception from many long-time black residents who feared the newly arrived blacks, whom they characterized as uneducated, abrasive, and 'lower-class,' would jeopardize their tenuous position in Richmond's economic and social hierarchy." Those African Americans who had established themselves as respectable members of the Bay Area communities often cringed at the sight of the weary yet hopeful migrants. In 1943, black sociologist Charles Johnson headed a survey of the city's African American population during the war years, and he found that while the migrants had a favorable view of the established black population, the long-time black residents held largely negative views of the migrants. The survey showed that nearly half of the native black population viewed the migrants unfavorably, while only about one-third had positive impressions of the newcomers. One long-time African American resident confessed that "I was really against some of them. I mean, that's the first feeling you have of these people coming in because they weren't...their culture wasn't the same as ours.... They brought a lot of things from the rural South with them here (chuckle), and their actions and the way they acted and everything and I wasn't used to it and it kind of frightened me (chuckle)."[7]

While certainly not all established residents rejected the newcomers, many were surprised and unnerved by the southerners' behavior, and they frequently complained of the migrants' loudness and bad manners on the streetcars. Sadie Calbert remembered that "there were some of them who were sort of loud and wrong. So, of course, you couldn't quite approve of some of the things that they did. Because some of those women were so kind of, oh, they were so loud and uncouth. You kind of wished that they would tone down sometimes, you know." Alma Brooks agreed, and she recalled that "they made a lot of *noise* on the streetcars...umm!" Edward Alley had similar memories of the southern migrant children he met: "Well, I was a little against them because some of them were so bad. See, we were more...like White kids. We had a White culture and they were coming here and there seemed to be more swearing and certain words they used, 'm-f' and all of that." Other residents told stories of the migrants' unrefined manners, creating a body of "hayseed" tales that paralleled the "Okie" fables about the white migrants from the Midwest who had come to the Bay Area during the Dust Bowl crisis of the 1930s. The new tales of the black migrants' misbehavior portrayed the southerners as unsophisticated and hopelessly uncultured. Marguerite Williams of Richmond was disturbed by the migrants' rowdiness, and she noted that "the kids would go around all day and they wouldn't be fed. They would look like they needed to be bathed and their heads combed.... They were just seedy people, the ones that we saw." Lora Toombs Scott remembered stories about the women factory workers who took their wartime pay and went directly to large department stores to buy fine furs and clothes:

> They were really something. They would go in in their work-clothes, say, [to] the Emporium.... But they would go in and want to try on clothes unkempt, unbathed, and so forth. And, of course, that caused a little flurry. Because you can't try on things unless you are properly prepared to try on clean, new clothes. Nobody else could use them if you have perfumed them. (Laughter).

The migrants' behavior was unacceptable to long-time residents because it challenged the norms and mores that Bay Area blacks and whites had carefully constructed and preserved for over a century. Established African Americans feared that flaunting the old rules would result in the deterioration of race relations and the fall in status of black residents. Their fears proved prophetic.[8]

## AN ARSENAL OF DEMOCRACY?

A booming wartime economy and desires for better lives outside of the South drove African Americans in their decisions to migrate to the Golden State. Hearing of the great opportunities in the shipyards of Oakland, Richmond, and San Francisco from railway workers and porters, friends, relatives, and labor recruiters scouring the South for able-bodied men and women for the worker-starved markets of the West, African Americans packed up their belongings and their hopes and dreams and headed down what they hoped would be the road to freedom. Established black residents stood in amazement as they beheld the newcomers' instant wealth. "I'd see these ladies in their shipyard clothes putting down *cash* for mink coats," remembered Johyne Beverly Osborne. "It was mindboggling for the amount of time they had been here. They were buying Cadillacs. Which, of course, even then that was a status car. And they were buying them with cash, which was blowing the sales people's minds downtown." The chance to gain such economic freedom was a great incentive for African Americans in the South to leave their homes to build new communities in the West. But their motivations were not solely economic; they also hoped to enjoy the reportedly liberal race relations and freer social environment of northern California. Their journey would be a long and arduous one, however, and the "promised land" that awaited the migrants would not easily yield the sweet fruits of liberty.[9]

The massive federal spending of the Second World War transformed the American West. Cities doubled, tripled, and quadrupled in size, new smokestacks sprouted from the landscape, and hundreds of thousands of interstate migrants moved into the region from the Midwest, South, and East. National defense dollars drove the rapid changes in the society, politics, and economy of California and its neighboring states. From the attack on Pearl Harbor until the final armistice in 1945, Washington pumped more than $35 billion into California's war industries, including more than $5 billion for the Bay Area's fledgling shipbuilding plants. The massive Kaiser shipyards in Richmond, which had not even existed prior to the Lend-Lease Act of 1941, used the government money to employ more than 90,000 workers at its peak and produce more than 700 cargo ships during the war. This federal presence was especially evident in the East Bay cities of Oakland and Richmond, but San Francisco also benefited from the largesse of the U.S. naval base at Hunter's Point. The swollen pipeline of federal money flowing into the West had run for nearly a century, starting with the huge grants of land to railroads in the nineteenth century and continuing with the enormous water projects of the twentieth. During the 1940s, however, California was able to further capitalize on Washington's bloated coffers, and unprecedented sums of cash were doled out to wartime contractors, factory owners, municipal governments, and war-industry workers. For example, the Richmond construction magnate Henry Kaiser turned from paving roads in the 1920s to building federally funded dams and bridges in the 1930s to operating the most successful shipbuilding company in the Bay Area in the 1940s. Kaiser and other Bay Area industrialists jumped on the federal bandwagon during the war to fulfill their patriotic duty and pad their wallets.[10]

The thousands of ordinary Americans who moved to the Bay Area also benefited from Uncle Sam's deep pockets. Reaping high wages for their labor, male and female workers of all races and nationalities were eventually welcomed into the factories by owners and managers desperate to fill the frantic orders for more war machines and supplies. The government also funded the construction of temporary wartime housing projects to ease the strain on overcrowded cities like Richmond, Oakland, and San Francisco. Ultimately, many of these "temporary" housing projects would come under the jurisdiction of the local municipal housing authorities, and they would house many of the former black workers, their families, and their descendants once the pool of industrial jobs had dried up after the war. The federal government, then, played a large role in creating the social disorder that would plague the Bay Area communities for decades after the war's end.

The federal government was not solely responsible for the infusion of thousands of African Americans into the Bay Area during the war, however. The blacks themselves made the ultimate decision to quit Dixie and make the long trek across the continent. Hoping to escape the shadow of Jim Crow and the lingering economic crisis that the agriculturally dependent South had entered during the Great Depression, African Americans scraped together their meager resources and lit out for the West Coast. Following the traditions of their predecessors who led the exodus to Kansas and the Trans-Appalachian West after Emancipation or who followed the great railroads to the urban North during the First World War, southern black migrants cast their lot with a new region in the hopes that it would be less infected with the poison of American racism. Continuing a long tradition of "voting with their feet," the blacks who left the South for California used what was for them the greatest and most powerful symbol of their rejection of the southern way of life and an affirmation of their rights to and hopes for equality and economic independence.[11]

During their journey west, African Americans utilized kinship, friendship, and employment networks to traverse the country, find jobs, and set up new homes and communities in the Bay Area. Often, the male heads of a family left the South to get industrial jobs in California, and once they had established themselves there, they would save enough money to bring the rest of their family to join them. Other relatives might then be persuaded to make the move away from their roots in the South, staying with their brothers, sisters, cousins, uncles, aunts, and friends until they found a place to live and a job to earn a livelihood. As a child, David Hilliard, future chief of staff of the Black Panther Party, moved from Rockville, Alabama, to Oakland with his family. His brothers, Van and Bud, had left for Oakland to get jobs in the burgeoning war industries, and their successes there lured the rest of the Hilliard family to California. The same was true for the family of Willie Stokes, a 27 year-old black man from Desha County, Arkansas. Stokes was a tenant farmer who earned $1.25 a day in credit at the plantation store owned by his landlord, and his meager earnings were poorly supplemented by a small plot near his house on which he grew what food he could. Disgruntled with this exploitative farming arrangement, Stokes arrived in Richmond in 1943 to work at the Kaiser Shipyards for $10 a day. He "doubled up" with a friend who had migrated to the Bay Area a year earlier, and when he finally secured a place in the government-owned housing projects near the Kaiser yards, he sent for his wife and two children. Loading her family and her belongings on a bus, Mrs. Stokes followed the now-legendary Route 66 west to her new home.[12]

Most of the African American migrants to the Bay Area came from the Old Southwest states of Texas, Louisiana, Arkansas, and Oklahoma; Mississippi and Alabama also sent their share of migrants to Oakland, Richmond, and San Francisco. According to Katherine Archibald, the majority of black workers at the Moore Dry Dock Company in Oakland hailed from Texas, Louisiana, and Mississippi. One small Louisiana town of 5,000 inhabitants was so well represented at the shipyard that a personnel assistant remarked: "You ask them where they're from and almost every one of them replies, 'Ah's f'om Bastrup, ma'am.'" Also among the migrants from the states of the Old Southwest were the first three members of the Black Panther Party for Self-Defense (BPP), which from its founding in 1966 attracted many of the sons and daughters of the wartime migrants. Bobby Seale, chairman and co-founder of the party, hailed from Dallas, Texas. In 1945, Seale's father, a carpenter, left to take a job in the defense industries and his family settled in a temporary wartime housing project in Berkeley. Named after the famous southern populist Huey P. Long, Huey Percy Newton, minister of defense and the other Panther founder, was originally from Oak Grove, Louisiana. His father went to Oakland in the early 1940s to work in the Naval Supply Depot, and Newton's family settled on 47th Street. Finally, Bobby Hutton, the first member inducted into the BPP in 1966, was born in Pine Bluff, Arkansas, in 1950. His parents, John and Dollie Hutton, moved to Oakland in 1953, where John worked in a cannery and was a part-time Baptist preacher. The Pacific states, and especially California, proved an enticing target for black migrants from the Old Southwest seeking to answer the national call for wartime workers. Their numbers would swell the population of the Bay Area in particular, and the demographic map of Berkeley, Oakland, Richmond, and San Francisco would be forever changed.[13]

In the decade between 1940 and 1950, the Bay Area population of African Americans would explode from a little over 17,000 to more than 117,000 inhabitants. Willie Brooks remembered that before the war there "weren't too many [blacks] here. But then after the War got started good, then the shipyards opened and they came by the boatloads, by the trainloads, by the planeloads. Anyway they could get here: walking, crawling, creeping, anything. Anyway they could get here...piggyback...they came." In Oakland alone, the black population grew by an astounding 463% from 8,462 to 47,610, and the percentage of African Americans in the city's total populace jumped from 3% to 12%. In 1940, four of five residents of Oakland were white; by the beginning of the next decade, the ratio had shrunk to only three in four. By 1960, the African American population of San Francisco and Oakland numbered in excess of 237,000. The East Bay cities of Berkeley and Richmond also witnessed the spectacular growth of their black populations. In Berkeley, there was a nearly four-fold increase in the number of blacks living in the city by 1950, and in Richmond, the postwar black population was fifty times larger than it had been in 1940. The great tide of wartime migrants made one long-time white resident of Richmond wistfully note: "All of a sudden there were too many people in town, and it was a twenty-four-hour-a-day business area.... People just seemed to come from everywhere.... In a sense, little Richmond was invaded, overrun, and overwhelmed by a mass of people from elsewhere — never to be the same again." Such dramatic growth had a profound effect upon life in the Bay Area.[14]

The African American migrants who invaded the Bay Area during the war were hardly the "hayseeds" of local legend, and many of them possessed education and job skills that were often far superior to those of the long-time black residents. According to a survey conducted in 1943, African American migrants had completed roughly the same number of years of schooling as their Bay Area counterparts, and the quality of instruction was judged by one black scholar as being essentially equal. Furthermore, although 36.9% of the southern blacks came as unskilled laborers, nearly a third of the black migrants were skilled workers, which was a much higher proportion than could be found in the native African American population. Likewise, many of the black migrants who ended up in the Bay Area hailed from southern cities rather than from the vast expanses of rural Dixie. Following a trend from the Great Migration during the First World War, African Americans completed part of a long, complex process of migration that started in rural areas, then staged to small towns, large southern cities, and that finally ended in the large industrial cores of the North and West. The resulting migrant population to the Bay Area was therefore significantly more urbane and proletarian than the picture painted by the tales of the long-time black residents would suggest.[15]

Whatever their origins, African American workers discovered that unprecedented opportunities awaited them in the wartime factories. Their instant wealth astounded those established residents, both black and white, who did not take jobs in the frenzied war industries. While many workers used their wages to purchase luxury goods, including automobiles and fur coats, that they could never have previously afforded, other African Americans saved their earnings to purchase homes or build nest eggs for the postwar era. In addition to their newfound riches, African Americans also gained entrance to new fields of employment and made important inroads into some unions. Black workers broke out of their domestic service role in the Bay Area economy, and many of them took skilled and semi-skilled positions in the shipyards. The severe shortage of welders, electricians, and other skilled tradesmen left white employers with little choice but to hire qualified African Americans. Although most unions segregated blacks into dependent auxiliaries, African American workers were able to use their collective strength to serve their communities' needs and press forward in the fight against discrimination and segregation. Auxiliary Lodge No. 36 of the International Brotherhood of Boiler Makers, Iron Ship Builders and Helpers of America, for example, pushed for more jobs for black women in the Richmond Recreational Department, agitated for improved recreational facilities for youngsters in Richmond and San Pablo, and purchased United States War Bonds to support America's war effort. The National Union of Marine Cooks and Stewards (MCS) was perhaps the most liberal workers' organization on the West Coast, however, and it allowed full and equal membership for African Americans. Affiliated with the Congress of Industrial Organizations (CIO), the MCS was a leftist union headquartered in San Francisco whose liberal anti-discrimination policy announced that "it is also part of our program to eliminate discrimination because of race, color or creed. We believe that all workers should have equal opportunities. Pay should be **for work done**, not for color of skin." The MCS's *Delegate's Handbook* from 1945 included a series of penalties, ranging from a $10 fine to expulsion from the union, for "discrimination against other members because of race, color or creed." The MCS blasted other union leaders for failing to address the needs of black workers and its 1951 *Officers' Report* declared that "at the present time, more than half of the paid officials of MCS are Negroes or members of other racial minorities. No other union in America, except those whose membership is entirely non-white, can match this record." Although not all Bay Area unions were as welcoming as the Marine Cooks and Stewards, African American workers did find some allies among the industrial working class and a few potent vehicles for change among labor organizations.[16]

Black leaders also trumpeted the successes of black workers in the shipyards and factories, and many long-time residents pointed to the quality workmanship of black laborers as proof of the equality of the races. African American printers produced pamphlets describing the skills of black workers in glowing terms, and one such booklet noted that the "contributions [of black workers] to the war effort have [done] much to destroy the myth that the Negro is lazy and incompetent, and has no place in the industrial life of the country except that of a common laborer and a 'flunky.'" Heralding the numbers of "Negro carpenters, painters, shipwrights, shipfitters, electricians, riggers, welders, burners, drillers, chippers, caulkers, stage riggers, engineers, co-ordinators, accountants, stenographers, [and] clerks," the pamphleteer concluded that the war had provided the opportunity for African Americans to gain the long-sought equality of the workplace, and he was assured that "the results will be lasting." Indeed, in the bustling war years, progress on the racial front seemed to be proceeding at a rate that had rarely been matched in American history. African American men and women entered the industrial workforce in record numbers, and old employment barriers crumbled before the onslaught of wartime need. Oakland hired its first five black policemen during the war, for example, and black men and women sporting welders' helmets and suits became a common sight on the streets of the East Bay. The workers' uniforms even became symbols of prestige in the Bay Area, and one established black resident recalled that "those hard-hats [became] you know, like a hat of honor. Sometimes you'd see the men fully dressed in suits, and they'd have on their shipyard hats. They'd be all dressed up, but they'd wear that hat."[17]

African American women also found many opportunities for work in the war industries, but their access was the most limited of any segment of the working class. Constrained by racial and sexual prejudice, black women workers discovered that white employers often summarily dismissed their applications for employment. Although many black families depended upon the wages earned by black women workers, hiring barriers for African American women were the last to fall during the war years. Few employers switched readily and easily to black women if no white men were available, and the shipyards set up elaborate hiring systems to limit the types of jobs African American women could take. When they were hired, African American women received the hardest and dirtiest jobs. According to a Department of Labor survey, nearly two-thirds of the black women working in the wartime shipyards were "engaged as welders trainees and laborers.... In contrast only 6 percent of white women were engaged as laborers, 9 percent worked as welder trainees, and 9 percent as electrician trainees." Unlike their white sisters who often held clerical positions in the war industries, black women found themselves in many of the most dangerous and difficult jobs in the shipyards. Reflecting upon their occupational status, one historian concluded, "black women were typecast by the general working population and major employers—they were seen as suitable only for menial labor. It was one thing to hire a black woman to scrub a toilet, yet quite another, as several employers indicated in their refusal to hire black women, for black women to share toilet facilities with white women." Some black women, however, did manage to succeed during the war and protect their prosperity in the postwar era. Despite the limits placed upon African American women workers, Mattie Jackson, a black woman from Livingston, Texas, prospered in this wartime atmosphere, and she owned a coffee shop and a music store before going to work in the Koret California Manufacturing Plant. She began as a garment worker, but she quickly rose to special machine operator and then shop steward. By 1974, she had become International Vice

## Table 1
### Population Change in the Bay Area during WWII

| City | Total Population 1940 | Total Population 1950 | Percent Increase |
|---|---|---|---|
| San Francisco | 634,536 | 775,075 | +22.1% |
| Oakland | 302,163 | 383,200 | +26.8% |
| Berkeley | 85,547 | 113,805 | +33.0% |
| Richmond | 23,642 | 99,545 | +321.1% |

SOURCES: Marilynn S. Johnson, *The Second Gold Rush: Oakland and the East Bay during World War II* (Berkeley: University of California Press, 1993), 34, 53; Albert S. Broussard, *Black San Francisco: The Struggle for Racial Equality in the West* (Lawrence: University Press of Kansas, 1993), 133; United States Department of Commerce, *Sixteenth Census of the United States: 1940; Population*, Vol. II, Part 3 (Washington, D. C.: United States Government Printing Office, 1943), 636, 657; and United States Department of Commerce, A *Report of the Seventeenth Decennial Census of the United States, Census of the Population: 1950*, Volume II, Part 5 (Washington, D. C.: United States Government Printing Office, 1952), 206-07.

## Table 2
### African American Population Change in the Bay Area during WWII

| City | Black Pop. 1940 | Percent of Total Pop. 1940 | Black Pop. 1950 | Percent of Total Pop. 1950 | Percent Increase |
|---|---|---|---|---|---|
| San Francisco | 4,846 | 0.8% | 43,460 | 5.6% | +796.8% |
| Oakland | 8,462 | 2.8% | 47,610 | 12.4% | +462.6% |
| Berkeley | 3,395 | 4.0% | 13,289 | 11.7% | +291.4% |
| Richmond | 270 | 1.1% | 13,374 | 13.4% | +4853.3% |

SOURCES: Marilynn S. Johnson, *The Second Gold Rush: Oakland and the East Bay during World War II* (Berkeley: University of California Press, 1993), 34, 53; Albert S. Broussard, *Black San Francisco: The Struggle for Racial Equality in the West* (Lawrence: University Press of Kansas, 1993), 133; United States Department of Commerce, *Sixteenth Census of the United States: 1940; Population*, Vol. II, Part 3 (Washington, D. C.: United States Government Printing Office, 1943), 636, 657; and United States Department of Commerce, A *Report of the Seventeenth Decennial Census of the United States, Census of the Population: 1950*, Volume II, Part 5 (Washington, D. C.: United States Government Printing Office, 1952), 206-07.

President of the International Ladies Garment Workers Union (ILGWU).[18]

Although they possessed knowledge and skill, however, African American migrants found that ignorance and prejudice awaited them at the entrance to the Bay Area factories and shipyards. A severe labor shortage forced white factory owners and white workers to accept the necessity of black labor in the wartime industries, but their acquiescence was neither total nor permanent. African American workers were kept in low-skill, low-wage jobs unless there was no other alternative, and white employers and supervisors resisted giving black workers much autonomy or control over their own labor. In her study of the wartime shipyards, Katherine Archibald noted that African Americans did mostly "clean-up and maintenance work, rigging, welding, plate handling, and other crafts of ship building as contrasted with those of outfitting and repair." Most white unions segregated black workers into dependent auxiliaries, and although the black members paid equal dues, they did not have equal representation in union elections and union decision-making. One white official at a Bay Area utilities company noted that "electricity is a complicated product and requires skill to handle. Many Negroes have a tendency to shirk responsibility and be lazy, in addition to their lack of opportunity for technical training." The same white man argued that his company's reticence to place African American workers into jobs that required a great deal of contact with the public was the result of widely held attitudes about the proper place of black people in Bay Area society, and his explanation reveals a great deal about the sexual politics of wartime life: "Many jobs such as collectors, meter readers, servicemen, and the like take employees into homes of customers. The company recognizes that such men must be acceptable to the people at home. The employee must look honest and impress the housewife with his integrity. Many Negroes would therefore not be trusted by customers." Although unparalleled opportunities for black employment existed during the war years, the barriers to full equality in the workplace remained stubbornly entrenched.[19]

The boundaries to equal access also reached out to the neighborhoods that surrounded the wartime factories. The large numbers of wartime migrants put a heavy strain on available housing, and overcrowding in the East Bay meant that many families, black and white, went without suitable housing for long periods of time. Popular anecdotes tell of people sleeping in all-night movie theaters during the early 1940s, and the practice of sleeping in shifts in boarding houses and renting beds for eight hours remained fairly commonplace until the end of the war. Some migrant families were fortunate enough to find rental housing in the private sector or in the new government-built temporary housing projects, but many others had to find makeshift shelter in trailers, automobiles, and shacks until more permanent housing could be completed. Harry and Marguerite Williams, a native African American couple from Richmond, recalled that Harry's aunt whitewashed her chicken coup and rented it out to a migrant family during the height of the housing crisis. Due to white attitudes, moreover, the housing market for black migrants was even more constrained. White real estate agents and white homeowners hesitated to rent rooms or houses to black customers, and some white homeowners wishing to move faced threats and intimidation from their white neighbors if they considered selling their houses to black families. White homeowners feared that their property values would plummet if blacks moved in next door, and many whites were simply repulsed by the idea of living near African Americans. One white San Franciscan quipped: "I wouldn't even want Marion Anderson as a neighbor." White racism made the difficult task of finding suitable housing during the wartime crunch even more arduous for African Americans. Although wartime prosperity exceeded what many of them had imagined, the black migrants found that their dreams of equality in the Golden State remained far from being realized. Ruth Gracon, a black woman migrant, noted that "...things were going to be different out here, but they weren't like we thought they'd be. They didn't have 'No Colored' signs or anything like that, but they had other ways of telling you they didn't want you."[20]

The kind of racism characteristic of the prewar established white population of the Bay Area is perhaps best exemplified by the case of the Port Chicago Mutiny. Port Chicago was an U.S. naval base situated northeast of Berkeley at the mouth of the Sacramento River where enlisted men, mostly black, loaded supply ships with bombs and ammunition that were destined for the Pacific Theater.

Conditions at the base were unsafe, and the black enlisted men frequently complained to their white superior officers that a disaster
at the base was imminent unless measures were taken to train the
workers, increase loading times, and halt officer-encouraged "com-
petitions" between loading crews.  On July 17, 1944, a huge explosion at the ammunition loading facility at Port Chicago killed 320
servicemen, 202 of whom were black, and injured 390 soldiers and
civilians, 233 of whom were black.  The totals represented more
than fifteen percent of African American naval casualties during the
Second World War.  Three weeks later, when 328 men, again mostly
black, were ordered back to work under nearly the same conditions
as before the explosion, 258 of them refused to load ammunition.
Fifty-eight of the men were charged with mutiny, court-martialed,
convicted, and imprisoned from eight to fifteen years.  The judge
advocate, Lt. Comdr. Keith Ferguson, concluded after the testimony in the case:

> The consensus of opinion of the witnesses |125 total, of whom
> only 5 where black|—and practically admitted by the interested
> parties—is that the colored enlisted personnel are neither tem-
> peramentally or intellectually capable of handling high explo-
> sives....  These men, it is testified, could not understand the
> orders which were given to them and the only way they could be
> made to understand what they should do was by actual demon-
> stration....  It is an admitted fact, supported by the testimony of
> the witnesses, that there was rough and careless handling of the
> explosives being loaded aboard ships at Port Chicago.

While only one instance, the racist assumptions about the intellectual capacity of African Americans in this statement are representative of the attitudes held by many, if not most, long-time white
residents of the Bay Area.  The myth of black intellectual inferiority
shaped war policy on naval bases and in civilian shipyards, where
managers and owners relegated African Americans into unskilled
jobs and denied them access to the most difficult and challenging
tasks of ship construction despite the dire need for capable war
workers.  Most whites simply assumed that blacks were inferior.[21]
  The white migrants who came to the Bay Area seeking employment in the war industries also embraced these notions, but their

hatred was more unrefined and brutal.  During her two-year study of the conditions at the Moore Dry Dock Company in Oakland, Katherine Archibald found that racism among southern white migrants ran at a fever pitch.  Forced to work in close quarters with African Americans, the white laborers developed a near mania about the inferiority of blacks.  When Archibald tried to convince one old white man that blacks deserved equality, he coldly retorted: "Well, a nigger may be as good as you are, but he sure ain't as good as me."  White workers constantly complained of the blacks' proclivity to violence, their hyper-sexual nature, their intellectual and physical inferiority, and their laziness.  Several white southern migrants advocated lynchings and other forms of racial violence to keep the blacks "in their place."  "What you need round here," noted one white migrant, "is a good old-fashioned lynching.  Back in my home state we string a nigger up or shoot him down, every now and then, and that way we keep the rest of them quiet and respectful."  Although this white war worker's words were more blunt than those of his upper-class counterpart, his fears and hatred would resonate among the hearts of many Bay Area white residents.  The poison of white racism fouled the air in northern California and the postwar era would be a time of continued conflict and racial discord.[22]

## A NEW CULTURAL LANDSCAPE

In the face of white racism and hostility, African American migrants relied on the survival strategies that they had crafted in the southland for more than three centuries.  The rich cultural heritage of the southern blacks would provide the means for the migrants to form a sense of identity and community in the urban West, and it would offer them a weapon against the dehumanizing forces of racism and segregation that they found there.  The southern roots of the newcomers' speech, dress, religion, food, and music would sink deep into the soil of the Bay Area and transform its social and cultural landscape.  The established black and white residents of the Bay Area often resisted and resented the alien lifeways of the migrants, but eventually the awesome tide of humanity that swept into the cities of Berkeley, Oakland, Richmond, and San Francisco overwhelmed its opposition.  The migrants' contributions to Bay Area culture would be persistent and pervasive, and the signatures of the first southern black migrants can still be discerned on the crowded canvas of northern California. The migrants slowly settled down into the routine patterns of daily life, and they built new communities throughout the Bay Area that would eventually produce a hybrid of southern and western elements.

The southern migrants' speech differed greatly from that of their California brethren. Having adopted the "correct" English of the white majority, long-time residents of the Bay Area were frequently disconcerted by the "lower-class" speech patterns of the newly arrived war workers. Although many old-timers attributed the southerners' speech to the paucity of schools for black children in the South, a hint of condemnation crept into many accounts of their dialect. Mrs. Toronto Cannaday Marshall noted that some of her southern-born friends had "been here a long time and all that but their English is very poor.... [S]ometimes this one woman, she'll say, 'Is you' and 'I is.' And they are well fixed [wealthy]. She belongs to clubs and all that. So, oh, I said, if I could only get Alberta...and so I say, 'Oh, they *are*,' you know. But I've never had a chance at her (chuckle)." Aurelious P. Alberga also recalled that the southerners' "English, naturally, was very, very bad. And they took—quite a bit of repeating, almost, on all—nearly all occasions, to understand what they were endeavoring to try and impress you with." Incorrect verb conjugations were not the only, or most shocking, new linguistic twist the southern migrants brought to the Bay Area, however. The litany of curse words that southern blacks seemed to know also reddened the faces of many established African Americans, despite the fact that San Francisco had long been a haven for sailors. Many established residents were aghast at the off-color commentary they heard on the streetcars and sidewalks from black newcomers. Even Bobby Seale, who would later use profanity to such great effect in the protest movements of the 1960s, claimed that he learned how to swear from other migrant children on the playground of a government-owned wartime housing project in Berkeley. "I first learned how to curse when I got to California," recalled Seale. When he tried to convince another black boy that his brother and sister had a right to play on the "big, gigantic, thick-rope swing," the boy "called me a MF, 'you old motherfuckin' sucker you.'" Surprised, Seale confessed that "I didn't know what he called me because remember, I'm...raised around a Christian family, [and I] had not heard these words [before]."[23]

The black migrants also challenged the existing social codes about appropriate dress in public. "Old-timers" held to a certain formality when going out on the town; they wore gloves, hats, and fine clothes for an afternoon excursion. The newcomers, however, cast off old conventions and donned an eclectic and pragmatic assortment of multi-colored and expressive clothing. Edward Alley remembered seeing the new arrivals riding the streetcars with "nets" on their hair to preserve their "conks," which would have been an egregious faux pas for long-time residents of San Francisco, who would certainly have taken their hats off when they boarded the trolleys. "[W]e always dressed up to go downtown and had on our white gloves and hats," recalled Alma Thomas Brooks. "And we always *dressed* going downtown. I wasn't used to seeing people with bandanas [sic] and...(Chuckle). I said, 'Where did all these *bandana* people come from?' We never...we *never* dressed that way." Despite the established residents' condemnation, however, the dress of the wartime workers and their families would remain a part of life in the Bay Area, and even on the streets of the more formal San Francisco, clothing styles would change and the city would eventually gain the reputation of being a center of avant-garde fashion.[24]

The migrants brought with them long-established patterns of worship and religion as well. Although some newcomers would be welcomed in the established churches, most of the migrants created their own houses of worship and continued to practice their religion in the centuries-old manner of their predecessors. Even some established Bay Area evangelical churches did not draw in many migrants because of the restrained nature of their preachers' sermons. The Rev. G. J. Wildy of the Allen Temple Baptist Church, for example, did not approve of the emotional style of religious worship practiced by many black southerners, and he lost many converts to the Bethel Missionary Baptist Church and the Star Bethel Church because they both had ministers "who were known as great 'whoopers.'" During the war years, itinerant ministers and southern evangelicals roamed among the temporary camps of wartime workers, and when things became more settled, storefront churches sprang up and quickly became fixtures in the new urban landscape. According to several established residents, the Baptist faith seemed to draw in most of the population of religious migrants, and Pentecostal churches attracted many others. Sadie Calbert, a long-time member of the Cooper Zion Church in San Francisco, remembered that a "great many" of the migrants "are Baptist. You know there are more Baptist Blacks than there are Methodist. So many of them were Baptist or else they joined these Pentecostal churches. No, we didn't get all of them. I think the Baptists and the Pentecostals and those different people, I think, got most of them." Johyne Beverly Osborne recalled that Baptist churches "just sprung up...a lot of these little store-fronts and Holiness and Pentecostal churches.... A lot of them belonged to those. There weren't that many [here] at that time. Many, many were Baptists, because there have always been a lot of Baptist churches [in the South]." The expressiveness of religious worship in these new churches was alien to the long-time black inhabitants of northern California, but the energy of southern black Protestantism weathered the storm of discontent and became one of the central factors in African American Bay Area culture.[25]

Southern cuisine was another contribution that black migrants added to the cultural mix of Berkeley, Oakland, Richmond, and San Francisco. The "strange" foods preferred by blacks from the South soon found their way onto grocery-store shelves. The migrants demanded access to their traditional staples, and store owners responded by bringing in products that many native black residents had never seen before. Confounded by the seemingly endless procession of southern meats and vegetables, Alma Brooks confessed that she had "never heard of greens or nothing like that until the War time, because the only greens we ever ate were spinach and Swiss Chard. We never heard of mustard greens and turnip greens. And never heard of chiterlings [sic], and never heard of pig ears and pig nose and all that (Chuckle)." Johyne Osborne remembered that before the war fresh pork and chicken were readily available in Chinatown, but after the arrival of thousands of black southerners, "the stores started stocking black-eyed peas, okra, that Louisiana coffee with all of that chicory,...more pigtails, more pork, cornbread,

cornmeal by the sack, chicken and ribs. It changed the entire shop-
ping in this particular area.... |A|nd what else? Oh, and greens.
Lots and lots of collard greens.... And yams." The distinctiveness
of the regional cuisine that the migrants brought with them left its
stamp on the new African American communities that were sprout-
ing up in the Bay Area, and it helped to reinforce a growing sense
of unity among them.[26]

The migrants' musical traditions were another gift they brought
to northern California. Steeped in the long traditions of blues and
jazz, many blacks from the Old Southwest prized their rich heritage
of musical expression. In the East Bay, jazz and blues clubs like the
Kozy Kafe Cabaret, the Swing Club, Harvey's Rex Club, Slim Jenkins'
Place, Mother Smith's, and Raincoat's Pinochle Parlor in Oakland
and Club Savoy, Fred's Place, the B and L Club, Tappers Inn, and
Minnie Lou's in Richmond offered down-home southern soul music
and food for the growing black population during and after the war.
Charles and Elizabeth Smith had operated Smith's Buffet, an eatery
frequented by railroad workers, before the war, but after the arrival
of the war workers, they opened the Kozy Kafe at 1783 7th Street in
Oakland. The nightclub employed a large black staff, including
musicians for its orchestra, entertainers for a floor show, a master
of ceremonies, a chef, waitresses, bartenders, a porter, a cashier,
and several photographers. These hot nightspots and others like
them scattered throughout the Bay Area attracted such noted per-
formers as Cab Calloway and Duke Ellington, and they established
a strong base of black musical expression that would continue in
the 1950s under such jazz luminaries as Dizzy Gillespie, Wes
Montgomery, and Theloneous Monk. The rage of "cool" that developed from this jazz and blues culture would later attract the eye of
a group of young white radical writers and artists: the Beat
Generation.[27]

The appearance of vast numbers of southern black migrants with
such a vibrant and electric culture shook up the established African
American communities and helped to fuel the fire of racial protest
in the Bay Area. A new wave of energy came out of the masses of
wartime migrants that would energize the struggles for equality and
justice, which older residents had waged with, what seemed in ret-
rospect, such reserve. According to San Francisco native Toronto

Marshall, the southern wartime migrants were the ones who "made it better. So many that have come in here, they are the ones. It wasn't the people that were here or the Northern people. The Southern people are the ones.... I give them credit for that. They are the ones. I really think so. In fact, I know so." Edward Alley, another San Francisco native and a musician, agreed. He conceded that the migrants "were the ones to begin to do the fighting here. For some reason they were the fighters. It wasn't the people that lived here that caused all those changes. It was the new people that came here." The native residents of the Bay Area, according to Marshall and Alley, had become complacent with their lives and the racial order that they had created with the whites. The newcomers often criticized the established black population for not doing enough to fight discrimination and segregation before the war. Alley confessed that "I think they thought we were...we didn't have any backbone. I think they thought we were...here we've been here all our lives and haven't got anything, what were we doing? You know what I mean. We didn't have much get up about us which we didn't. We were very complacent. We were law abiding and complacent and we accepted what they had but we weren't militant and so, man, I guess they were kind of disgusted with us." The arrival of new African Americans, however, made the old system obsolete, and the migrants pushed hard to create a new society where freedom, liberty, and equality for all residents were accepted and ensured.[28]

The pressure of thousands of new black bodies in the cities of Berkeley, Oakland, Richmond, and San Francisco challenged the status quo and demanded a new set of racial mores be devised between the white majority and growing black minority. Almost overnight, the racial dynamic of the Bay Area was completely changed. With the internment of large numbers of Japanese Americans, Asian Americans became a tiny minority compared with the expanding African American population. Consequently, in the eyes of white residents, blacks became in the postwar years the new social problem. Long-time white residents and the numerous white migrants who also flooded into the Bay Area during the war quickly circled their wagons and traded stories about the inferiority of the black "invaders" and created a new racial mythology that grew out of the "benignly" racist prewar attitudes of the established white residents of the Bay Area and that particularly virulent strain of race-based hatred that is frequently found among working-class southerners. The lines between the races were sharply redrawn in the wartime shipyards, and the long-term causes of the racial violence of the 1960s were clearly evident two decades earlier.[29]

## THE ORIGINS OF THE BLACK REVOLUTION

As the winds of war died out in Europe and the Pacific, wartime hysteria and economic excitement began to quickly fade in the Bay Area. Production in the shipyards fell off dramatically, and large numbers of returning veterans meant that competition for what jobs were left would be increasingly fierce. Established white and black residents also began to realize that many wartime migrants had resolved to remain in the Bay Area and start new lives there. The population pressures and housing shortages that characterized the war years would continue to plague local governments in Berkeley, Oakland, Richmond, and San Francisco, and the disappearance of federal war dollars meant that local charities and municipalities would be stretched to the breaking point. Public fears of a growing crime problem brought by the war migrants raised calls for "law and order" campaigns designed to protect "honest" citizens and solidify the racial boundaries that separated white and black. The unsolved problems of the war years would leave a long and bitter legacy for African Americans in the San Francisco Bay Area, and they would be the seeds of the Black Revolution of the 1960s.

As the wartime entrepreneurs sensed the coming end of the war, they began to scale back production and gear their capital for the civilian market as early as 1944. Far-sighted white war workers also fled the shipyards for peacetime jobs in technical and skilled fields in factories that sprang up in the lily-white suburbs that surrounded the old industrial quarters of Oakland and Richmond. Black workers, however, were locked out of skilled positions in new construction and manufacturing jobs, and they held out in the defense industries until the well ran dry. As in the rest of the nation, blacks in northern California faced the problem of being the "last hired, first fired" segment of the labor market. With the return of white GIs and the slowdown in production, African Americans were the first ones to get pink slips in 1945. Due to their intimate knowledge of employment discrimination before the war, many established black residents foresaw the problems that migrants would face after the war industries closed their doors. Johyne Osborne admitted, "I just couldn't believe...I mean, the money they had! And the way they were spending it. I was thinking, you know, 'I hope they are saving some of this money.'" Other long-time residents also realized that the postwar economy would require African Americans to be more frugal, and according to Sadie Calbert, "some of those [workers] possibly who had not been provident were on welfare. And some of them bought their homes. They had made a new place for themselves and planted their roots out here in California, and did very well because they were provident and conservative." Many of the black old-timers proved prescient, for by 1950, the postwar position of blacks in the labor market was shockingly similar to their prewar status. Pushed out of technical and manufacturing jobs, African American men and women returned to the service sector. Only about one in six black men were able to remain in industrial jobs after the war. While more than 127,000 white men continued to work in manufacturing jobs in San Francisco and Oakland, only 5,580 black men were so employed by 1950. African American women fared little better. Of the 17,884 black women employed in San Francisco and Oakland, more than half of them, 9,456, worked as domestic servants five years after the end of the war.[30]

Black women in particular felt the sting of racism. Occupying the lowest rung of the economic ladder before the war, black women hoped to improve their status during the war's heyday and protect their gains in the postwar years. Alma Thomas Brooks, a long-time black resident of San Francisco who went to work in a nursery school during the war, recalled that many black women wanted to remain in the workforce after 1945: "I stayed for a while longer because the mothers were still...they got used to working and so the mothers kept on working." Unfortunately, however, African American women's hopes were quickly dashed by postwar conservatism, and as white women were pushed back into the home as housewives, black women returned to the familiar role of maidservant. One scholar has noted that "for black women, especially, what is significant about the war experience is the extent to which [employment] barriers remained intact." The postwar effort to send white women back into the home became a double burden for black women. In the Bay Area and the rest of the nation, African American women had commonly worked outside of the home before and during the war. Many African American families depended upon the wages earned by black women, and a large number of black women counted on their earnings outside of the home as their only means of support. In the Bay Area's glutted postwar labor market, black women toiled at the bottom of the employment pyramid, and they suffered with the highest jobless rates of any group. Although many African American women had hoped that their wartime gains would translate into postwar prosperity, the decades after the end of the Second World War would see the long decline in the status of black women workers. Assessing the employment situation of American women after the war, one historian concluded: "Despite the wartime expansion of women's economic roles, women of the postwar era simply were not equal participants with men in the labor market." Their losses in the job market would parallel a similar crisis for black women in their own communities, and their position within black families and black organizations would come under increasing attack during the 1950s, and it would reach its nadir during the Black Revolution of the late 1960s.[31]

Despite the grim economic picture of the postwar years, many black migrants from the Old Southwest were determined to stay in the Bay Area. Willie Stokes, the intrepid former sharecropper from Arkansas, preferred the freedom he enjoyed in the West over the limitations put on a black man in the Jim Crow South. The absence of segregation in public facilities and the right to vote were enough to keep Stokes from being too discouraged by the postwar economic downturn. Most established white and black residents, however, had viewed the newcomers as "temporary citizens" only to be suffered during the wartime boom, and most of them apparently expected the migrants to return to their home states when the war was over. Driven to distraction by the prospect that the southern black migrants were there to stay, established residents feared that many of the newcomers would end up on the public dole.  Sadie Calbert, a long-time black resident, noted that public officials even offered to pay return fares for some migrants "to keep them from going on welfare."  This one-way ticket policy was popular among welfare agents, and it lasted well into the 1950s.  For example, local officials offered to send Mrs. Montronia Brown and her five children back to Columbia, Mississippi, in 1954, after her husband, Raymond, abandoned the family when he could not find carpentry work in the Bay Area.  Mrs. Brown and her children had arrived in San Francisco in the summer of 1953, but Raymond was denied entrance into the all-white Carpenters' Union, and he was unable to find work to support the family.  He left Montronia and their children in September 1953.  Nearly a year later, members of the Third Baptist Church raised money to help the woman and the five children after they had been evicted from their home because they were unable to pay the rent.  Welfare officials then stepped in to offer the family passage back to Mississippi, but Mrs. Brown preferred to stay in San Francisco and struggle to make ends meet in her new home.[32]

Although many black migrants hoped to stay in northern California after the war, finding homes remained a nagging problem.  Housing shortages in Berkeley, Oakland, Richmond, and San Francisco continued after the war, and the lack of suitable dwellings for blacks was intensified by residential segregation.  "Redlining" and restrictive real estate covenants kept African Americans from buying or renting housing throughout the Bay Area, and distinct lines between white and black neighborhoods became much more clear after 1945 than they had been before the Second World War.  Although few established residents were eager to push for new housing projects for the black migrants, developers lined up to participate in the white suburban housing boom that created Bay Area "Levittowns" up and down the coast.  According to one established black resident, the migrants "drove a lot of the White people out of the city.  You know, White people...all my friends that I went to school with don't live here anymore."  Black customers were not welcome in these new subdivisions, and black populations in the East Bay and in San Francisco were increasingly concentrated into neighborhoods like West Oakland and Hunter's Point.  Of the more than 75,000 building permits for new houses that were issued in the Bay Area from 1949 to 1951, only 600 were available to African Americans. Even for blacks who could afford them, the new suburban homes were clearly off limits.[33]

The public housing situation was particularly desperate. Cramped temporary wartime housing units were transferred from the federal government to local governments in Berkeley, Oakland, Richmond, and San Francisco, and these dwellings formed the core of the postwar public housing system. Although many whites were able to leave the "temporary" units after the war, African Americans had little choice but to stay in public housing due to their financial straits and the closed Bay Area housing market. Furthermore, not only did public housing carry the stigma of "public assistance," but public housing authorities throughout the Bay Area segregated blacks and whites in different developments. Despite the small supply of public units for black families, no officials moved to integrate the public housing facilities even on a temporary basis, and many African Americans were left on waiting lists and in cramped quarters with families and friends. J. Maceo Green, a columnist for the black weekly newspaper, the *Sun-Reporter*, blasted San Francisco for its discriminatory housing policies: "The city of San Francisco, is in the minds of its smug-minded residents, the most liberal city in all North America, has perhaps the worst housing record in the country when it comes to admission of Negroes to houses erected with public funds."[34]

In addition to their attempts to segregate the black migrants into closed communities, white Bay Area residents also started a "law and order" campaign after the war in order to control the behavior of the working-class and unemployed blacks who had seemingly overrun the cities. Many Bay Area whites believed that African Americans had a predilection toward crime, and one white shipyard worker proclaimed that "[N]iggers take to murder and cutting people up with knives like a duck takes to water. They're natural-born gangsters and criminals." Of course, organized crime within black communities was substantially different than the unorganized black crime that spread into surrounding white areas. Local police forces overlooked local black gambling clubs, numbers rackets, and the like, according to one reformer, because they "felt there was really no harm in allowing these fellows to gamble in their 'clubs' since it provided them an outlet for the 'native, immature gambling instincts of uneducated colored people.'" A reform movement led by middle-class blacks, however, targeted the working men's gambling dens in order to wipe out the growing sin in the black community. Frequent targets of the reformers' ire were the Pageant Club on Post Street, the Janitors Association, Inc., the American Legion Club on O'Farrell Street, the Pacific Social Club in the Edison Hotel, the Fidelity Social Club on Geary Street, Just Peanuts, and other "Chinese" lottery joints throughout the city of San Francisco. Official force was infrequently and unevenly applied against these establishments, so the black elite fought against them in the realm of public opinion.[35]

When blacks transgressed the boundaries of race in more public forums, however, police officers quickly resorted to force to quell what they considered to be potentially riotous situations. Police were especially vigilant in controlling gangs of black youths, and frequent conflicts between officers and black teen-agers erupted throughout the 1940s and 1950s. In January 1954, for example, seven young black men were arrested at the New Orleans Drive-In in Richmond, and police charged them with disturbing the peace and resisting arrest. Apparently, a fracas between the police and black men broke out when the white officers approached the crowd of blacks and ordered them to disperse. This incident, and many others like it, reveals the tensions between the police and young blacks in the Bay Area that characterized the era. Despite various civil rights groups' attempts to improve relations between the police and black youths, official racial violence continued to be a major problem in the Bay Area through the 1960s. Black community-police relations, like the postwar crises of black employment, limited housing, and segregated schools, continued to drive a wedge between the white majority and black minority. As conditions deteriorated during the 1950s and 1960s, northern California's liberal façade crumbled under the onslaught of racial turmoil.[36]

By the time of the *Brown v. Board of Education* decision of May 1954, the San Francisco Bay Area had witnessed a profound economic, social, and cultural upheaval. The arrival of thousands of black migrants from the Old Southwest woke small, sleepy towns like

Berkeley and Richmond and shook larger cities like Oakland and San Francisco out of their states of complacency. The humdrum of everyday life was drowned out by the roar of wartime factories. Crowded streets and trolleys busting at the seams with people destroyed the relative tranquillity of the prewar era. Established white and black residents alike had to renegotiate and redefine racial barriers, and the newcomers threw their exotic spices into the mix. The conflicts that arose out of these tumultuous years, and the failures to address the problems that came with them, would create a bitter legacy for the next generation. Southern black migrants transformed life in the cities of Berkeley, Oakland, Richmond, and San Francisco, and their arrival touched off a series of crises and created a bundle of issues so contentious that no veil of fog, no matter how thick, could conceal.

# Notes

1.   The best overview of wartime migration to the East Bay cities of Oakland, Berkeley, and Richmond is Marilynn S. Johnson, *The Second Gold Rush: Oakland and the East Bay in World War II* (Berkeley: University of California Press, 1993). An older, yet excellent, account of war workers at the Moore Dry Dock Company in Oakland is Katherine Archibald, *Wartime Shipyard: A Study in Social Disunity* (Berkeley: University of California Press, 1947). A good study of African Americans in the East Bay City is Shirley Ann Moore, "The Black Community in Richmond, California, 1910–1963" (Ph.D. diss., University of California, Berkeley, 1989). A more recent study of the lives of black women industrial workers in the East Bay is Gretchen Lemke-Santangelo, *Abiding Courage: African American Migrant Women and the East Bay Community* (Chapel Hill: University of North Carolina Press, 1996). For a general overview of black life in the East Bay since the nineteenth century, see Lawrence P. Crouchett, Lonnie G. Bunch, III, and Martha Kendall Winnacker, *Visions toward Tomorrow: The History of the East Bay Afro-*

*American Community, 1852–1977* (Oakland: Northern California Center for Afro-American History and Life, 1989).

2.    United States Department of Commerce, *Sixteenth Census of the United States: 1940, Population*, Vol. II, Part 3, (Washington, D. C.: United States Printing Office, 1943), 636; Albert S. Broussard, *Black San Francisco: The Struggle for Racial Equality in the West, 1900–1954* (Lawrence: University Press of Kansas, 1993), 134; Shirley Ann Moore, "Getting There, Being There: African American Migration to Richmond, California, 1910–1945," in *The Great Migration in Historical Perspective: New Dimensions of Race, Class, and Gender*, ed. Joe William Trotter, Jr. (Bloomington: Indiana University Press, 1991), 106.

3.    Broussard, *Black San Francisco*, 6.  Broussard skillfully undermines the notion that San Francisco was a haven for liberal interracialists in his recent study.  For the views of two established white residents of the East Bay city of Richmond, see Alan Clarke, "Recollections of Point San Pablo and San Francisco Bay," an oral history conducted in 1985 and 1986 by Judith K. Dunning, Regional Oral History Office, The Bancroft Library, University of California, Berkeley, 1990; and Stanley Nystrom, "A Family's Roots in Richmond: Recollections of a Lifetime Resident," an oral history conducted in 1985 by Judith K. Dunning, Regional Oral History Office, The Bancroft Library, University of California, Berkeley, 1990.  For two long-time black residents' views on life in the same city, see Harry and Marguerite Williams, "Reflections of a Long-time Black Family in Richmond," an oral history conducted in 1985 by Judith K. Dunning, Regional Oral History Office, The Bancroft Library, University of California, Berkeley, 1990. Quotation is from Maya Angelou, *I Know Why the Caged Bird Sings* (New York: Bantam, 1970), 181.

4.    Charles S. Johnson, *The Negro War Worker in San Francisco* (n.p., 1944), 3. See also, Douglas Henry Daniels, *Pioneer Urbanites: A Social and Cultural History of Black San Francisco* (Philadelphia: Temple University Press, 1980), 75–82, 98–99.

5.    Ben Watkins, *We Also Serve: 10 Per Cent of a Nation Working and Fighting for Victory* (San Francisco: The Tilghman Press, n.d.), 5. Broussard, *Black San Francisco*, 39–47.  See also, Edward Everett France, "Some Aspects of the Migration of the Negro to the San Francisco Bay Area since 1940" (Ph.D. diss., University of California, Berkeley, 1962), 20.  Quotations are from Edward Alley, Interview by Jesse J. Warr, 19 September 1978, transcript, San Francisco African American Historical and Cultural Society, Research

Library and Archives, 52; and Willie Brooks, Interview by Jesse J. Warr, 19 June 1978, transcript, San Francisco African American Historical and Cultural Society, Research Library and Archives, 44.

6.    Quotation is from Willie Brooks, Interview, 47. See, Moore, "The Black Community in Richmond," esp. Chps. 1 and 2; and Hubert Owen Brown, "The Impact of War Worker Migration on the Public School System of Richmond, California, from 1940 to 1945" (Ph.D. diss., Stanford University, 1973), esp. 308–09. The best treatment of African Americans in the Bay Area in the first half of the twentieth century is Broussard, *Black San Francisco*. The first six chapters of his book deal with the growth and development of black society in the city, and although he would disagree with some of my generalizations about the homogeneity of black life before 1940, both of us see the Second World War as a major watershed in the history of black San Francisco. Another solid account that goes back into the nineteenth century is Daniels' *Pioneer Urbanites*. He also stresses the classlessness of black life and points to the level of cooperation necessary for the black community in San Francisco to function.

7.    Moore, "Getting There, Being There," 115. See also, Daniels, *Pioneer Urbanites*, 132 passim. This pattern of opposition from established residents was a common theme in the history of black migration to the North and West. For example, in Chicago and Pittsburgh, black "old-timers" tried to keep their social distance from the migrants by denying them entry into clubs, churches, and mutual-aid societies, and they criticized the migrants' "uncouth" behavior and alien southern customs. See, James Grossman, *Land of Hope: Chicago, Black Southerners, and the Great Migration* (Chicago: University of Chicago Press, 1989); and Peter Gottlieb, *Making Their Own Way: Southern Blacks' Migration to Pittsburgh, 1916–1930* (Urbana: University of Illinois Press, 1987). Johnson, *Negro War Worker in San Francisco*, 18–19. See also Broussard, *Black San Francisco*, 170–71; Daniels, *Pioneer Urbanites*, 171–73. Quotation is from Alley, Interview, 50–51.

8.    Alma Thomas Brooks, Interview by Jesse J. Warr, 17 October 1978, transcript, San Francisco African American Historical and Cultural Society, Research Library and Archives, 14; Williams, "Reflections of a Longtime Black Family in Richmond," 97–98; Sadie Calbert, Interview by Jesse J. Warr, 11 July 1978, transcript, San Francisco African American Historical and Cultural Society, Research Library and Archives, 55; Alley, Interview, 50; Lora Toombs Scott, Interview by Jesse J. Warr, 23 August 1978, transcript,

San Francisco African American Historical and Cultural Society, Research Library and Archives, 41.

9.    Johyne Beverly Osborne, Interview by Jesse J. Warr, 18 August 1978, transcript, San Francisco African American Historical and Cultural Society, Research Library and Archives, 69, 71.

10.   Gerald D. Nash, *The American West Transformed: The Impact of the Second World War* (Bloomington: Indiana University Press, 1985); Johnson, *The Second Gold Rush*, esp. Chp. 2; and Lemke-Santangelo, *Abiding Courage*, esp. Chp. 2; William Sokol, "Richmond during World War II: Kaiser Comes to Town," (Berkeley: University of California, 1971, typescript; copy in Richmond Collection, Richmond Public Library), cited in Johnson, *The Second Gold Rush*.

11.   A large body of literature chronicles African Americans' attempts to better their station by moving to different parts of the nation.  The first large-scale movements of blacks out of the South came close on the heels of emancipation during and after the Civil War.  A good overview of this period of migration is William Cohen, *At Freedom's Edge: Black Mobility and the Southern White Quest for Racial Control, 1861–1915* (Baton Rouge: Louisiana State University Press, 1991).  A classic case study of black migration to Kansas during the late 1800s is Nell I. Painter, *Exodusters: Black Migration to Kansas after Reconstruction* (New York: Alfred A. Knopf, 1976).  A study of the black town movement of the nineteenth century is Kenneth M. Hamilton, *Black Towns and Profit: Promotion and Development in the Trans-Appalachian West, 1877–1915* (Urbana: University of Illinois Press, 1991).  Studies of the Great Migration of blacks from the South to the industrial North during the WWI era are more numerous.  They include Grossman, *Land of Hope*; Gottlieb, *Making Their Own Way*; Kenneth Kusmer, *A Ghetto Takes Shape: Black Cleveland, 1870–1930* (Urbana: University of Illinois Press, 1976); Carole Marks, *Farewell—We're Good and Gone: The Great Black Migration* (Bloomington: Indiana University Press, 1989); Gilbert Osofsky, *Harlem: The Making of a Ghetto; Negro New York, 1890–1930* (New York: Harper & Row, 1966); Allan H. Spear, *Black Chicago: The Making of a Negro Ghetto, 1890–1920* (Chicago: University of Chicago Press, 1967); Joe William Trotter, Jr., *Black Milwaukee: The Making of an Industrial Proletariat, 1915–45* (Urbana: University of Illinois Press, 1985); and Trotter, ed., *The Great Migration in Historical Perspective*. Studies of black migration during the WWII era are less common, but they include Broussard, *Black San Francisco*; Daniels, *Pioneer Urbanites*; Johnson, *The Second Gold Rush*; Nicholas Lemann, *The Promised Land: The Great Black*

*Migration and How It Changed America* (New York: Alfred A. Knopf, 1991); Lemke-Santangelo, *Abiding Courage*; and Quintard Taylor, *The Forging of a Black Community: Seattle's Central District from 1870 through the Civil Rights Era* (Seattle: University of Washington Press, 1994).

12.  David Hilliard and Lewis Cole, *This Side of Glory: The Autobiography of David Hilliard and the Story of the Black Panther Party* (Boston: Little, Brown and Company, 1993), 51 passim; Cy W. Record, "Willie Stokes at the Golden Gate," *Crisis* 56 (June 1949): 175–76.  For a similar story, see Eddie Eaton, "In Search of the California Dream: From Houston, Texas to Richmond, California, 1943," an oral history conducted in 1986 by Judith K. Dunning, Regional Oral History Office, The Bancroft Library, University of California, Berkeley, 1990.

13.  Archibald, *Wartime Shipyard*, 60; Bobby G. Seale, *A Lonely Rage: The Autobiography of Bobby Seale* (New York: Times Books, 1978), 18–19 passim; Bobby Seale, Interview by Ronald Jemal Stephens and Clyde Robertson, 1989, transcript in possession of the author, n.p.; Gene Marine, *The Black Panthers* (New York: New American Library, 1969), 12–13, 137.

14.  Willie Brooks, Interview, 44; Nystrom, "A Family's Roots in Richmond," oral history, 32.  Even these totals probably underestimate the amount of growth.  Due to limitations of the federal census and the difficulty of finding accurate records about such a spectacular rate of growth in a short time frame, the figures presented here account for only those African Americans counted in the official census for the cities of Berkeley, Oakland, Richmond, and San Francisco.  See also tables 1 and 2.

15.  Johnson, *Negro War Worker in San Francisco*, 7, 16–17.  See, especially, Johnson, *The Second Gold Rush*, and Lemke-Santangelo, *Abiding Courage*, and the works cited in note 11 above.

16.  Watkins, *We Also Serve*, 25.  The *A Word to the New Men in the National Union of Marine Cooks & Stewards*, CIO, *Delegate's Handbook*, MCS *Officers' Report*, and other pamphlets and materials on the National Union of Marine Cooks and Stewards are in Papers of the National Union of Marine Cooks and Stewards, Ephemera Collection, Labor Archives and Research Center, San Francisco State University [hereafter cited as SFSU Archives].

17.  Watkins, *We Also Serve*, 5; Osborne, Interview, 69.

18.  The Department of Labor survey is quoted in Lemke-Santangelo, *Abiding Courage*, 108; the other historian is Broussard, *Black San Francisco*, 152.  See also, Sheila Tropp Lichtman, "Women at Work, 1941–1945: Wartime Employment in the San Francisco Bay Area" (Ph.D. diss.,

University of California, Davis, 1981); Karen Tucker Anderson, "Last Hired, First Fired: Black Women Workers during World War II," *Journal of American History* 69 (June 1982); Johnson, *The Second Gold Rush*, 46, 48; and the images in *Selections from the Henry J. Kaiser Pictorial Collection*, BANC PIC 1983.017–019, 027—PIC, The Bancroft Library, University of California, Berkeley. Watkins, *We Also Serve*, 39, 3; the information on Mattie Jackson is from a folder from Box 1993/070, International Ladies Garment Workers Union, San Francisco Joint Board Records, 1931–1969, SFSU Archives.

19. Archibald, *Wartime Shipyard*, 60–61; Quotation is from Johnson, *Negro War Worker in San Francisco*, 68, 61–75. See also, Brown, "The Impact of War Worker Migration," 174–77.

20. Williams, "Reflections of a Longtime Black Family in Richmond," 48. For other stories of the migrants' housing difficulties, see Johnson, *The Second Gold Rush*, esp. Chp. 4; Lemke-Santangelo, *Abiding Courage*, esp. Chp. 3; Johnson *The Negro War Worker in San Francisco*, 20–33; and Brown, "The Impact of War Worker Migration," 178–80. White San Franciscan is quoted in Johnson, *The Negro War Worker in San Francisco*, 32; Ruth Gracon is quoted in Lemke-Santangelo, *Abiding Courage*, 67.

21. The most comprehensive study of the Port Chicago disaster is Robert L. Allen, *The Port Chicago Mutiny* (New York: Warner Books, 1989). The quotation from the naval officer is on pgs. 70–71.

22. Archibald, *Wartime Shipyard*, 58–99; quotations are from 65, 75. In all, the attitudes demonstrated by the white workers conform to patterns evident in southern society as a whole in the late nineteenth and early twentieth centuries. For an overview of racial attitudes in the Jim Crow South, see Joel Williamson, *The Crucible of Race: Black-White Relations in the American South since Emancipation* (New York: Oxford University Press, 1984).

23. Toronto Cannaday Marshall, Interview by Jesse J. Warr, 5 October 1978, transcript, San Francisco African American Historical and Cultural Society, Research Library and Archives, 37; Alberga quoted in Daniels, *Pioneer Urbanites*, 171; Seale, Interview, n.p.

24. Alley, Interview, 51; Alma Brooks, Interview, 14.

25. J. Alfred Smith, *Thus Far by Faith: A Study of Historical Backgrounds and the First Fifty Years of the Allen Temple Baptist Church* (Oakland: Color Art Press, 1973), 32; Moore, "The Black Community in Richmond," Chp. 5; Calbert, Interview, 55; Osborne, Interview, 71.

26. Alma Brooks, Interview, 16; Osborne, Interview, 70. For a provocative discussion on the power of southern cuisine and how kitchens became

focal points in migrant homes, see Lemke-Santangelo, *Abiding Courage*, Chp. 5.

27.  Watkins, *We Also Serve*, 67; Moore, "The Black Community in Richmond," esp. Chp. 5; Johnson, *The Second Gold Rush*, 138–40, 240; Angelou, *I Know Why the Caged Bird Sings*, 174–75; Allen J. Matusow, *The Unraveling of America: A History of Liberalism in the 1960s* (New York: Harper & Row, 1984), Chp. 10.

28.  Marshall, Interview, 37; Alley, Interview, 51–53.  See also, Williams, "Reflections of a Longtime Black Family in Richmond," 103–04; Broussard, *Black San Francisco*, 180–92.

29.  According to Marilynn S. Johnson in her study *The Second Gold Rush*, the majority of white wartime workers also came from the states of the Old Southwest.  The intensity of their distaste for working with and living near African Americans is well chronicled in Archibald, *Wartime Shipyard*.

30.  Johnson, *Second Gold Rush*, 210 passim; Osborne, Interview, 69, 71; Calbert, Interview, 55; United States Department of Commerce, *Seventeenth Census*, 1950, 272, 420.

31.  Alma Brooks, Interview, 12; Anderson, "Last Hired, First Fired," 97. Joe William Trotter, Jr., in his study of black migrants in Milwaukee, Wisconsin, during the first Great Migration of blacks in the WWI era, argues that the "proletarianization" of African American workers was a major watershed in black history.  He points to the entrance of black workers in industrial employment as a major break from the long history of low-skill, low-wage agricultural labor that typified black life in the South.  While Trotter is correct to note the new issues that African Americans faced with the transition to urban life in the North, and especially the possibility to obtain manufacturing jobs, his suggestion that this marks a major shift in black history is exaggerated.  Most African Americans, either during the WWI era or the WWII era, had relatively brief periods of employment in high-paying, skilled, industrial jobs.  When the immediate labor crises caused by the two world wars ended, blacks were ushered out of northern and western factories with all deliberate speed.  The failure of "proletarianization" to really improve the economic conditions of African Americans, not to mention the absence of a truly interracial labor movement, did ultimately contribute to a change in the Black Freedom Struggle, but not in the way that Trotter suggests.  See, his *Black Milwaukee*; and Thomas J. Sugrue, "The Structures of Urban Poverty: The Reorganization of Space and Work in Three Periods of American History," in *The "Underclass" Debate: Views from*

*History*, ed. Michael B. Katz (Princeton: Princeton University Press, 1993). Lichtman, "Women at Work," 3 passim; Lemke-Santangelo, *Abiding Courage*, 124 passim.

32.  Record, "Willie Stokes at the Golden Gate," 187; Calbert, Interview, 55; "Church Members Rescue Evicted Family of 6 from Slum Conditions," *Sun-Reporter*, 13 November 1954, 1.  See also Eaton, "In Search of the California Dream," 49.

33.  Alley, Interview, 51; Johnson, *Second Gold Rush*, 214.

34.  J. Maceo Green, "The Weekly Report," *Sun-Reporter*, 23 January 1954, 12.

35.  Johnson, *Second Gold Rush*, 151–81; Moore, "The Black Community in Richmond," 106–15; Brown, "The Impact of War Worker Migration," 183–87; Archibald, *Wartime Shipyard*, 62; Reginald Wood, "Gambling Clubs Fleece People," *Sun-Reporter*, 30 June 1951, 1, 15.

36.  "Juveniles Riot in Richmond," *Sun-Reporter*, 9 January 1954, 1; "7 Youths Arrested at Riot Scene," *Sun-Reporter*, 16 January 1954, 1.

CHAPTER 2

# Crisis

The war left as quickly as it had come.  With the fall of Germany and Japan in 1945, Uncle Sam put down his sword, called home the troops, and silenced the war factories.  The tide of humanity that had washed into the Bay Area, however, did not recede.  Some of the white and black migrants did return home, but most of the wartime workers had come to stay.  Their presence meant that natives could not return to the lives they had known and that, together, the newcomers and old-timers would have to fashion a new social fabric from the threads left behind by the war juggernaut.  The euphoria of the war years quickly wore off, and residents of the San Francisco Bay Area were left breathless in its aftermath.  The crisis of war faded, and whites and blacks alike faced the even more formidable challenges of carrying on their lives amidst the buzz of everyday tedium and strain.  For African Americans especially, the struggle against fascism and totalitarianism abroad would become much less formidable in the face of the obstacles they confronted at home.

By the mid-1950s, racial boundaries in the Bay Area had been clearly redrawn, and minorities found themselves in worse straits than they had been in before the war.  West Oakland's African American community, for example, was the center of black life in the Bay Area during its heyday after the 1906 earthquake.  Until the Second World War, West Oakland bustled with a growing population, a dynamic black leadership, and a healthy dose of businesses and industries.  Yet by 1955, one observer noted that "West Oakland is sick with a nearly fatal illness. Her streets are dirty and deserted, her businesses failing rapidly, her leaders scattered...and her children growing up without the physical requirements for community pride, inspiration and hope which can result in a sense of personal achievement." West Oakland mirrored a trend occurring throughout African American communities in the urban North and West. In the postwar years, urban centers that had witnessed dramatic booms during the 1940s sank into decline. Emerging post-industrial economies, rising unemployment, crumbling infrastructures, deteriorating housing, rampant crime, failing educational systems, and exhausted welfare networks plagued cities across the United States, and the urban hubs of the Bay Area were no exception.[1]

These burdens would fall most heavily upon the shoulders of the generation of young blacks who would come to maturity nearly two decades after their parents had made the fateful wartime trip to the industrial centers of the North and West. According to social scientists Peter Marris and Martin Rein, "a third of them were soon to be out of school and out of work — a whole generation of misfits, driven from the poverty of the South to the more humiliating frustrations of an urban ghetto." This generation of young African Americans, however, would be more resourceful than Marris and Rein allow, and the conflicts they generated in the San Francisco Bay Area would blossom into a wholesale Black Revolution. Confronted by unemployment, poor housing, segregated schools, and police brutality, these young blacks rejected the social system that placed them at or near the bottom and they abandoned the tactics of non-violence for the politics of rage. This "generation of misfits" would shake the foundations of the Establishment and change the meaning of "blackness" in America.[2]

## DEPROLETARIANIZATION AND UNEMPLOYMENT

Major cities throughout the United States retooled their economies following the Second World War. The immediate drop-off in wartime production signaled a longer decline in heavy manufacturing in the United States, and large cities shifted their economic bases to accommodate an increasingly technology-driven marketplace. The industries that did remain followed the white working classes to suburban industrial parks that sprang up on the outskirts of former manufacturing strongholds like Chicago, Detroit, and Oakland. The pattern of "white flight" from inner cities that occurred throughout the urban North and West following World War II was part of a larger realignment of American society and was a response both to postwar opportunities and to the demographic and social shifts that had happened during the war itself. The GI Bill and Federal Housing Authority loans coupled with massive consumer spending and a vigorous economy allowed many working-class whites access to home ownership in growing suburbs with good schools, paved sidewalks, and community little league baseball teams. A more sinister side to the dramatic changes in urban landscapes was the desire of many white Americans to turn back the clock and regain the racial homogeneity that had characterized many manufacturing centers before the Second World War. In the San Francisco Bay Area in particular, working-class whites had long dominated most high-skill, high-wage industrial jobs, and they resented the influx of hundreds of thousands of African American competitors.[3]

The burdens of this postwar economic and demographic realignment fell, of course, upon the feared, scorned, and hated black working-class families who had "invaded" the cities during the war. As inner-city factories closed or relocated to the surrounding suburbs, blacks in San Francisco and the East Bay were left in the burned-out city centers where economic activity had slowed to a crawl. U.S. military bases closed or laid-off thousands of civilian workers, and shipbuilding plants trimmed their payrolls and most had shut their doors for good by the mid-1950s. One Urban League official later noted that

> the problems of [black] workers were manifold...in 1946. A large segment of industrial opinion was proclaiming that the Negro would be returning to his former place of residence, [and] many labor unions were withdrawing their work permits to Negroes and closing their memberships to these workers. To greatly aggravate the problem, federal installations were cutting back on their personnel requirements. Far too many Negro workers were being

made victims of this procedure without recognition of tenure, employment stability and job performance.

Blacks who had come to the Bay Area in search of the highly touted war-industry jobs were left bitter and disillusioned, and the promise of racial uplift and the hopes of thousands of "bootstrappers" were left crushed under the rubble of empty promises.[4]

Willie Stokes, a young former tenant farmer from Arkansas, typified the legions of desperate black workers. Stokes enjoyed a $10-a-day job at the Kaiser Shipyards until the end of the war. His affair with skilled, industrial labor was short lived, however, and like many other black workers, he lost his prized position in the shipbuilding industry in 1945. By June 1946, he had found a job unloading trucks, sweeping, and cleaning vats for a chemical company located just outside of Richmond. Here, his unskilled position won him $6.40 a day. Despite the dramatic pay cut, Stokes was pleased just to be working. One year later, he was unemployed and had been for six months. Few companies in Richmond were hiring and competition among white and black workers for the available jobs was increasingly fierce. Unions locked out black workers and employers tenaciously held on to stereotypes that painted black workers as lazy, deceitful, and stupid. Throughout the East Bay, the demise of the wartime shipyards meant hard times for thousands of African American workers. By 1950, black women in Richmond suffered from the highest unemployment rate of any segment of the industrial working class, and their 39% jobless rate was three times that of white women. African American men fared little better, and their 25% unemployment rate was more than double that of their white counterparts. As white laborers reaped the benefits of the outburst of consumer spending in the 1950s, black laborers in the inner city were once again reminded of their inferior status in the American economy and in American society.[5]

Throughout the 1950s, the disparity between black and white workers worsened. The national figures are startling. In 1940, black unemployment was 20% higher than white unemployment, but by 1953, it was 71% higher, and by 1963, the gap had grown to 112%. In 1959, as a consequence of their higher rates of unemployment, African Americans only earned 52% of what white Americans earned. By 1960, the employment problem had become a major crisis for several predominantly black communities in the Bay Area. In Hunter's Point, for example, black male unemployment stood at 12.2%, which was nearly double the unemployment rate for white males. The jobless rate for black women was even higher, and the median family income for African Americans in Hunter's Point was a measly $4,639, which was barely above the federal government's standard $4,000 poverty line. Those black men who were fortunate enough to find jobs in Hunter's Point rarely held skilled positions. The leading Bay Area black newspaper reported that only 500 black men were skilled workers, whereas 840 were semi-skilled, 530 were service industry workers, and 950 were common laborers. While white working- and middle-class incomes took off during the post-war economic boom, black incomes lagged far behind. Whites in the Bay Area, who instead enjoyed the prosperity of the Ike Age, largely ignored the economic crisis that black Americans faced. The ignorance of most whites prompted one black journalist to note: "This may come as a shock to some whites who are in touch with few Negroes in their daily lives, but there is not a Negro in the Western sections of the United States who is not conversant with the fact that jobs for Negroes just do not exist in plentiful numbers."[6]

The paucity of jobs was worsened by the discrimination that could be found in most Bay Area workplaces throughout the 1950s and 1960s. Black leaders and civil rights organizations in San Francisco and the East Bay, especially the West Coast branch of the National Association for the Advancement of Colored People (NAACP), agitated for a Fair Employment Practices Act from the war years, and they frequently pressured employers and white political leaders to embrace fair and non-discriminatory hiring policies. During testimony in front of the San Francisco Board of Supervisors in 1951, witnesses complained of bias in the hiring and promoting of African American workers in local businesses. They called for a legal ordinance requiring non-discrimination to replace the "voluntary plan" that relied on the good will of businesses to comply with fair hiring guidelines. The complainants blasted white business owners who refused to hire blacks, requested white workers only, or used minority workers as a tool against lily-white unions to lower wages. One witness recounted the story of a young black man who had been employed at the Foster Corporation commissary. Hired as a cook's helper, the young black worker quickly mastered his job and then began to take on the additional tasks of a cook, yet he still received the lower wages of a helper. When the union learned of this practice, they protested and filed a claim that would force the Foster Corporation to raise the black man's salary and pay him for the additional work he had already completed. The company responded by revoking the black worker's extra duties and returning him to the role of cook's helper. "In other words," noted the witness, "the employer was happy to allow the man to do the work indefinitely, provided it was not necessary to give him the wages or recognize his ability openly.... [I]t is indicative of the practice in the [food-services] industry and especially in the chain restaurants."[7]

African American shipyard workers voiced similar complaints of employer bias throughout the 1950s. Jobbie L. Johnson, a black worker at the U.S. Navy's Hunter's Point shipyard, charged his white supervisors with failing to promote black workers and assigning white foremen to oversee the work of all-black teams of laborers. During his long tenure at the shipyard from 1943 until 1957, Johnson mastered many jobs and he demonstrated the ability to lead crews in dangerous repair work, but his attempts at promotion were always stymied. He recalled one particularly perilous assignment where he and a team of four other men removed a twelve-ton propeller from a ship. "I was the only man in the group that knew this particular job," Johnson noted. The leading rigger "was a white man name Mr. Taylor. He was put in charge of the other four colored men after which he admitted he didn't know how to pull the wheel.... [T]he supervisor, Mr. Fred Lyons, didn't know so they put me in the lead to get the work done. This I did." After the job, however, Johnson did not receive a promotion or a subsequent increase in pay or responsibility. Such incidents were unfortunately commonplace in the Bay Area's shipyards, and they reflected a much larger trend that characterized the employment market of the region as a whole. A survey conducted in 1958, for example, showed that while most businesses in San Francisco had adopted a merit hiring system, few of the firms actually made sure that the policies were fairly enacted. Essentially, they paid lip service to their claims of equal opportunity. Many firms had no black employees, and those that did usually concentrated them in low-wage, low-skill jobs, like janitorial services. Likewise, few companies had blacks in public service or sales positions.[8]

Despite the Bay Area's history of militant labor activism, most unions in San Francisco and Oakland were unresponsive to the needs and complaints of African American workers. As more and more African American laborers fell out of the ranks of the industrial proletariat in the 1950s, unions closed the doors behind them and returned to their largely lily-white status of the prewar era. Black laborers remained segregated into powerless auxiliaries of the main unions, and white labor leaders continued to favor other white workers in employment, placement, and promotion decisions. White labor leaders began segregating black workers into auxiliaries during the Second World War, and they designed the separate groups to be completely subordinate to the existing white unions. Although African American workers resented this arrangement and agitated for full equality in the unions, the white workers doggedly held onto the privileges that their racial identity afforded them. African American leaders sued several Bay Area unions, including the International Brotherhood of Boilermakers, Iron Shipbuilders and Helpers of America, to force them to open their ranks to black workers. Several prominent labor lawyers, including Thurgood Marshall, represented Joseph James and more than one thousand other black workers who refused to join the Boilermakers' segregated black auxiliary, and they argued that "the Boilermakers are trying to force the Negroes, under penalty of losing their jobs, to join an auxiliary A-41 which is not in fact a labor organization but is a racket and a scheme and device whereby the Boilermakers extract tribute in the form of 'dues' and 'initiation' fees from Negroes without giving them membership rights or other privileges in the union, although white workers who pay initiation fees and dues have rights and privileges in the union." Despite African American workers' attempts to break down the barriers to union membership, the exclusionary policies of these established organizations remained largely intact throughout the 1950s and 1960s.[9]

African American laborers in the segregated auxiliaries paid full union dues yet they often had to work under more stringent rules of conduct, had inferior health and insurance benefits, and had no voice in union elections.  Shortly after the end of the war, Lucius Winn, an African American worker at the Moore Dry Dock Company in Oakland, complained to the NAACP that his union discriminated against black workers when it gave work assignments and that "when it come to the showdown they work the colred [sic] 2 or 3 days and lay off.  Then when they send more men it will be all white.  We are Americans.  We all fought for the same thing.  We all pay union dues."  Winn's complaints were well known by most black workers in the Bay Area, and many African Americans had to wait more than a decade before the walls separating the auxiliaries and the main unions would begin to crumble.  Black musicians had run the segregated Local 669 of the San Francisco Musicians Union since 1946, yet they operated under the constitution and wage scales of the white Local 6.  The state of California finally sued the white union under the Fair Employment Practices Law, and the two unions merged in 1960.  Although a few Communist-oriented unions affiliated with the Congress of Industrial Organizations (CIO) did protest lily-white unions in the shipping industries, African American workers were largely left to their own devices to fight against workplace discrimination and what amounted to union fraud.[10]

Workers and activists who dared speak out against the white unions or tried to integrate their ranks faced violent reprisals and scathing verbal attacks.  In 1942, members of the Amalgamated Association of Street, Electric Railway, and Motor Coach Employees of America, Division 518, apparently assaulted and seriously injured one white man, Spencer Rogers, and threatened several of his co-workers when they attempted to break the union's color barrier by training a black man, Audley Cole, to work as a motorman on the Municipal Railway in San Francisco.  When several thugs ambushed Rogers on the corner of Van Ness Avenue and Market Street and struck him on back of his head, the other white workers quickly fell into line and all talk of integrating the union became a whisper.  A decade later, black workers feared a resurgence of labor violence if the Seafarers International Union (SIU), a lily-white organization affiliated with the conservative American Federation of Labor (AFL), won its bid to become the bargaining agent before the National Labor Relations Board (NLRB) for stewards department employees on the West Coast. Many observers feared that the SIU hoped to eventually force all African American workers out of the industry. The leftist International Longshoremen's and Warehousemen's Union (ILWU) also desired to represent stewards before the NLRB, and the union's paper warned black workers that "the SIU...has not dispatched a Negro to any job in the past 40 years. The ILWU constitution forbids any kind of discrimination because of race or national origin. The issue is vital because approximately 1,700 of the 2,000 jobs in the stewards department are held by Negroes or Orientals. The objective of the SIU is to replace these workers and make West Coast ships all white." In a similar vein, Russel Ryvers, a black steward for forty years, remembered the hostility between black and white marine workers during the 1920s and 1930s, and he told stories of the whites using violence to try to drive black workers off of the ships. White union leaders who opposed integration also engaged in a verbal war with their opponents, and they often charged that their foes were Communist sympathizers. Harry Lundberg, head of the Sailors Union of the Pacific, desperately tried to keep black workers out of his union in the 1950s, and he frequently red-baited those activists who pressed for equal membership and equal opportunities for minority workers. Rather than being champions of the rights of all workers, unions in the San Francisco Bay Area were largely enclaves of white working-class power.[11]

During the postwar years, unemployment and deindustrialization were major problems for blacks in the Bay Area. The jobless rate rose steadily throughout the 1950s and 1960s, especially for black teenagers, and the outlook for many blacks trapped in postindustrial inner cities was grim. The dramatic economic changes that occurred in the cities of San Francisco, Richmond, and Oakland in the postwar era and the continuing history of discrimination against black workers created a crisis situation among black communities in the Bay Area. The dream of industrial jobs that had lured the migrants to northern California had turned into a nightmare by the mid-1950s, and mounting frustrations among black workers and the growing legions of the black unemployed would not forever be held in check.

## HOUSING PROBLEMS AND URBAN RENEWAL

In addition to the discriminatory policies that kept blacks in the Bay Area out of highly skilled and lucrative positions in the postwar economy, a new system of residential segregation developed after the war that concentrated black populations into small, inner-city neighborhoods that were characterized by deteriorating housing, the absence of public services, and segregated and inferior schools. By the mid-1950s, urban ghettos had formed around historically black-majority neighborhoods and also around the numerous "temporary" wartime housing structures that became public housing units in the late 1940s. Unable to purchase homes in the expanding white suburbs on the outskirts of Berkeley, Richmond, Oakland, and San Francisco, and segregated in the most dilapidated public housing units in the Bay Area, African Americans quickly found themselves locked into neighborhoods that were shut off economically, politically, and socially from the larger society around them. In 1956, Franklin H. Williams, secretary-counsel for the West Coast Region of the NAACP, noted that "builders, contractors, realtors and lending institutions still, with rare exception, form a solid phalanx against the Negro and other minority groups on the West Coast." Although the low economic status of African Americans was somewhat responsible for their ghettoization, the engine of residential segregation had been cast in the red-hot furnace of racial hatred.[12]

African American customers were shut out of the Bay Area postwar housing boom. Developers refused to sell their homes to black customers, real estate agents discouraged African American clients from viewing homes in white neighborhoods, and white home owners threatened and intimidated any blacks who sought to purchase houses in all-white areas. In 1952, for example, white residents of Richmond burned a cross on the lawn of a black GI who had recently purchased a home in previously all-white Rollingwood. The San Francisco Urban League tracked the problem of residential segregation from the end of the war, and by the mid-1950s, its officials considered the lack of housing to be a major crisis for African American families. Jacqueline Myles Smith, the community relations secretary of the San Francisco Urban League, noted that "although the production of new homes in San Francisco has been tremendous, only a negligible amount has been made available to the Negro. It is therefore not surprising that the Negro has found his major housing outlet in existing structures in older parts of the city and in temporary war housing."[13]

The most public example of white San Franciscans' aversion to having black neighbors struck the Bay Area in the fall of 1957. Willie Mays, the star centerfielder for the San Francisco Giants, met spirited resistance when he tried to purchase a home on Maraloma Drive in the lily-white Sherwood Heights district. White residents in the elite neighborhood tried to convince the white homeowner, Walter Gnesdiloff, not to sell his house to Mays. In an attempt to save face for his beleaguered city, San Francisco Mayor George Christopher quickly offered his apologies and invited Mr. and Mrs. Mays to stay at his home until they found housing, but in the end, Mays was able to purchase the home. Shortly after the baseball hero closed the deal on the house, area newspapers reported that Mays's purchase price had been grossly inflated over the real value of the home. The Village Realty Company had listed the home for $32,500, but Mays paid $37,500 in cash for the house. The NAACP and other civil rights groups denounced the deal and they used the case to illustrate the patterns of segregation and discrimination that existed throughout northern California. The San Francisco *Sun-Reporter* compared the Mays case to that of another black professional who paid $26,500 for a house on Los Palmas Drive that had been offered to a white customer for $19,500.[14]

The problem of residential segregation persisted into the 1960s, and a telephone survey conducted by the Japanese American Citizens' League in February 1962 found that discrimination had even infected the purportedly liberal haven of Berkeley. The Citizens' League called Berkeley property owners to see if they would rent or sell to black buyers, and the League discovered that prejudice ran deep in the East Bay. Out of 126 managers or owners with apartments or rooms for rent, only twenty-three agreed to rent to African Americans; none of the eight white homeowners would sell to black customers. The Citizens Committee to the Community Welfare Commission announced similar findings in its 1962 report,

"Housing Discrimination in Berkeley," and the committee included testimony from property owners who claimed that other tenants or neighbors would be upset and would leave the area if they rented to African Americans. In one case, "one manager told |us| she didn't rent to 'Negroes or beatniks.'" Across the bay, African Americans seeking quality rental property faced similar challenges. Larry J. Logan complained to the San Francisco Branch of the NAACP that one of his friends, a professional black woman, was having difficulty finding an apartment "because she is Negro and she has been rebuffed many times previously in her attempts to locate housing that suits her." In 1962, a white member of the Congress of Racial Equality (CORE) reported that when she went to a rental agency to find an apartment, she overheard an agent explaining to a white couple why there were no "For Rent" signs in good neighborhoods in San Francisco. The agent said: "I'll tell you what the problem is. There are so many Negroes moving in, and people don't want them. You know, you can't say no in California, it's against the law. You can't say no so you have to figure out some other means, you know, another gimmick."[15]

African Americans quickly tired of this white resistance and racism and they pushed harder to break open the closed housing market. In 1961, for example, Willie Brown, an African American attorney and the future mayor of San Francisco, led a sit-in outside a model home in the Forest Knolls subdivision. Developers had refused to show the home to prospective black buyers. The Bay Area Catholic Interracial Council censured the developer, the Standard Building Company, and the NAACP passed a resolution supporting Brown's sit-in. The following year, the Bay Area's leading black newspaper, the *Sun-Reporter*, ran another story on the discriminatory policies of local developers. Bradrick Developers, owned by Bradford Ricks, refused to sell a home in its new 28 Palms development to Selton Price, a black Korean War veteran and an auto mechanic. Although Price and his family owned a home on Deerwood Street in Fremont, they were refused the opportunity to move to the new suburban subdivision. A real estate agent representing Bradrick Developers told the Prices that "he had 250 new houses to sell in the tract, and he would have small chances of selling any of them if he sold to a Negro family." Mrs. Price wryly noted that the family had just returned from a vacation trip to Alabama, and she felt whites in California were worse than the southerners she had met.[16]

In the arena of public housing, African Americans fared little better. Blacks had long known that they would need every available tool to fight against the indifferent and hostile public housing bureaucracies in the Bay Area. Overlooked and ignored when they first arrived in the crush of wartime migrants, African Americans were assigned to overcrowded, all-black housing units in Berkeley, Oakland, Richmond, and San Francisco. Officials refused to place black families into all-white units at the war's end, when whites were moving out of public housing and into newly constructed homes in suburbia. Not until almost all of the white families had left a complex were African Americans allowed to move in. Furthermore, the black housing units were often in disrepair, and officials were slow to respond to maintenance complaints. When the government-owned temporary housing projects were transferred to local housing authorities after the war, the municipal bureaucrats were even less responsive to the needs of African American residents. When the NAACP appealed to the Oakland Housing Authority Commission to open more units to black families, the Commission responded that "Negroes have been given a share of housing out of porportion [sic] to their numbers; that Negroes should appreciate the fact that integration must be a gradual process and that the Authority has given a quota of housing to Negroes." In Berkeley, the Codornices Village public housing development was built during World War II to house factory workers, but it never measured up to state or federal specifications due to the strains of wartime need. After the war, its mostly black population was dislocated as Berkeley public officials moved quickly to rid their community of a large public housing project. Without seriously trying to find new homes for the residents of Codornices Village, the bureaucrats signed the demolition orders and the projects were leveled by 1956. Despite help from other welfare agencies, black families found it very difficult to relocate since they did not have access to adequate home loans, few could buy new houses in the segregated, all-white suburbs, and many of them were not able to gain full-time employment and save enough money to make the move.  Although the Community Welfare Commission later concluded that the housing officials had acted correctly and justified the decision by claiming that living conditions had much improved for the residents despite higher housing costs, they essentially admitted that they had done little to help the low-income residents survive the strain of relocation: "In the main, families helped themselves.  They made their own choices."  This abdication of responsibility by public officials for the welfare of the poor was only one example in a long history of neglect.[17]

The debate over open housing, both private and public, came to a head in 1964, with the passage of Proposition 14.  Conservative groups initiated the referendum to counter recent victories by civil rights groups and African American leaders, especially California Assemblyman William Byron Rumford, in the struggle against segregated housing.  Rumford and his allies were responsible for the "Rumford Fair Housing Bill" of 1963, which prohibited discrimination against minorities in the sale and rental of housing.  Soon after the passage of this civil rights legislation, various real estate organizations and conservative politicos organized a public campaign to offer a referendum to California voters to decide the fate of "choice" in the sale or rental of private property.  The California Real Estate Association noted in a propaganda pamphlet that the Rumford Bill was a violation of the rights of the Golden State's citizenry, and the association concluded that "such control of private property by the State is what distinguishes the Communist form of government from our own system.  The Communist approach assumes that public welfare always takes precedence over individual desires." White Californians responded to this call to protect their liberties, and in 1964, they voted to uphold their sacred right to discriminate. The leading black Bay Area newspaper editorialized that "the passage of Proposition 14 is no shock to California Negroes.  Since early childhood, Negro Californians have known that the average white Californian does not really believe in democracy with its emphasis on equality, justice and individual freedom.  A majority of white people are only concerned about the freedom which permits them to discriminate against non-whites."  Although Proposition 14 would later be declared unconstitutional by the courts, the law slowed down progress on the open housing front, delayed federal moneys for important public housing projects, and added to the bitter legacy of distrust and hostility that separated black and white communities as much as the imaginary lines that real estate agents and home sellers drew around their property.[18]

One of the greatest challenges of the 1950s and 1960s that confronted those African Americans who depended upon public housing was the fiasco of urban renewal. Spurred by the federal housing acts of 1949 and 1954, urban renewal quickly gained favor among urban planners, city bureaucrats, and urban politicians who were eager to revive crumbling city centers and rebuild the tax base in cities across the United States. Urban renewal demanded the "relocation" of the inner-city poor to new public housing projects that were theoretically going to be cost-efficient, sanitary, and pleasant dwellings. Unfortunately, few of the planned public housing projects were ever completed, although in many cities bulldozers leveled vast amounts of the inferior housing that was literally the only resource for thousands of low-income residents. Having no where else to turn, poor families had to either crowd further into substandard housing adjacent to the units they had vacated or flee the city in search of affordable housing elsewhere. According to some of its critics, "urban renewal became, for the city's poor, a cynical expropriation in the interests of business, real estate, and the tax base."[19]

In the San Francisco Bay Area, African Americans suffered disproportionately at the hands of urban renewal planners. In San Francisco and Oakland, black neighborhoods were targeted for urban renewal programs that would replace the temporary wartime housing units and older private housing with high-rise apartments, office towers, and retail shopping centers. In 1957, Oakland received a $2 million grant from the federal government to clear 250 blocks of slum housing in the western part of the city. Unfortunately, the city never developed a program to deal with the families who would have to be relocated because of such projects. In 1958, San Francisco city officials announced that more than 8,600 people would be displaced by an urban renewal project in the predominantly black Western Addition. According to Julia Smith, senior relocation specialist for the Redevelopment Agency, the city planned to "get people rehoused in better homes than what they

had in the blighted houses" that filled the Western Addition.  The
Redevelopment Agency estimated that 91% of the people to be
relocated did not own their own homes, and 98% of them would
need rental housing that cost $50 per month or less.  Although
Joseph Alioto, chairman of the San Francisco Redevelopment
Agency and future mayor of the city, assured community leaders
and residents that they would be moved to better dwellings, bitter
feelings would hinder later efforts at urban renewal as public housing residents felt cheated by the city.[20]

Charges of corruption quickly surfaced in the Western Addition
redevelopment plan, and African Americans saw through the promises of better homes to the realities of graft, corruption, and greed.
As early as May 1958, the *Sun-Reporter* urged black homeowners in
the Western Addition to hold out for better prices on their property if they were unsatisfied with the offers made by the
Redevelopment Agency.  Suspicious of the intentions and actions
of the city government, the editor noted that the courts could set
fair selling prices if the owners and the Redevelopment Agency
could not agree on terms.  The paper's warnings seemed justified,
for in October 1958, Arthur J. O'Connor, an appraiser in the
Assessor's Office, was charged with conflict of interest since he and
some of his cronies, including Chief Administrative Officer Chester
R. MacPhee and Harold Ropers, had invested in slum property in
the Western Addition.  O'Connor and his friends speculated in the
Western Addition apparently in the hope of selling the condemned
properties to the city for a healthy profit.  Criticism of the Western
Addition redevelopment plan continued throughout the following
year, and Jack Morrison, a candidate for city supervisor, urged the
city to make sure that affordable housing was included in the project.  "At the present time the city has no settled plan for trying to
maintain reasonable rents in an area that was populated largely by
low- and middle-income families," he said.  "Though the
Redevelopment Agency is well aware of this problem, other divisions of the city government have not shown a proper interest in
it."[21]

By 1960, concern over redevelopment in the Western Addition
had grown, and a series of damning editorials appeared in the
*Californian* that denounced the project as a way for the rich to "wax

fat off the poor." The paper attacked the San Francisco city government for mismanaging the project, and it noted that "at a cost to
the taxpayers of $8 million (so far), a slum housing area has been
torn down, poor families have been thrown out, and a batch of
streamlined apartment houses designed for the upper one-third
income brackets are about to be erected by private contractors who
will reap fat profits at the city's expense. The project is being han-
dled with total disregard for lower and middle income groups, and
when it is completed rents will rise all over the city." Families
whose incomes fell below the poverty line were moved to the
already overcrowded Diamond Heights area as high-rise apartment
buildings with high-rise rents went up to serve wealthier patrons in
search of in-town dwellings. According to the *Californian*, "most of
the displaced moved into other slums on the fringes of the Western
Addition, thus perpetuating the nasty process and creating new
slums of a more crowded and nauseating nature than those from
which they came." Slum landlords raised rents on the dilapidated
buildings that were jammed to the rooftops with low-income tenants who could not afford to live elsewhere. Reflecting on the
urban renewal projects throughout the Bay Area, the NAACP concluded that redevelopment agencies had "consistently pursued a
policy of redeveloping areas which have a high percentage of non-
whites, but especially Negroes. While Negroes constitute only
eleven per cent of the population, seventy-two per cent of those
evicted in urban renewal projects are Negroes." It is no wonder
then that among African Americans, "urban renewal" became syn-
onymous with "Negro removal."[22]

Another urban renewal project slated for the African American
Hunter's Point district drew similar criticism. The population of
Hunter's Point had doubled between 1955 and 1965 due to urban
renewal projects and the destruction of low-income housing in
other San Francisco neighborhoods, and its overcrowded apartment buildings were fit prey for the officials of the San Francisco
Redevelopment Agency. Many of the black residents forced out of
the Western Addition by its urban renewal project resettled in
Hunter's Point. One disgruntled man recalled that the San
Francisco Housing Authority promised "that they were going to better the buildings and make conditions so as we could live in high

type apartment buildings. They did what they said they was goin' to do, they built them alright, but after they did, I couldn't afford to move in the things. I was staying with some friends, paying when I could to help out, but the rent cost about sixty dollars more, and, well, hell, we just couldn't cut it." Fears that similar projects in Hunter's Point would force all blacks out of San Francisco kept most residents against the idea of urban renewal. Skeptical African Americans mistrusted the intentions of the Housing Authority and the Redevelopment Agency, and many critics protested that most of the area's current black residents could not afford the higher rents of the new developments. One long-time resident suggested that the ideal location of Hunter's Point and its impressive view of the San Francisco skyline accounted for the whites' interest in the area. "Before the Housing Authority started kicking people out, you'd see big black Cadillacs come up to the hill on Sunday, and these fat old guys get out and look at the city, and then they'd smile like they were going to break their faces. It's no secret why the Housing Authority wants us out." Housing officials and urban renewal planners ignored the residents' protests, however, and the cranes and bulldozers wiped out block after block of minority housing. One puzzled white official, San Francisco Supervisor William Blake, offered the following heartless solution for the disgruntled residents of the Western Addition and Hunter's Point: "Let them go — Let them live in Oakland. Maybe they will be happier."[23]

As unlikely as the idea of blacks being made happier by going to Oakland seems, it was made even more absurd by the controversial redevelopment projects underway in that city. Although the Oakland Redevelopment Agency announced in December 1958, that it opposed residential segregation, it did much to further ghettoize African Americans in the East Bay. The agency urged white Oaklanders to open the housing market to all minorities, but it did relatively little to ensure that blacks displaced by redevelopment projects would indeed have someplace else to go. Urban planners in the Redevelopment Agency hoped to renovate the predominantly black areas of West Oakland through their "Project Acorn." Despite its benign name, Project Acorn would grow an entire forest of problems. Targeting an area of generally well-kept African American-owned homes and apartment buildings, Project Acorn, according to its critics, did nothing to remove the real slums in West Oakland that were filled with homes that had boarded-up windows, trash-filled yards, and tenants crammed into every nook and cranny. Black residents in the target area had no desire to sell their homes, and they argued that the 1949 Federal Housing Act required that they first be given the opportunity to take out loans to improve their properties. Homeowners despaired of getting a fair price from the Oakland city government, and many felt that since they were retired and living off their pensions they were too old to take on a new mortgage for another home. Suspicious of the intentions of the city leaders and developers pushing for the project, many African American residents concluded that the program was designed to remove them from an area that was close to downtown Oakland and that would make an excellent shopping district and a fine place for exclusive apartments and condominiums.[24]

Angry and fearful, black residents and business owners sued the city to try to stop the project. The United Taxpayers and Voters Union, which represented the residents in the lawsuit, had over 2,000 members and was supported by donations and monthly dues from members, Twist contests and other social gatherings organized by the women's auxiliary, and aid from local churches. Although Redevelopment Agency officials tried to quell the fears of black West Oakland residents, the Taxpayers and Voters Union and local business owners vowed to fight on. Their attempts were only partially successful, however, and in 1962, city workers rolled in with army-surplus Sherman tanks and bulldozers to level vast tracts of what had once been the Bay Area's most important African American community. Despite the developers promises, the land lay barren for several years until the city handed the project to an enterprising collection of black investors who finally arranged for low-income housing units to be built more than a half-decade after the inception of the project.[25]

The plans continued to unravel in the 1970s and 1980s, and the area around Project Acorn became a quagmire of poverty, drug abuse, petty crime, and murder, and it was the scene of the violent death of Black Panther leader Huey P. Newton in 1989. The battle over Project Acorn lasted until well into the 1990s, and the bitter taste it left in the mouths of black Oakland residents would linger

for many years. For several decades, West Oakland would deteriorate as urban renewal projects and the construction of the Bay Area
Rapid Transit System (BART), the Nimitz Freeway, and an United
States Postal Distribution Center ate away the heart of the old black
community and dispersed its citizens throughout the ghettos of the
East Bay. The gulf between the desires of the white urban planners
and city officials and the black homeowners and tenants throws
into sharp relief the social, political, and economic distances that
separated the races in the Bay Area.[26]

Years of miscommunication, broken promises, and segregationist policies added to African Americans' heavy burden of finding
affordable and decent housing. Locked out of much of the Bay Area
housing market because of the color of their skin, African
Americans struggled to build their communities and house their
families. The racist attitudes of white developers, real estate
agents, homeowners, and city officials conspired to drive black residents into closed ghettos or out of the cities altogether. Public
housing facilities were hardly a refuge, and blacks trapped within
their walls were subjected to constant ridicule and disdain from the
white majority. The fiasco of urban renewal further undermined the
self-sufficiency of African American communities, and the miscon-
ceived and poorly executed projects reduced the total amount of
affordable housing that was available for blacks in the Bay Area. By
the mid-1960s, the housing crisis had reached the boiling point,
and from the depths of these ghetto slums would arise a call for liberation.

## EDUCATION AND SEGREGATED SCHOOLS

African Americans' inferior position in Bay Area society was also
illustrated by the segregated schools found throughout the cities of
Berkeley, Oakland, Richmond, and San Francisco. Most of the
school segregation resulted from the residential separation of
blacks and whites, and white Bay Area residents fought doggedly to
maintain the *de facto* segregation caused by their insistence upon
neighborhood schools. While many black migrants hoped that the
education of their children would be much better in the urban West
than it had been in the rural South, the promise of western liberal-

ism proved to be more illusory than real, as in the cases of employment and housing.  Although the San Francisco *Sun-Reporter* would
hail the May 1954 *Brown v. Board of Education* decision as "the equiv-
alent of a second Emancipation Proclamation," blacks would face a
long struggle to integrate public schools in the Bay Area.  African
American calls for more integrated schools and the inclusion of
black history in elementary and secondary education echoed
throughout the 1950s, and by the early 1960s, African American civil
rights groups protested against and sued local school boards to
force them to undo the policies of *de facto* segregation that kept their
children locked into underfunded and inferior schools in San
Francisco and the East Bay.  Bay Area schools failed to help many
young blacks graduate from high school, and those who did stay
long enough to earn their diplomas found that they had often been
poorly trained and inadequately prepared for the tight urban job
market.[27]

A survey completed by Charles S. Johnson during 1943 revealed
that segregated educational facilities had long been the norm in
San Francisco.  Of the total school population of 26,687, African
Americans made up about five percent of the student body, or
1,432.  More than half of the black students in the San Francisco
school system, however, attended schools where over one-quarter
of the students were African American.  At Emerson Elementary,
black students made up nearly fifty percent of the total enrollment
of the school, and at Pacific Heights and Raphael Weill, they
accounted for about one-third of the schools' student bodies.  At
Girl's Junior High and Girl's High in the Fillmore District, black students accounted for about one in four of the total enrollment.  The
racial imbalance in San Francisco's schools did not dramatically
improve over the next two decades, and in 1962, Superintendent
Harold Spears admitted that residential segregation was responsible for the educational segregation in the city's neighborhood-
based schools.  He pointed in particular to the problems caused by
urban renewal projects in the Western Addition, and he noted that
"the clearance of property did not diminish the school population
in the area.  Two schools, the Benjamin Franklin Junior High and
the Raphael Weill Elementary are operating at capacity in the middle of this wasteland, and the John Swett Elementary [is] on its

edge." Just as African Americans were crowded into smaller and smaller neighborhoods, so were black children concentrated into fewer and fewer schools.[28]

Conditions across the bay in Oakland were not much better for African American students. Hostility greeted black students at the thresholds of East Bay schools, and on February 28, 1955, a race fight broke out at the noon recess between about forty black and white students at Castlemont High. The two groups of boys fought with rocks and knives in a vacant lot across from the school, and an "officer said some of the Negro boys revealed during the questioning that they felt the whites were trying to run them off the school grounds." In 1963, the United States Commission on Civil Rights reported on educational segregation in the All-American City. The commission found that out of a total of 64 elementary schools, 21 had more than 50% black enrollment, and twelve had more than 90% black enrollment. The pattern was similar in junior high schools, where in six of sixteen junior highs African Americans accounted for more than half of the schools' populations, and in four junior highs they were more than 90% of the student bodies. The same was true for the city's McClymonds High School, which had a student body consisting of 97% African Americans. African American teachers were almost exclusively stationed at schools with large enrollments of black students, and the whole situation suggested more than a casual relationship between desires for neighborhood schools and the fact of educational segregation.[29]

The city of Berkeley was more responsive to the needs of its black population and it was one of the few northern or western cities to peacefully integrate its schools in the 1960s, yet the limitations of its reforms highlight the obstacles that African Americans in the Bay Area faced in their efforts to gain access to equal education. By the late 1950s, African Americans accounted for nearly a third of Berkeley's public school enrollment, and by 1970, black students made up forty-five percent of the city's student body. The dramatic increase in the population of young African Americans in Berkeley resulted in overcrowding in the black neighborhood schools and calls for a redistribution of the school-age population to different facilities throughout the city. In December 1957, Americans for Democratic Action asked the Berkeley School Board to switch from its policy of geographically assigning children to schools, and the following month, the Berkeley NAACP made a similar request.  The school board appointed a committee of ten whites and four blacks to study the problem later that year.  In its benignly racist report, the committee often pointed to cultural and familial weaknesses in the black community to explain, in part, the poor performance of black children in Berkeley's schools. "Although there are Negro families in this City [sic] with an excellent educational background," the committee noted, "the brief schooling of many Negro parents importantly affects, on the average, the performance of their children, and the public schools here are confronted with many pupils who, because of home deficiency, are apt to encounter difficulty in school."  In October 1959, the board decided to adopt a "color blind" approach to hiring and promoting teachers and encouraged ethnic diversity in the classroom, but they did nothing to address the *de facto* segregation of the city's schools.  Protests by the Congress of Racial Equality (CORE) and the NAACP followed, and the two civil rights organizations issued reports denouncing Berkeley's segregated schools in the early 1960s.[30]

As throughout northern California's urban centers, residential segregation led to educational segregation in Berkeley's neighborhood schools.  In 1958, 18,000 of the city's African Americans lived in seven census tracts where the proportion of blacks was 34% or higher.  More than 4,500 African Americans lived in one tract, which was 91.5% black.  Consequently, 2,275 of the city's 2,682 black elementary-age children were in four of the city's seventeen schools. Nine of the other elementary schools had less than two percent black populations.  Lincoln Elementary had the highest concentration of black children, at 95%, and the three other elementary schools with large black enrollments had figures at 88%, 54%, and 43%.  At the junior high level, one school had only two percent African American enrollment, while two others had 57% and 39%. By the early 1960s, Berkeley's African American schoolchildren were effectively segregated into a few of the city's schools, and many critics began to question the direction of public education in Berkeley. Civil rights groups and concerned black citizens were alarmed when a report from the autumn of 1963 revealed that educational segregation in Berkeley was getting worse. In 1963, African American students accounted for about one-third of the district's school-age population. Berkeley had seventeen elementary schools, of which only three were considered integrated. Nine of the city's elementary schools were white majority, and five of the schools had between 62% and 97% black student populations. Incredibly, segregation at Lincoln Elementary actually increased in the five years since the previous student population report, as black students accounted for 97% of the school's total enrollment in 1963. The report noted that 6,968 of 8,811 black students attended segregated elementary schools and that they tested one year or more below their grade level on language achievement tests. Segregation also increased in the city's junior high schools. Burbank and Willard junior highs now had 76% and 46% black student bodies, respectively, and only five in one hundred students were black at the predominantly white Garfield Junior High. As in Oakland, African American teachers in Berkeley almost exclusively taught at black-majority schools.[31]

In 1964, the Berkeley School Board conducted a survey of public opinion to discover the support for and opposition to redrawing its school boundaries to ensure greater diversity in its schools. A slim majority of the city's whites accepted the idea, and an overwhelming number of blacks embraced the plan. Older, established white residents were more likely to oppose the plan, but they were in the minority, and the board went ahead with its desegregation project. One major hurdle that remained before African American residents, however, was the white public's dogged defense of "ability groupings" in the public schools. One white parent in favor of the ability groupings argued that "brighter children should not be brought down to the level of achievement of less bright children...." Another parent concluded that "eliminating them [the ability groupings] would neither benefit the slow nor the more advanced student. The latter would be left without challenge and the slow would have a very hard time to follow. Give special teaching to all children who need extra help — the integration will follow in time." The "ability groupings" system resulted, however, in the *de facto* segregation of white and black students within the same schools. According to one critic of the program, white students were more likely to be placed in the "advanced" classes as black students often filled the ranks of remedial courses and special education programs. "This solution suggests that 'time' will solve the problem," noted the crit- ic, "but how 'time' will do this is not indicated. That adults adhere to this belief is somewhat naive, since past history shows that unaided 'time' has a rather poor performance in the solution of social problems."[32]

Despite their limitations, however, Berkeley's reform efforts were much more impressive than those of neighboring cities. San Francisco and Oakland ignored the repeated calls for integrating black history into their schools' curriculum, yet the Association for the Study of Negro Life and History (ASNLH) continued to issue the demand for more openness through its annual "Negro History Week" each February. A few teachers had embraced the idea of allowing their black students to research the lives of famous black figures, and the interest such projects generated among all stu- dents led the ASNLH to call for further diversity in the classroom. Such small victories did not overshadow the continued problem of school segregation, however, and in 1962, thirty demonstrators par- ticipated in a CORE-sponsored all-night sit-in to protest plans to fill the new temporary Central Junior High School with sixty percent black students and forty percent white students. Black parents at the protest demanded more integration of the city's schools and improved conditions at predominantly black institutions.[33]

Throughout the Bay Area, African American students in segre- gated schools complained that white students were often treated better than blacks, that whites had more access to advanced cours- es, that whites were not punished as frequently or as severely as black students, and that whites dominated positions in student activities and leadership. The radical neighborhood newspaper, *Flatlands*, reported that Oakland schools disciplined black students at a much higher rate than their white counterparts, and they demanded reforms in a system where 753 black pupils had been suspended from school for behavioral problems in 1965. In San Francisco, one alarmed teacher complained to the NAACP that her colleagues at the black-majority Pelton Junior High School were often not trained in the subjects that they taught. She noted five cases of math teachers who had no formal college-level training in mathematics, and she claimed that these faculty had been "select-ed for skill in disciplining youngsters" rather than for their teaching qualifications. She argued that not only was such a situation alarming, but according to California law, it was illegal.[34]

In September 1962, both the NAACP and CORE issued reports denouncing segregation in San Francisco schools. The NAACP noted that seventeen elementary and two junior high schools had over sixty percent black student enrollment, and both the NAACP and CORE argued that district boundaries should be redrawn to ensure integration in the city's schools. The following month, the NAACP sued the San Francisco School Board to end segregation in public schools, and the civil rights group asked for an injunction against the School Board to force it to submit a plan for desegre-gation, redraw school attendance boundaries, and re-open Central Junior High School as an integrated school by February 1963. Conditions had not significantly improved by the end of the decade, however, and at a tumultuous school board meeting in March 1969, a riotous crowd of white parents protested the board's decision to implement a busing and desegregation plan. The mob severely beat a San Francisco *Chronicle* reporter and a black teenag-er, and a group of eight black women had to be escorted out of the meeting by police after they were confronted by a large group of angry white men. Complaining of the "organized" violence by whites against blacks at the meeting, Mary Rogers noted that: "We feel that police protection was totally inadequate. Where was the Tac Squad [San Francisco's elite anti-riot police unit]?" White par-ents were incensed by the busing plan, and Maurine Koltugin of Parents and Taxpayers argued that "unless we stand together and organize, minorities can overrun us." Another white present claimed that "there was a communist conspiracy behind all this," and tensions at the meeting ran at a fever pitch.[35]

African American residents continued to feel that they were being short-changed with their children's education, and rightly so. *De facto* segregation in Bay Area schools continued to be a major problem for black communities in San Francisco and the East Bay, and despite Berkeley's limited successes in dealing with the prob-lems of public education, the most difficult crises remained unsolved by 1969. The large numbers of low-income black teenagers who left the Bay Area's public schools usually had not enjoyed the same benefits that their white counterparts had received, and the entire public school system faced severe obstacles that no one seemed to know how to overcome. Nerves were stretched taut as officials studied busing plans and began to experiment with classroom integration and changes in the basic core curriculum at Bay Area schools. The school campuses themselves would be the sites for increasing interracial conflict in the late 1960s, and in Richmond, a full-scale riot would explode in 1966 after black and white students scuffled at the city's high schools. If black students were learning anything at the Bay Area's public schools, it was just how deeply entrenched racism was in northern California society.

## SOCIAL CONTROL AND POLICE BRUTALITY

The appearance of hundreds of thousands of black wartime migrants from the Old Southwest sparked fears of social turmoil in the minds of established residents. Surrounded by throngs of "uncouth" and "potentially violent" foreigners, black and white long-time inhabitants of the Bay Area called for anti-vice campaigns and a return to the comfortable, prewar status quo. As juvenile delinquency and gang activity became chronic problems in African American communities from Richmond to San Francisco, black leaders and their white counterparts called on community organizations and the police department to restore order and protect the public. The white boys in blue quickly proved to be an unwieldy tool in black communities, however, and by the mid-1950s, a steady stream of police brutality complaints transformed concerns about juvenile delinquency into fears for juvenile safety. Although relations between the police and African American residents had never been rosy, the postwar era would see a marked deterioration in trust and cordiality on both sides, and by the end of the Eisenhower Administration, black residents would increasingly feel that Bay Area police officers were on the wrong side of the law.

Cries from white observers for a return to social order and a campaign for social control of the black masses were first voiced during the war itself.  It did not take long for established white residents to call for "reasonableness" from the black migrants and increased diligence from the law enforcement establishment.  The white press sensationalized black crimes and editorials demanded that the black migrants accept "their place" in the Bay Area social order.  In 1944, the *Oakland Observer* concluded that the recent rise in racial tensions was

> brought about by the influx of what might be called socially-liberated or uninhibited Negroes who are not bound by the old and peaceful understanding between Negro and white in Oakland, which has lasted so many decades....  Thus, we see, in Oakland, white women taxicab drivers serving Negro passengers, and white women waitresses serving Negroes in white men's restaurants.... [I]f that is not a potential source of trouble, we do not know what is.  Right there is where the Negro is making his big mistake.  He is butting into white civilization instead of keeping in the perfectly orderly and convenient Negro civilization of Oakland....  It might be as well for the more orderly and respectable Negroes to tell the newcomers about the facts of life.

The ominous tone in this editorial was unfortunately typical of the kind of responses from established whites.  African American migrants could expect nothing more from the thousands of white southwesterners who also poured into the Bay Area during the war, for their acceptance of rigid Jim Crow mores and proclivity to violent resolutions of racial problems were even more threatening than the attitudes of the white northern Californians.[36]

Although black migrants to the Bay Area witnessed little civility from the white residents and probably expected less, the more surprising response came from established blacks.  African American leaders were on the front lines of the "social order" campaign, and many established residents resented the increase in gambling, prostitution, and petty crime that followed the newcomers.  In a NAACP-sponsored study, "The Negro and Crime in San Francisco," R. J. Reynolds concluded that the rise in arrests of blacks in the 1940s was a result of the introduction of a criminal element among the migrants who came to work in the shipyards and factories: "It appears that at the peak of San Francisco's wartime production Negro elements with pronounced criminal backgrounds were brought in to help do the job, and the projection of their criminal activities into this area is still apparent." Reynolds argued that a small, alien group of petty thieves and repeat offenders was responsible for the increase in crime in African American neighborhoods, and he desperately tried to distance respectable black citizens from the tiny band of crooks and swindlers. Reynolds and other middle-class African Americans were concerned that while blacks only made up five percent of San Francisco's population, they accounted for about thirteen percent of all arrests. Fearing a white backlash, Reynolds emphasized that most black criminals were not violent offenders, but he lamented the increase in prostitution, the narcotics trade, robbery, burglary, gambling, and larceny. He also pointed a finger at the white establishment's failure to secure decent housing and regular employment for many blacks, some of whom he confessed had been forced into criminal activity after the war in order to survive. Other established residents and local ministers voiced their fears of growing criminal activity in black neighborhoods like Fillmore and Hunter's Point, and the editors of the leading black newspaper even tentatively requested the hiring of a special detachment of black police officers to help restore order.[37]

By the mid-1950s, the patience of some established residents had worn thin and they abandoned any pretense of civility and encouraged a separation of the working-class and low-income blacks from the more prosperous, cultured, and better sort of African Americans. James F. Wood, a long-time black resident of San Francisco, sent a letter of complaint to the Bay Area's black weekly newspaper in 1956 to criticize the paper's "Go-To-A-Concert-Month" contest where readers could win tickets to a theater or musical performance. He argued that the respectable element of the city that actually enjoyed such entertainment should have the right to attend "without being confronted by the rough element of the city." Having worked hard all week, Mr. Wood did not wish to sit amongst a crowd of rowdy, uncouth black patrons. "It is bad enough encountering this element on our streets and at work or in the services," he wrote. "We really do not want them in our concert halls, or in our libraries or art galleries, opera houses and theaters. These people are not ready for a life of culture, so is it not better to leave them in their present surroundings?" Although not representative of the attitudes of all long-time black residents, Wood's concerns illustrate how much established Bay Area African Americans had tired of the social upheaval brought by the thousands of wartime migrants.[38]

Of special concern to most Bay Area blacks was the rise in gang activity and juvenile delinquency. The mid-1950s witnessed a spate of outbreaks of gang violence, and concerned black citizens called on their leadership and the white establishment to restore order in the streets. Gang fights and robberies in North Richmond, San Francisco, and Oakland filled the headlines of black newspapers, and readers and reporters alike were shocked at tales of teenage boys knifing each other and attacking passersby. In January 1956, five teenage black boys were arrested after they started a knife fight in a bar on Divisadero Street in San Francisco. The teens, ranging in age from 15 to 18, killed one man. Roaming gangs of black youths also plagued the East Bay, and in July 1960, Berkeley police officers arrested about thirty teenagers wielding knives in Tilden Park after a married couple claimed the group had accosted them. By the early 1960s, highly organized street gangs, like the Magnificent Seven and the Savoys of Hunter's Point, terrorized black communities in the summer months with frequent armed clashes and frightful violence. In September 1961, the San Francisco Housing Authority (SFHA) tried to evict twelve families who had teenagers involved in gang fights between the Magnificent Seven and the Savoys, but a residents' protest, supported by the NAACP, forced the SFHA to complete a thorough investigation first. Letters to the local black weekly newspaper expressed growing concern about the problems of gang violence and teenage crime. Kenneth M. Freeman, a black resident of San Francisco, noted that "something must be done by us about the juvenile delinquency in our city.... We don't want to see our kids being shot up. But neither do we want a city where it is not safe to attend a theatre or walk the streets for fear of being involved in a scramble between the kids or between the kids and the police."[39]

Just as there was an escalation of conflicts between gangs of black youths in the postwar era, there were also an increasing number of violent confrontations between African Americans of all ages and white police officers. Rumors, witnesses' recollections, and newspaper stories recorded an alarming trend in police actions in black communities throughout the Bay Area. As with the problems of gang violence and juvenile delinquency, many blacks blamed the increase in claims of police brutality on the arrival of so many migrants during the war years. By the middle of the 1950s, however, all African American residents realized that they were targets of the "official violence" of the policemen who patrolled their neighborhoods. Community leaders began to demand investigations into cases of apparent police brutality, and by the end of the decade, many African Americans were skeptical about the behavior and motivations of the men who were supposedly there to serve and protect ordinary citizens. In early 1955, for example, the editors of the *Sun-Reporter* complained that mistreatment at the hands of the police "has happened to so many Negroes, over and over, without any action on the part of the department heads, [that] the feeling has grown that Negroes can look for nothing better at the hands of the police."[40]

The stories that circulated in black neighborhoods told of average black people going about their daily affairs until they were harassed by police officers, arrested on trumped-up charges, and then severely beaten after they were handcuffed or locked in a jail cell. Tensions ran so high between police and civilians in black communities that even routine traffic stops could escalate into dramatic encounters. Sensational headlines and tragic accounts of the police departments' official violence in the Bay Area ran frequently in the black press. In 1954, for example, the leading black newspaper reported that James and Dolores Eliston were beaten by two police officers following a dispute that Eliston had with his neighbors. The NAACP agreed to file a civil case against the arresting officers for using unnecessary force and violating the civil rights of Mr. and Mrs. Eliston. More lawsuits were filed against San Francisco police officers the following year when Charles J. Murray said that he was beaten by three police officers after being stopped for a traffic violation, and George L. Rice accused police of assaulting him during a traffic stop after he objected to their calling him a "nigger." In a disturbing account from November 1959, the paper reported that a black man was brutally beaten in front of a group of school children. All witnesses said the victim did not resist and that he was assaulted after he was handcuffed. Similar reports appeared throughout the late 1950s, and they increased dramatically following the harassment of the editor of the paper, Dr. Carlton B. Goodlett, in July 1959.[41]

Initially, it seems, the police vented their ire only on working-class and low-income African Americans. By the late 1950s, however, even respected black community leaders were not immune from embarrassing and dangerous encounters with the police that could end in arrest and physical abuse. Goodlett was arrested after he resisted a police officer's attempts to inspect several packages he was carrying. Otis Rauls, a 38 year-old insurance agent, accused officers of beating him at the Central Police Station in San Francisco on the morning of May 18, 1958, after he was arrested for public intoxication outside of a black jazz club in the early morning hours. Rauls claimed that he was not drunk at the time of the arrest. In a more bizarre story from December of the following year, Harry Eberhardt charged that three cops had invaded his store, harassed his employees, and then savagely beat him for illegally broadcasting Christmas carols out of his storefront. Similar confrontations between middle-class black citizens and the police continued in the 1960s, and in 1964, Harold B. Greenleaf, a teacher and occasional reporter for the *Sun-Reporter*, complained that police had used excessive force when they arrested him after a minor traffic violation. The respectability of a middle-class position was no longer a defense against police brutality, and many middle-class blacks demanded that police departments take steps to ensure that officers did not wantonly employ force when arresting black citizens. In a bitter letter to the editor in 1963, Robert E. Treuhaft attacked Oakland Police Chief Edward Toothman's remark that "We have a get tough policy around here. When force is necessary, our officers are instructed to use force." Treuhaft noted that "this policy is being followed, it is clear, at least in dealing with the Negro population of Oakland," and then proceeded to recount the story of how two black youths were so savagely beaten by police after their arrests that they both suffered broken jaws and numerous other injuries.[42]

To heighten its critique and apply more pressure to Bay Area police departments to enact real reforms, the *Sun-Reporter* began running gruesome front-page photos of the victims of police brutality. In June 1960, the paper placed the picture of Benny Rankins on the cover after police had beaten him and his acquaintance outside of a bar in San Francisco. Similar grisly photos appeared in January, March, and November of 1961. Forty-one year-old William M. Sherron was pictured with a swollen left eye and multiple cuts and lacerations across his face. He needed four stitches to close a gash in his head before police booked him for being drunk and in his car. Lauren Trotter, a twenty year-old black man, suffered eye and ear cuts and lost two teeth at the hands of police. Annette Goudeaux, a twenty-four year-old African American woman, had been slapped by the arresting officer following a traffic accident. These front-page pictures drove home the reality of police brutality for African Americans throughout the Bay Area. The *Sun-Reporter* concluded that many policemen in the Bay Area "believe that the best way to deal with any Negro...is to first crack him across the head so as to get his attention, second to knock him to his knees, and finally to place the Negro under arrest. This is the usual treatment given a stubborn mule in the Southland."[43]

Relations between black communities and police forces in the Bay Area continued to worsen during the tumultuous 1960s. Reports of illegal break-ins by police officers and their indiscriminate use of force against young people and the elderly inflamed black tempers and made an already tense situation more dangerous. In January 1965, San Francisco's finest severely beat an elderly black epileptic, Leonce H. Locks, following his arrest on Fillmore Street. Mr. Locks received a nasty gash on the back of his head near an earlier injury sustained during a seizure. A white officer had previously arrested Locks for public drunkenness when his mistook a seizure for disorderly conduct. The following month, police in Oakland sent two black women to the hospital after they illegally broke into their apartment to break up a tenants' meeting. Lucille Roberston and Geneva Johnson had organized their fellow tenants to protest the landlord's refusal to make needed repairs to their apartment complex. The women stated that police beat one of them senseless during the attack and that they were denied medical attention for four hours while they were in jail. The black press soon began comparing Bay Area police officers to Nazi stormtroopers, and more stories of reckless police behavior continued to fill black papers for the rest of the decade. Numerous confrontations between black residents and white policemen widened the gulf between the races, and charges of wanton police brutality further emphasized the message that African Americans were second-class citizens whose rights no white man was bound to respect.[44]

By the early 1960s, the battle lines between black residents and white policemen had been drawn throughout the Bay Area. The bonds of trust that had linked, however weakly, private citizens and law enforcement officials in the prewar era were stretched taut. Resentment grew on both sides as African Americans demanded more accountability from police departments and officers resisted any constraints on their authority. The situation deteriorated throughout the decade as the campaign of official violence waged against African Americans from police headquarters continued unabated. It is not surprising then that when a small band of young black revolutionaries began patrolling the African American neighborhoods of West Oakland to monitor police activity in 1966, their real and symbolic protest would strike a chord with so many black residents, young and old, middle class and working class. When the first nightstick struck a black body in the shadow of the wartime shipyards, the die was cast. The war had begun.

The 1950s, a decade of supposed prosperity and consensus, saw the rise of racial tensions in the San Francisco Bay Area. As the growing legions of middle-class whites settled into comfortable suburbs, thousands of African American residents were stranded in the deindustrializing urban cores. Plagued by problems of unemployment, housing shortages, segregated schools, and official and criminal violence, black communities throughout the Bay Area struggled to create safety and security within their borders. Long and bitter campaigns for fair employment and housing laws, equal schooling for black and white children, and local control of police forces taxed the resources of black neighborhoods and soured the atmosphere of race relations in northern California. The relatively limited gains that the moderate civil rights groups won during the 1950s opened the door for more radical black political organizations in the 1960s. The generation of African Americans that came of age after the wartime migration would create this militant turn in the black freedom movement, and the Bay Area's and the nation's future would be forever altered by its course.

# Notes

1. Newell Johnson, "Inside West Oakland: California's Oldest Negro Community," *Sun-Reporter*, 12 November 1955, 3. Johnson continued his account the next week in the 19 November issue, page 4.

2. Peter Marris and Martin Rein, *Dilemmas of Social Reform: Poverty and Community Action in the United States*, 2nd. ed. (Chicago: Aldine Publishing Co., 1973), 13.

3. See Thomas J. Sugrue, "The Structures of Urban Poverty: The Reorganization of Space and Work in Three Periods of American History," in *The "Underclass" Debate: Views from History*, ed. Michael B. Katz (Princeton: Princeton University Press, 1993); and Sugrue, *The Origins of the Urban Crisis: Race and Inequality in Postwar Detroit* (Princeton: Princeton University Press, 1996). A good general survey of the prosperity of the 1950s is William H. Chafe, *The Unfinished Journey: America since World War II*, 2nd. ed. (New York: Oxford University Press, 1991), esp. Chp. 5.

4. D. Donald Glover, "Review of a Decade of Progress on the Job Front," *Sun-Reporter*, 6 October 1956, 6.

5. Cy W. Record, "Willie Stokes at the Golden Gate," *Crisis* 56 (June 1949), 175-79; Gretchen Lemke-Santangelo, *Abiding Courage: African American Migrant Women and the East Bay Community* (Chapel Hill: University of North Carolina Press, 1996), 124.

6. Marris and Rein, *Dilemmas of Social Reform*, 11-12; Lee Soto, "What Is there Left for Hunter's Point?" *Sun-Reporter*, 18 January

1964, 27; J. Maceo Green, "The Weekly Report," *Sun-Reporter*, 23 January 1954, 12.

7.   "Fair Employment for San Francisco?   'Voluntary Plan' vs. FEPC," transcript of testimony presented to Board of Supervisors, City and County of San Francisco, May 14, 1951, Carton 45, NAACP West Coast Region Papers, Bancroft Library, University of California, Berkeley [Hereafter cited as NAACP Papers].

8.   Statements by Jobbie L. Johnson, n.d.; James A. Fisher, 21 August 1957; LeVell McClain, 24 August 1957; Grant Garrett, 24 August 1957; Wilson Simien, 23 August 1957; Curtis L. Cummings, 24 August 1957; and David A. Carter, n.d., all in Carton 26, NAACP Papers; Press Release, "Survey Finds Racial Bias in San Francisco Private Employment," 30 July 1958, Carton 3, William Byron Rumford Papers, Bancroft Library, University of California, Berkeley [Hereafter cited as Rumford Papers].

9.   For general descriptions of union discrimination against African American workers, see, Amory Bradford, *Oakland's Not for Burning* (New York: David McKay Company, Inc., 1968), 106-110, 150; Edward Everett France, "Some Aspects of the Migration of the Negro to the San Francisco Bay Area since 1940" (Ph.D. diss., University of California, Berkeley, 1962), 66-76; Lemke-Santangelo, *Abiding Courage*, 113, 121-24; Shirley Ann Moore, "The Black Community in Richmond, California, 1910-1963" (Ph.D. diss., University of California, Berkeley, 1989), 94-95; Wilson Record, *Minority Groups and Intergroup Relations in the San Francisco Bay Area* (Berkeley: Institute of Governmental Studies, 1963), 16-17; and Ben Watkins, *We Also Serve: 10 Per Cent of a Nation Working and Fighting for Victory* (San Francisco: The Tilghman Press, n.d.), 25.   George R. Andersen, Herbert Resner, and Thurgood Marshall, "Brief for Respondent," S.F. No. 17,015, 1944, In the Supreme Court of the State of California, Joseph James v. Marinship Corporation, Local Union No. 6 of International Brotherhood of Boilermakers, Iron Shipbuilders, and Helpers of America..., Labor Archives and Research Center, San Francisco State University [hereafter cited as SFSU Archives].

10.   Letter, Lucius Winn to Legal Defense Educational Fund, NAACP, n.d. [1946?], Carton 16, NAACP Papers; *Centennial History of San Francisco Musicians Union, Local 6, 1885-1985* (San Francisco:

American Federation of Musicians, 1985), Papers of the American Federation of Musicians, Ephemera Collection, SFSU Archives. The International Longshoremen's and Warehousemen's Union (ILWU) and the National Union of Marine Cooks and Stewards (MCS) were two left-leaning unions that did agitate for black workers' rights in the Bay Area during the 1950s and 1960s. African Americans were particularly well represented on the membership rolls and in leadership positions in the MCS, and the union adopted policies for equal pay for equal work and rules against racial discrimination by its members. Both of these unions, however, were locked in heated battles with conservative, white-controlled American Federation of Labor (AFL) unions, and each organization suffered serious setbacks in the face of white workers' hostility to minority laborers in the postwar era. See the ILWU's papers and the MCS's papers in the Ephemera Collection of the SFSU Archives.

11. Richard Grant, "The Case of Audley Cole: Racial Policy in the AFL and the CIO," unpublished paper, SFSU Archives; Letter to the Editor, Morris Watson, *The Dispatcher*, 3 February 1955, ILWU papers, SFSU Archives; J. Maceo Green, "The Weekly Report," *Sun-Reporter*, 16 July 1955, 8.

12. "NAACP Lists Assets & Liabilities for 1955," *Sun-Reporter*, 7 January 1956, 8.

13. Richmond Branch, NAACP, "Annual Report of the Richmond Branch of the N.A.A.C.P.," 4 January 1953, Carton 26, NAACP Papers; Jacqueline Myles Smith, "Adjustment to Urban Living," *Sun-Reporter*, 6 October 1956, 10.

14. The Mays housing flap created a minor sensation in the local media, and representative clippings can be found in Carton 39, NAACP Papers. See also, France, "Some Aspects of the Migration of the Negro to the San Francisco Bay Area," 41-42; and Max Silverman, "Urban Redevelopment and Community Response: African Americans in San Francisco's Western Addition" (M.A. Thesis, San Francisco State University, 1994), 50-51.

15. Citizens Committee to the Community Welfare Commission, "Housing Discrimination in Berkeley," (Berkeley, 1962), Carton 37, NAACP Papers. The Japanese American Citizens' League survey is included as Appendix B of this report. Letter, Larry J. Logan to San Francisco Branch of the NAACP, 8 August

1966, Carton 17, NAACP Papers; CORE, "Statement on Discrimination in Housing in the State of California," April 1963, Reel 37, Series 5, File 269, The Papers of the Congress of Racial Equality, 1941-1967, Microfilm, Sanford, NC: Microfilming Corporation of America, 1980 [Hereafter cited as CORE Papers].

16.    "Catholic Council Censures Forest Knolls Builders; NAACP Urges More 'Sit-Ins,'" *Sun-Reporter*, 3 June 1961, 2; James Richardson, *Willie Brown: A Biography* (Berkeley: University of California Press, 1996), 73-76; Thomas C. Fleming, "Developer Refuses to Sell Negro Couple Home," *Sun-Reporter*, 4 August 1962, 5.

17.    For representative concerns about public housing in the Bay Area, see, Letter, Richard W. Dettering to Shirley Adelson Seigel, 22 December 1949, Box 3, California Federation for Civic Unity Records, 1945-1956, Bancroft Library, University of California, Berkeley; Memo, "Oakland Housing," 8 March 1954, Carton 16, NAACP Papers; City of Berkeley, "The First Fifty Years of the Community Welfare Commission" (Berkeley, February 1959), 40-44; Letter, Herman Schein to Franklin H. Williams, 18 May 1955, Carton 37, NAACP Papers; France, "Some Aspects of the Migration of the Negro to the San Francisco Bay Area," 48-51.

18.    California Real Estate Association, "Freedom of Choice vs. Forced Housing," pamphlet, n.d., Carton 3, Rumford Papers; "*Backlash Apparent*: Only in California," *Sun-Reporter*, 7 November 1964, 2; "Vote on 14 No Surprise to California Negroes," *Sun-Reporter*, 7 November 1964, 7; "California's Shame," *Sun-Reporter*, 7 November 1964, 8; Memo, Harry C. McPherson, Jr., to the President, 30 March 1966, FA 4, Housing, WHCF, Box 16, Lyndon Baines Johnson Presidential Library, Austin, Texas [Hereafter cited as LBJL]; Donald Canter, "Hunters Point a Crisis for Shelley," San Francisco *Chronicle*, 12 December 1965, 1, 7; and W. J. Rorabaugh, *Berkeley at War: The 1960s* (New York: Oxford University Press, 1989), 54-61.

19.    Marris and Rein, *Dilemmas of Social Reform*, 13-14. See also, Martin Anderson, *The Federal Bulldozer: A Critical Analysis of Urban Renewal, 1949-1962* (Cambridge, MA: The MIT Press, 1964).

20.    Two excellent recent studies on urban renewal in San Francisco argue that African Americans shaped the course of rede-velopement policy throughout the 1940s, 1950s, and 1960s. While

this was undoubtedly true, blacks in the Bay Area were often over-powered by white real estate magnates, and they ultimately suffered severe setbacks at the hands of city redevelopment agencies and white speculators. See, Eric Fure-Slocum, "Emerging Urban Redevelopment Policies: Post-World War II Contests in San Francisco and Los Angeles" (M.A. Thesis, San Francisco State University, 1990), esp. Chp. 2; and Silverman, "Urban Redevelopment and Community Response," esp. Chp. 3. "$2 Million for Oakland Slums," *Sun-Reporter*, 30 November 1957, 2; "8600 to be Moved in Western Addition," *Sun-Reporter*, 1 March 1958, 3; "Redevelopment Problems Studied in Western Add.," *Sun-Reporter*, 23 August 1958, 3.

21. "It's Your Property—Get the Best Price You Can!" *Sun-Reporter*, 24 May 1958, 10; "Slum Property Dealings by City Officials Questioned," *Sun-Reporter*, 18 October 1958, 1, 3; "Candidate Urges Middle-Rent Dwelling Units for W. Addition," *Sun-Reporter*, 3 October 1959, 1, 16.

22. "'Goodbye Slums, Hello Corruption,'" *Californian*, reprinted in the *Sun-Reporter*, 16 July 1960, 5, and 23 July 1960, 5; "Ghettos Have to Go," *Sun-Reporter*, 28 September 1963, 20.

23. Western Addition resident quoted in Neil Arthur Eddington, "The Urban Plantation: The Ethnography of an Oral Tradition in a Negro Community" (Ph.D. diss., University of California, Berkeley, 1967), 19; Hunter's Point resident quoted in Arthur E. Hippler, *Hunter's Point: A Black Ghetto* (New York: Basic Books, 1974), 173. See also, "Redevelopment for Hunter's Point," *Sun-Reporter*, 17 March 1962, 12. "'Let Them Live in Oakland,'" *Sun-Reporter*, 28 April 1962, 10; San Francisco Redevelopment Agency, "Proposed Redevelopment Plan for Hunter's Point Redevelopment Project Area," 10 December 1968, Carton 17, NAACP Papers.

24. "Racial Ghettoes Are Opposed by Oakland Agency," *Sun-Reporter*, 27 December 1958, 1; Thomas C. Fleming, "The West Oakland Story," *Sun-Reporter*, 7 July 1962, 5; Fleming, "West Oakland Story: Project Acorn at Wrong Site!" *Sun-Reporter*, 14 July 1962, 3; Redevelopment Agency of the City of Oakland, "Revised Relocation Section of the Eligibility and Relocation Report, Acorn Project Area," 3 February 1960, Carton 16, NAACP Papers.

25.    Thomas C. Fleming, "West Oakland Story: West Oakland Negroes Fear Redevelopment," *Sun-Reporter*, 21 July 1962, 3; Fleming, "West Oakland Story: Negro Fears Are Groundless, Says Agency," *Sun-Reporter*, 28 July 1962, 2; Fleming, "Weekly Report," *Sun-Reporter*, 28 July 1962, 8; Fleming, "West Oakland Story: West Oakland Resident Finance Own Fight," *Sun-Reporter*, 4 August 1962, 13; Fleming, "West Oakland Businessmen Fear Redevelopment and Tell Why," *Sun-Reporter*, 2 February 1963, 2; Fleming, "West Oakland Businessmen Form Relocation Committee," *Sun-Reporter*, 9 February 1963; Fleming, "Relocation Committee Formed," *Sun-Reporter*, 16 February 1963, 2; "Mighty Oaks? Thomas Bell Interviewed by Elsa Knight Thompson," cassette E2BB0320, Pacifica Radio Archive, North Hollywood, California, 1962; Bradford, *Oakland's Not for Burning*, 6; "Acorn: Where Bunnies Hop," *Flatlands*, 9 April 1966, 1, 3; Marion Fay, "Acorn — A Symbol of Progress," *Sun-Reporter*, 30 December 1967, 12; "East Bay News: Project Acorn," *Sun-Reporter*, 20 September 1969, 31, 38.

26.    Hugh Pearson, *The Shadow of the Panther: Huey Newton and the Price of Black Power in America* (Reading, MA: Addison-Wesley Publishing Co., 1994), 238-40, 313-14; "Nowhere to Go," *Flatlands*, 18 November to 2 December 1966, 1, 3; "Minority Workers and BART Jobs," San Francisco *Chronicle*, 18 February 1966, 2.

27.    "Death of School Jim Crow NAACP's Crowning Glory," *Sun-Reporter*, 22 May 1954, 10.

28.    Charles S. Johnson, *The Negro War Worker in San Francisco* (n.p., 1944), 34-35; Harold Spears, "The Proper Recognition of a Pupil's Racial Background in the San Francisco Unified School District," 19 June 1962, Box 45, San Francisco Labor Council Records, 1902-1976, SFSU Archives.

29.    "Race Fight in Oakland Hi. School," *Sun-Reporter*, 5 March 1955, 1; Ira Michael Heyman, *Civil Rights U.S.A.: Public Schools, Cities in the North and West, 1963, Oakland* (Washington, D. C.: United States Commission on Civil Rights, 1963), 52-54, Carton 4, Rumford Papers.

30.    Rorabaugh, *Berkeley at War*, 173; Advisory Committee of Citizens, "Interracial Problems and Their Effect on Education in the Public Schools of Berkeley, California," 19 October 1959, Carton 36, NAACP Papers.  The history of the Berkeley school desegregation

fight is in Leonard A. Marascuilo, *Attitudes Toward de facto Segregation in a Northern City* (Berkeley: University of California, 1965), 5-17 passim. See also Rorabaugh, *Berkeley at War*, 61-70.

31.   Advisory Committee of Citizens, "Interracial Problems and Their Effect on Education in the Public Schools of Berkeley"; Record, *Minority Groups and Intergroup Relations*, 10-11; Citizens Committee, Berkeley Unified School District, "De Facto Segregation in the Berkeley Public Schools," Fall 1963, Reel 5, Series 1, File 75, CORE Papers.

32.   Marascuilo, *Attitudes Toward de facto Segregation*, Appendix C, 22-24.  For similar complaints against such tracking in Richmond's public schools, see Harry and Marguerite Williams, "Reflections of a Longtime Black Family in Richmond," an oral history conducted in 1985 by Judith K. Dunning, Regional Oral History Office, The Bancroft Library, University of California, Berkeley, 1990, 127-31.

33.   See, for example, "The Challenge of Negro History Week," *Sun-Reporter*, 8 February 1958, 12.   "CORE Stages Sit-In on S.F. School Segregation," *Sun-Reporter*, 11 August 1962, 2.

34.   Robert Wenkert, John Magney, and Ann Neel, *Two Weeks of Racial Crisis in Richmond, California* (Berkeley: Survey Research Center, 1967), 34-42; "Oakland's 'Side Walk Cases': Products of Discipline in Oakland's Public Schools," *Flatlands*, 7 May to 21 May 1966, 1, 5; Letter, Anonymous Teacher to San Francisco Regional Office of the NAACP, 21 June 1966, Carton 17, NAACP Papers.

35.   Linda Grant, "De Facto Segregation Aired: Background of School Situation in San Francisco," *Sun-Reporter*, 22 September 1962, 2; "SF NAACP Sues in School Case," *Sun-Reporter*, 6 October 1962, 4; "Insults and Violence: School Board Meeting Disrupted," *Sun-Reporter*, 3 March 1969, 3.

36.   *Oakland Observer*, 1 March 1944, quoted in Lemke-Santangelo, *Abiding Courage*, 71-72.  For a study of black and white migrants in a WWII shipyard, see Katherine Archibald, *Wartime Shipyard: A Study in Social Disunity* (Berkeley: University of California Press, 1947).  I cover this topic in more detail in Chapter 1.

37.   R. J. Reynolds, "The Negro and Crime in San Francisco, Final Report," 1 September 1947, Carton 44, NAACP Papers; Letters to the editor from Mr. and Mrs. A. J. Watson, Jim Crayton, Sammy J.

Johnson, and the Rev. A. L. Clement, *Sun-Reporter*, 9 June 1951, 8; "We Cry for Help," *Sun-Reporter*, 7 July 1951, 8.

38.    James F. Wood, letter to the editor, *Sun-Reporter*, 4 February 1956, 6.

39.    "Boy Badly Knifed in Gang Brawl," *Sun-Reporter*, 31 July 1954, 15; "Teen-Age Gang Arrested for Beating East Bay Man," *Sun-Reporter*, 21 April 1956; "Robberies Charged to Negro Gangs," *Sun-Reporter*, 6 April 1957, 1-2; "Two Gang Members Identify Knife Slayer in Bar Brawl," *Sun-Reporter*, 28 January 1956, 1; Tom Fleming, "Berkeley Cops Nip Near Riot by Teen Hoods," *Sun-Reporter*, 9 July 1960, 2; Thomas J. Fleming, "Ghetto Conditions Breed Violence at Hunters Point," *Sun-Reporter*, 2 September 1961, 4; "200 Attend Hunters Point Protest Meeting; Evictions Rescinded," *Sun-Reporter*, 2 September 1961, 14; Kenneth M. Freeman, letter to the editor, *Sun-Reporter*, 30 June 1956, 12. See also, Williams, "Reflections of a Longtime Black Family in Richmond," 140 passim.

40.    "Police Brutality, Old Story," *Sun-Reporter*, 26 February 1955, 8.    See also, Marvin Anthony, "Police Brutality in San Francisco," *Sun-Reporter*, 7 June 1958, 1, 3; "What's Wrong with Our Police Department," *Sun-Reporter*, 7 June 1958, 6; and Robert B. Powers, "Law Enforcement, Race Relations: 1930-1960," an oral history conducted by Amelia R. Fry, Earl Warren Oral History Project, Regional Oral History Office, The Bancroft Library, University of California, Berkeley, 1971, 39-40, 55-64.

41.    "Man and Wife Reported Roughed Up by 2 Cops," *Sun-Reporter*, 21 August 1954, 1; "Police Charged with Beating Youth, 19," *Sun-Reporter*, 1 October 1955, 1; "2 Policemen Accused of Brutality in Arrest," *Sun-Reporter*, 8 October 1955, 9; "School Children See Police Beat Negro," *Sun-Reporter*, 21 November 1959, 22; "Four Charge Brutal Treatment by Police," *Sun-Reporter*, 19 May 1956, 1; "East Bay Sportsman to Sue Berkeley Cops: Police Brutality Victim to Sue," *Sun-Reporter*, 22 August 1959, 1; "New Police Brutality Cases Anger Parents: Ask Police Chief and Mayor 'Stop Brutality,'" *Sun-Reporter*, 14 November 1959, 1; "Dr. Goodlett Arrested: 'Hey, Boy! Waddaya Got in Those Packages?' Cop Yells," *Sun-Reporter*, 1 August 1959, 1, 14.

42.    "Ins. Agent Charges Police Beating: Grand Jury Investigation Urged," *Sun-Reporter*, 24 May 1958, 1; "Christmas Caroler Beaten by Police," *Sun-Reporter*, 12 December 1959, 1;

"Teacher Says Cops Kicked Him," *Sun-Reporter*, 4 January 1964, 3; Robert E. Treuhaft, letter to the editor, *Sun-Reporter*, 9 February 1963, 7.

43.    Thomas C. Fleming, "Claim Cop Brutality," *Sun-Reporter*, 18 June 1960, 1, 2; "Charges Brutal Blows by Cops," *Sun-Reporter*, 28 January 1961, 1, 4; "Victim of Police Brutality?" *Sun-Reporter*, 4 March 1961, 1, 5; "Woman Claims Police Beat Her," *Sun-Reporter*, 18 November 1961, 1, 2; "Civil Rights: Now the Enforcement," *Sun-Reporter*, 15 August 1964, 6.

44.    "Policemen's Blind Alley: New Intrusion into Family Home," *Flatlands*, 16 July to 30 July 1966, 1, 3; "*Police Brutality*: Cops Beat Epileptic," *Sun-Reporter*, 16 January 1965, 3; "Two Women Beaten by Oakland Police," *Sun-Reporter*, 20 February 1965, 2; "Cahill's Storm Troopers Beat Another Negro; Surgery Necessary," *Sun-Reporter*, 31 July 1965, 1, 6; "Victim of SS Beating Still Hospitalized; Melvin Belli Will Represent Newman," *Sun-Reporter*, 7 August 1965, 1; "Man Accuses Police of Kicking His Door in and Attacking His Family," *Sun-Reporter*, 23 April 1966, 1, 2; Bradford, *Oakland's Not for Burning*, 131-37; "Cops Break Girl's Arm, Parents Sue for $100,000," *Sun-Reporter*, 26 August 1967, 3.

# CHAPTER 3

# Organization

Beneath the blanket of whiteness that covered the Bay Area, African Americans struggled constantly to forge strong organizations that would help them build and protect their communities in the face of great odds and fierce white opposition. From local neighborhood centers and churches to city-wide and regional civil rights groups, African American associations served as important resources for action and barriers for defense in the struggle for equality in northern California. Throughout the 1950s and early 1960s, these institutions provided leadership, funds, and workers for the civil rights struggle, and they created a vast safety net for African Americans who were otherwise ignored by or excluded from white-dominated social service agencies. Drawing from long traditions of African American community activism, Bay Area blacks organized new institutions and strengthened established ones to combat lingering problems in the areas of employment, housing, education, and police-community relations.

Despite their energies, however, these moderate groups were unable to solve the crises of the postwar era, and as tensions rose in the mid-1960s, a new group of younger, militant African Americans would come to the fore and offer a different kind of racial reform. The radicals' use of direct-action protest tactics would shift the freedom struggle into a higher gear, and they would set the stage for the rise of the Black Panther Party at the end of the decade.

## SOCIAL ORGANIZATIONS AND THE BONDS
## OF COMMUNITY

The crises of unemployment, poor housing, segregated schools, crime, and police brutality set substantial obstacles in the path that African Americans sought to take to full equality. As municipal agencies failed to confront these problems in any substantial manner, blacks were left to their own devices to develop solutions for the social problems they faced. Important weapons that African Americans had to use against these barriers were the civic organizations, mutual aid societies, and churches that had grown rapidly since the Second World War. Institutions like the Bayview Community Center and the Madame C. J. Walker Home railed against the segregationist and discriminatory policies found throughout the Bay Area and provided needed services for black residents who were frequently turned away from white-dominated social agencies. African American churches also supported civil rights activities by providing funds, meeting places, leadership, and moral support for the ranks of black demonstrators and activists. Established leaders and ordinary citizens pressed against the racial boundaries that separated whites and blacks, and although they faced overwhelming odds, the community-based organizations and churches won some important victories in the struggle for social justice.

At the core of many African Americans' conception of community were the kinship bonds that tied them to their relatives and friends. Although there were tensions between established black residents and the droves of migrants from the Old Southwest, many African Americans put aside their differences to focus upon the new society they created after the Second World War. Once the initial shock had passed, many African Americans realized that the key to racial uplift laid in cooperation and community. Black migrants, in particular, were aware of the importance of strong social bonds to unite them in common cause, and they relied upon the well-established mores that had protected African Americans in the Jim Crow South for centuries. The migrants' emphasis on pride, unity, and self-respect gave the Bay Area Black Freedom Struggle a southern flavor, and their enthusiasm energized black protest and black community building during the 1950s and 1960s. The migrants also preserved the ties to their kith and kin throughout the South, and the movement of African Americans from the West Coast to the South became an annual cycle. Oma June Scott and her husband regularly returned to the Southwest to visit friends she had left behind when her family migrated to the East Bay. "We have lots of friends who stayed back in Texas," she noted, "and we stay with them when we go back. In fact, the only vacations we took were back to Texas." African Americans also returned to the South for weddings, births, funerals, and other family occasions, which reinforced the ties the migrants had with their former homes. In the summer of 1951, for example, Naymon Shelbon made a quick trip to Louisiana to help his brother whose wife had recently passed away. Such journeys, in addition to the frequent letters that migrants exchanged with their southern kin, bound Bay Area blacks to their distant relatives and ultimately to one another.[1]

The fledgling sense of community that grew out of kinship and friendship ties strengthened as African Americans created new institutions to defend and improve their neighborhoods. The San Francisco Chapter of the Association for the Study of Negro Life and History (ASNLH), for example, focused on education, cultural awareness, and African American pride rather than on breaking down the barriers of discrimination that blocked blacks from jobs and housing. Founded by Mrs. Frances Miller in 1956, the San Francisco ASNLH coordinated local fraternal groups, colleges, churches, and libraries in a campaign to spread knowledge about black history to residents of the Bay Area. The first Negro History Week sponsored by the ASNLH was held February 10-17, 1957, and the series of lectures, seminars, and workshops became an annual fixture throughout the 1950s and the 1960s. Chronicling the long story of black achievement, the organizers of the history week program spread their knowledge of the African American past and hoped to instruct both blacks and whites alike on the important roles that African Americans had played in the history of the United States. One San Francisco teacher reported that a black student's project on the eighteenth-century black mathematician Benjamin Banneker sparked interest among black and white students alike, and the leading black newspaper editorialized that "an experience of this kind not only helps to instill pride in the minds of Negro youngsters but also serves to build the democratic precept in the minds of all our youth." The ASNLH leaders thought that an awareness of black history was an important weapon in the fight against the destruction of African American society. Nurturing a sense of cultural pride amongst black citizens undermined some of the hateful assertions of black inferiority that were so frequently broadcast from the centers of white power in the Bay Area.[2]

African American mutual aid associations and community centers, on a somewhat more practical level, catered to the social service needs of the Bay Area black population. Established black churches had, of course, provided spiritual and physical assistance to their members for nearly a century, and the new places of worship founded by the migrant blacks during the war also frequently aided orphans, widows, and victims of accidents, illness, and other tragedies. For example, the Mt. Zion Missionary Baptist Church in Berkeley gave money to aid the seven orphaned children of the late Rev. General Grant Greer and his wife, Ruby. The Greers were killed in an automobile accident in 1952, and the church collected funds for the orphans, who lived with their maternal grandmother in Richmond. The churches usually did not offer regular or systematic social-service programs, however, and that burden fell to the Bay Area's many black mutual aid associations and community centers. Black women's clubs, the YMCA, and the YWCA held summer classes and created youth groups for African American boys and girls, and the Madame C. J. Walker Home provided shelter for girls who came to San Francisco to finish school or find work. In the early 1960s, the Sutter Street YWCA had 284 members in its teenage clubs, and the organization sponsored a study hall program with San Francisco State College students. The Madame C. J. Walker Home, founded in 1920, offered room, board, and a "family atmosphere" for eleven girls, and it was supported by contributions from community members and the small rents that the female boarders paid.[3]

The largest African American neighborhood organizations in the Bay Area were the Bayview Community Center and Booker T. Washington Center in San Francisco and the De Fremery Center in

Oakland. To curb the mounting problem of juvenile delinquency, these associations often focused on youth programs, including the innovative Youth City program operated by the Bayview Center, as well as sports leagues, dance classes, arts and crafts courses, job-training seminars, and drug and alcohol workshops. Late in 1956, the Bayview Neighborhood Center started an ambitious "Youth City" program where black teens elected "officials" for a youth city council that would represent the interests of African American teenagers. Following the format of a successful youth city project that had been started in Pittsburgh in 1939, Frederick Marcus of the neighborhood center created the program and got the support of the mayor, the police chief, and local African American community leaders. In 1957, the Citizens Committee on Youth Problems scheduled a public meeting at the Booker T. Washington Community Center on Presidio Avenue in San Francisco to get teenagers to talk about juvenile problems and open a discussion in an attempt to curb juvenile delinquency in the Hunter's Point-Bayview and Western Addition neighborhoods. These programs had varying degrees of success in reaching out to disaffected and alienated African American teens, but none was able to completely stem the tide of juvenile delinquency in the Bay Area. Since these community centers received no public tax dollars, they constantly stretched their tiny budgets to keep their doors open and provide needed social services to black neighborhoods. The Bayview Center folded several times in the mid-1950s before it was able to somewhat stabilize its finances by the early 1960s. That African American communities in the Bay Area were able to keep any of these organizations afloat during the 1950s in the face of rising unemployment and white official indifference is a testament both to the strength of black resolve and the limitations of moderate reform in northern California.[4]

In addition to providing social services and support for African Americans in need, black churches were also notable for their advocacy of civil rights. Various Bay Area ministerial alliances frequently offered leadership and support for civil rights rallies and campaigns, and black churches often served as forums for speeches, meetings, debates, and other gatherings. For example, the Third Baptist Church on McAllister Street in San Francisco was the site of a rally in support of a state Fair Employment Practices Law in the spring of 1953, and the church served as the venue for public speeches by W. E. B. Du Bois and Martin Luther King, Jr., in 1958. Likewise, Oakland's Allen Temple Baptist Church, which was founded in 1919, grew to become a leading civil rights organization in the 1950s. Under the leadership of the Rev. C. C. Bailey, the church pulled out of the segregated General Baptist Association of the American Baptist Family and joined the multi-racial Oakland Area Association. The church also created scholarship programs, adult education classes, and other educational programs, and it remained a staunch supporter of the National Association for the Advancement of Colored People (NAACP) and the Urban League. Oakland's Taylor Memorial Methodist Church revealed its commitment to the Black Freedom Struggle during the dedication of its new, larger building in November 1954: "Racial integration is the goal toward which all Christian churches must aspire. But while we are achieving the objective, we must supply trained leadership, [a] well rounded religious program, and adequate facilities to effectively convey the Christian Gospel wherever urgent opportunity is calling." Many Bay Area churches opened their coffers and extended financial support for civil rights activities during the 1950s and 1960s, and in one particular case, the NAACP reported that twenty-two churches and religious organizations from Berkeley, Oakland, Richmond, and San Francisco donated in excess of $1,440.00 to help fund a public rally. A large number of African Americans throughout the Bay Area attended church regularly during the 1950s and 1960s, and one survey of blacks in Oakland found that nearly half of the respondents of all ages went to church "almost every week." African American churches, like other mutual aid societies and social organizations of the black community, remained an important vehicle of social reform, self-determination, and self-defense in the postwar era, and their energies and programs would create a positive legacy from which other African Americans would later draw.[5]

One of the crucial factors that explains the successes of African American community institutions and churches during the 1950s and 1960s was the leadership and activity of black women. African American women supported and led many of the neighborhood centers that dispensed what social services were available to black citizens. In 1952, for example, Dorothy Seal ran Oakland's De Fremery Recreation Center, and six of the other ten full-time staff were women. Black women were also active in local Parent Teacher Associations (PTA), and they often raised complaints about school segregation and poor conditions in black-majority schools. Black women's clubs sponsored the Madame C. J. Walker Home, the local YWCAs, and other African American community organizations. In 1965, Charlotte Lewis, program director for the Bay Area Urban League, led the campaign to create a Community Participation Center in East Oakland to serve as a communications hub for African Americans in need of social services. Many of the project's founders were also women, and they made up eight of seventeen board members. Black women also organized many of the social service projects offered by Bay Area churches, and female members of Oakland's Allen Temple Baptist Church served on the church's Nursery Committee and Library Committee and they participated in the Business and Professional Women's Society. Although their economic status had declined following massive lay-offs after World War II, black women continued to play important roles in African American families and in African American communities throughout the Bay Area.[6]

## THE NAACP AND MODERATE CIVIL RIGHTS REFORM

On the civil rights front, the oldest and most powerful black organization in the San Francisco Bay Area was the West Coast Branch of the National Association for the Advancement of Colored People (NAACP). From its origins in the early twentieth century, the NAACP would become an important force for racial reform after WWII. African Americans in the Bay Area founded the Northern California Branch of the NAACP in 1915, which consisted of members in San Francisco and Oakland. Black San Franciscans soon pushed for independence from their East Bay brethren, however, and the San Francisco chapter became autonomous in 1923. During the Second World War, however, the San Francisco group was paralyzed by internal strife and it failed to make much headway until after 1944. With the accession of new leadership after the war, the San Francisco chapter of the NAACP would launch several important campaigns in the late 1940s and the 1950s that pressed for fair employment and housing practices.   In Oakland, the Alameda County chapter witnessed a similar burst of energy in the mid-1940s, and the group saw its membership jump from 2,874 in December 1944 to 3,526 in September 1945.  In 1946, the Alameda County Chapter elected a slate of officers that included President C. L. Dellums, Vice-President Dr. B. G. Gallagher, Secretary Eugenia Greene, Treasurer Dr. C. C. Rhodes, Tarea Hall Pittman as head of the Membership Committee, and Joyce Cooper as head of Youth Work.  African Americans in Richmond responded after the war to create their own branch of the NAACP, and in January 1948, they elected officers including President Rev. I. C. Mickens, Vice-President Cleophas Brown, Secretary Juanita Wheeler, and Treasurer W. L. Pace.  By 1946, the new and old chapters of the NAACP apparently had solidified their foundations and were prepared for a fresh offensive against racism in the Golden State.[7]

All of the northern California branches of the NAACP benefited from spectacular growth in the years immediately following the Second World War.  Eager to secure the gains they had made during the war and to press forward on other fronts, African Americans joined the NAACP in record numbers.  The membership rolls in San Francisco and the East Bay swelled to impressive highs in 1946 and 1947, as African Americans invested their earnings in the campaign for racial equality.  Membership in Oakland's chapter swelled to over 3,000, and San Francisco nearly equaled that mark.  As wartime production sharply declined, however, membership in the leading civil rights organizations plummeted.  Few blacks in the Bay Area could afford to commit their shrinking resources to membership dues, and although interest in the NAACP and its projects did not greatly decline, the chapters faced a severe shortage of manpower and funds in the late 1940s.  By the end of the decade, the Alameda chapter had less than one-fifth of the membership that it had recorded at its peak, and the San Francisco and Richmond chapters teetered at the brink of extinction.  The precipitous decline in membership was apparently a state-wide phenomenon, as even the powerful Los Angeles chapter lost more than ten thousand members.  While the dramatic fluctuation in membership was perhaps

**Table 3**
**NAACP Membership, 1945-1951**

| Branch | 1946 | 1947 | 1948 | 1949 | 1950 | 1951 |
|---|---|---|---|---|---|---|
| Alameda | 3,207 | 3,227 | 2,451 | 596 | 614 | 1,682 |
| Richmond | 410 | 333 | 764 | 48 | 160 | 238 |
| San Francisco | 2,911 | 2,981 | 782 | 499 | 387 | 704 |
| Los Angeles | 14,012 | 10,121 | 7,390 | 3,939 | 2,570 | 4,179 |

SOURCE: Memo, "Comparative Study of West Coast Branches," n.d., Carton 7, NAACP West Coast Region Papers, Bancroft Library, University of California, Berkeley.

partly a correction from the enthusiasm of the war years, it was also certainly a reflection of the economic crises that African Americans faced after the wartime industries shut down and blacks were pushed out of the industrial working class in large numbers. After a period of frantic activity and grave concern, the NAACP leaders were able to stabilize their memberships, and by the early 1950s, several successful drives to pull more African Americans into the organizations had returned the rolls to relatively safe and stable levels. The chapters then began in earnest their assault against racial segregation and discrimination in the Bay Area.[8]

The NAACP remained a champion of African American workers throughout the postwar era by suing employers for the reinstatement of unjustly fired black workers or threatening pickets against businesses that refused to hire qualified blacks. The Alameda County Branch held only two mass meetings in 1949, but the chapter did convince the East Bay's Chevrolet auto plant to hire its first black worker that year. In 1953, Gladys Fermon of Oakland returned to her position at the Transportation Division of the Oakland Army Base after the NAACP came to her defense. Mrs. Fermon had been dismissed after she complained about her white civilian supervisors. She appealed to the NAACP, and it arranged a grievance hearing for Mrs. Fermon, who was subsequently reinstated to her old position. The NAACP continued its campaign, and a few years later the organization picketed outside the St. Francis Hotel in San

Francisco to protest against employment discrimination by the Yellow Cab Company. Roy Wilkins, national president of the NAACP, even made a special trip to the Bay Area to join the protests. In 1960, the NAACP undertook one of its most ambitious projects by threatening the Jack Tar Hotel in San Francisco. The new hotel, which had not yet opened, was to have 437 employees, only 40 of whom were black. Three of the black employees were to be doormen, and the other 37 were either cooks or maids. Of the eight thousand applicants interviewed, over one thousand were black, yet only one in ten of the final hires were African American. The NAACP threatened to hold a picket line outside of the hotel, but Terry Francois, president of the San Francisco NAACP, arranged a meeting with the hotel management. After winning concessions, Francois called off the protest. Several years later, the NAACP backed a group of nineteen African American housekeepers at the San Francisco Hilton Hotel after they were fired for refusing to clock in until they had a meeting with management to discuss their grievances. The maids complained of constant abusive language by their superiors, of being forced to always work during one of their two guaranteed days off, of being frequently "laid off" for a week if they asked for a day off, and of having to bring in a doctor's note if they missed a day for being sick. The NAACP organized a picket line in front of the hotel until the housekeepers' grievances were finally addressed.[9]

Other formal and ad-hoc civil rights groups also protested employment discrimination in the Bay Area. The interracial Council for Civic Unity (CCU) reported that African Americans were concentrated in menial employment and had little job security. Although most firms surveyed by the CCU claimed to have non-discrimination policies, the CCU complained that they often did not effectively communicate those policies to their supervisors and employees. In some instances, African Americans used boycotts and picket lines to demand that businesses in their communities offer jobs to black residents. For example, the San Francisco Negro American Labor Council and the Bay View Citizens' Committee joined forces in 1962 to protest outside the Super Save store of Justine Wong in the predominantly black Bayview area. Buckling under the picket lines, Mr. Wong agreed to hire two black workers for his store. Benjamin Christwell, a local community leader, noted that "elementary justice demands that Negroes be hired in businesses where they bank and spend their money. Our committee will continue to advise Negroes not to spend their money where they can't work."[10]

The Bay Area Urban League was another moderate civil rights organization that pressed for better employment opportunities for blacks. Originating in San Francisco and expanding to the East Bay following World War II, the Bay Area Urban League pushed for better job-training programs for African Americans and tried to persuade white employers to hire black workers. According to Director Kenneth Smith, the Urban League favored a non-confrontational approach when dealing with white employers: "The Urban League uses the conference method usually. When we find a Negro is having difficulty in securing a job, we talk to the prospective employer. We try to convince him that it is not bad business to hire a person of a minority race. An employer misses a good business opportunity when he refuses to hire a well-trained Negro." Led and controlled by middle-class black reformers, the Urban League sought to work within the legal and social system of the Bay Area to persuade the white establishment to grant access to black workers and business leaders. This approach was only successful if Bay Area whites were indeed willing to abandon their prejudices and their discriminatory hiring practices; not surprisingly, many white employers were unmoved by the Urban League's arguments.[11]

The most impressive victory won by the African American civil rights organizations on the job front came in 1959 with the passage of a Fair Employment Practices bill by the California legislature. Sponsored by the newly elected governor, Edmund G. "Pat" Brown, and a veteran state senator, William Byron Rumford, the FEP ordinance "prohibit[ed] employers or labor unions from discriminating on [the] grounds of race, creed, national origin or age." A five-person commission was established by the law to investigate claims of bias. After signing the bill on Thursday, April 16, 1959, Gov. Brown declared: "In guaranteeing equal job opportunities for all our citizens, regardless of race, creed or color, the State Legislature has taken a historic step forward in the ages long battle against prejudice and discrimination." The FEP victory had been a long time coming, as African American civil rights leaders and politicians had pushed for such a law since the Second World War. State assemblymen Augustus F. Hawkins and George D. Collins, Jr., had introduced the first FEP law in 1945, and the NAACP had mobilized its forces in 1952 for a long pro-FEP campaign. C. L. Dellums, a noted black leader from Oakland and the state chairman of the California Committee for FEP, was another major player behind the bill. In the spring of 1953, Tarea Hall Pittman wrote to Franklin Williams, chairman of the San Francisco chapter of the NAACP, that she had mailed letters to the authors of a FEP law in the California assembly, to the legislators who promised conferences on the bill, and to all the rest of the members of the assembly. "There hasn't been a night that I haven't worked until after midnight," she noted. "I'm going out now to mail some more letters." Their efforts finally paid off after nearly fifteen years of constant pressure, and employment discrimination became, in the eyes of the law at least, illegal and invalid.[12]

African American activists wasted no time testing the limits of the new FEP law, and they quickly brought their grievances before the Commission on Equal Employment Opportunity. In one case, a black cook was turned away from a one-month replacement job because the restaurant did not "work colored cooks." The black worker was awarded $195.00 by the commission, less his earnings from another job that he had worked for one week after he was refused the first job. William Byron Rumford, the black state senator who had sponsored the successful FEP bill, reflected on the importance of the act and concluded:

> There was a time a black person couldn't get a job in a service station. You never saw a black face working for, say, Shell Oil or any of those stations. I mean just an ordinary manual labor job, no particular skill, no particular profession. We weren't able to get those jobs. Then, when we got the Fair Employment Practices Act the whole thing changed completely!... When you go now, you see clerks in stores; you see them filling prescriptions.... We never saw a Negro girl, say, down at Kahn's Department Store doing anything! But the FEPC brought that all down. It was the law that did it....

With the Fair Employment Practices Act, moderate African American reformers finally had a law that prohibited discrimination in employment, and they had won a long and bitter legal battle to stomp out *de jure* discrimination against blacks.[13]

The NAACP also supported and often led the offensives to gain equal housing opportunities and decent living conditions for African Americans in the Bay Area. Throughout the 1950s, the NAACP tried to break down the walls that locked blacks out of lily-white neighborhoods in San Francisco and the East Bay. The organization was at the forefront of the Willie Mays controversy in 1957, and it used the publicity generated by that scandal to help other African Americans in their efforts to secure housing or rental property. In September 1958, for example, the NAACP appealed to San Francisco Mayor George Christopher to help a black entrepreneur obtain a location for her beauty salon. Juanita Bell had rented the storefront and had started preparing it for her grand opening when her landlord called and asked that Mrs. Bell return the key and accept her deposit back. The white owner confessed that she had received threatening phone calls from neighbors and had decided not to go through with the deal. The NAACP requested that the mayor step in to ensure "that our minority citizens will not have to continue to bear the burden of the ghettoized housing, unfair buying and rental policies, and insulting bigoted housing practices." The NAACP also attacked assertions that African Americans drove down property values, and moderate black leaders often wrote white politicians, builders, and real estate agents to argue that home prices would actually increase if the market was open to more eligible buyers. The civil rights group pointed to numerous studies that countered the "generally accepted theory that minority races depreciate property values," and the NAACP encouraged white property owners to sell to anyone who could offer them fair prices for their homes.[14]

Moderate civil rights leaders also joined in the effort to improve conditions in and access to public housing. Although the United States Supreme Court had ruled in May 1954, just weeks after the momentous *Brown v. Board of Education* decision, against the segregationist policies of the San Francisco Housing Authority (SFHA) and in favor of non-discrimination in public housing projects,

African Americans continued to face numerous obstacles in their quest to find decent, affordable housing. The NAACP enthusiastically received the news of the Supreme Court's ruling, which was to apply to all of California, but they soon found that enforcing the decision was a formidable challenge throughout the Bay Area. The NAACP spent many years trying to define the boundaries of the ruling, and in 1959, they threw their support behind a bill in the California legislature that would prohibit discrimination on the basis of race or religion in publicly assisted housing. Riding on the coattails of their success in the Fair Employment Practices fight, the NAACP and Augustus F. Hawkins pushed the bill through the legislature, and Gov. Pat Brown signed it into law. Although such a measure should have been unnecessary in the face of the 1954 Supreme Court ruling, the proponents of non-discrimination in public housing facilities now had another weapon at their disposal.[15]

The NAACP continued to agitate for equality in housing throughout the 1960s, and the organization offered support for the Rumford Fair Housing Act of 1963, and it represented those African Americans who were threatened with displacement by the policies of urban renewal. The NAACP monitored white resistance to the Rumford Fair Housing Act and lobbied for its passage during the early 1960s, and the moderate reformers maintained a vigilant guard over the rights defined in the bill once it had gained passage. When conservative forces organized support for Proposition 14, which would have bypassed the anti-discrimination measures of the Rumford Act, the NAACP countered with a series of fair housing initiatives. In Richmond, Mrs. William Stiles and Elton Brombacher headed the Fair Housing Committee, which planned a voter-registration drive, organized an educational campaign, and trained local speakers to oppose Proposition 14 in the November 1964 election. The civil rights organization also protested against urban renewal programs, and it defended the interests of low-income black residents whose homes were threatened by the projects. The NAACP argued that African Americans displaced by such projects often could not find suitable replacement housing due to discrimination and segregation, and the group demanded that "Negroes...be rehoused and relocated in standard housing on a non-discriminatory basis." The NAACP argued that urban renewal projects were "being used to extend and perpetuate rigid ghettos. Urban renewal should be used to realize the promise of breaking up the ghetto, and to create a free housing market where all can compete equally." The NAACP strongly opposed urban renewal and construction programs, like Project Acorn, the Grove-Shafter Freeway, and the construction of a new postal processing center in West Oakland, that demolished large tracts of black housing without first finding adequate replacement homes for the residents. During the 1950s and 1960s, the NAACP remained at the forefront of the charge against housing discrimination and segregation in the Bay Area.[16]

Closeiy related to the issue of residential segregation was, of course, *de facto* educational segregation in the Bay Area's neighborhood-based school system. The NAACP produced numerous reports and statements about the problem of school segregation in the 1950s and 1960s, and the organization frequently lobbied the school boards in San Francisco and the East Bay to change policies that concentrated African American students into inferior schools. In 1962, for example, the NAACP filed suit against the San Francisco School Board to end segregation in the city's public schools. The NAACP sought an injunction against the School Board and asked the court to force the board to submit a desegregation plan, redraw school attendance boundaries, and re-open Central Junior High School as an integrated facility by February of 1963. Several years later, Roy Wilkins, national executive director of the NAACP, criticized San Francisco school board officials for refusing to take a more active stance against school segregation. "I fear that [Superintendent] Dr. [Harold] Spears and San Francisco are given to the idea that segregation doesn't exist here as it does in the South and that in any case little can be done about it that is educationally sound," he said. "This is a widespread attitude among administrators in big cities, such as New York, Los Angeles, and to a monumental degree in Chicago. San Francisco is not unique." Through its activism, the NAACP played an important leadership role during the frequent and heated battles over segregation in public schools, and the organization helped to define the public agenda for educational reform in the Bay Area.[17]

Finally, the NAACP and other moderate civil rights groups also represented African American concerns over incidents of police brutality in the postwar era. Black citizens' frequent complaints of rough treatment at the hands of the police led civil rights leaders to call for community review boards of local law enforcement agencies that would have the power to hear cases and impose sanctions for excessive use of force or other illegal activities. Several activist groups, including the NAACP and the California Federation for Civic Unity (CFCU), pressed local governments to improve relations between police forces and minority citizens. In 1946, the CFCU disseminated a "Police Training Manual" throughout California that instructed officers on how to deal with racial issues. Several years later, a CFCU official noted that "it has been a long-time stand of this organization that minority group people in particular should not be placed at the complete mercy of local police administration.... [They], by dint of bitter experience, have been made uncertain whether they are the beneficiaries or the victims of law enforcement processes." In 1949, the Alameda County Branch of the NAACP convinced the city of Oakland to hire Dr. David McIntyre of the University of California to give the city's police department a course in human relations in order to curb police brutality and incidents of violent confrontation between black civilians and the largely white police force. Across the bay, black San Franciscans lobbied the city to hire more black officers who could better relate to the growing population of young African Americans. In the summer of 1956, after repeated appeals by black leaders and citizens, two African American police officers, John Finney and Henry Williams, were appointed to the Juvenile Division of the San Francisco Police Department after a "near riot" at the New Fillmore Theatre.[18]

Despite the moderate leaders' gains, however, police-community relations continued to worsen during the late 1950s and early 1960s. In 1962, the NAACP renewed its calls for a community police review board in San Francisco, but these were ignored by city officials. Frustrated by local bureaucrats' foot-dragging, the NAACP appealed to state and federal officials in 1968. Everett P. Brandon, field secretary for the NAACP, offered to testify on the problem of police brutality to the California Assembly Interim Committee on

Civil Liberties.  Cliffron R. Jeffers wrote a letter to United States Attorney General Ramsey Clark to protest the activities of the San Francisco Police Department's elite TAC Squad.  Jeffers claimed that the TAC Squad, which was originally created to prevent and quell civil disorders, was systematically violating the civil liberties of African Americans in San Francisco.  Their protests went largely unheeded, however, and the problem of police-community relations would remain a vexing one for the rest of the decade.  Indeed, violent confrontations between African Americans and white police officers would spark massive protests in the Bay Area during the 1960s, and the issue of police brutality would become a major rallying cry for black militants.[19]

To combat discrimination and segregation in the Bay Area, moderate civil rights groups like the NAACP relied mostly on the established tactics of persuasion, legal action, and, as a last resort, the threat of nonviolent protest.  Moderate civil rights leaders stressed the respectable nature of their campaigns for equality, and most activists preferred a reasoned, non-confrontational approach.  In 1946, Laurence I. Hewes, Jr., regional director of the California Federation for Civic Unity (CFCU), explained to the head of the California State Hotel Association that

> as professional people, working in the field of race relations, it is our judgment that the increased colored population of California and the frequency of incidents of a racial character indicate the need for intelligent handling of this problem and the development of a policy.  Otherwise, racial incidents, as they occur, tend to be handled on a piece-meal basis, without any sound procedure for mutual settlement....  [O]ther, more direct measures to secure equal treatment have been taken.  These are, in our judgment, evidences of the total lack of planning and careful thought on the matter.

The moderates' approach of polite persuasion characterized many of the actions by the CFCU and the NAACP during the 1950s and early 1960s.  In 1953, for example, Stanley S. Jacobs of the CFCU appealed to Harris Rickseeker of the Mill Valley Cub Scouts to have Pack II abandon their plan to put on a minstrel show in blackface.

Jacobs argued that "many schools and youth organizations throughout the country have taken definite stands against minstrel shows because they have come to realize that although seemingly harmless on the surface, actually they depict Negroes as shiftless, gambling, drinking, lazy people and make a profound impression on young minds." In a similar vein, Tarea Hall Pittman reported to a friend in Klamath Falls, Oregon, about the NAACP's successful campaign to remove the book *Little Black Sambo* from the libraries of public schools in Alameda County in the early 1950s. Moderate black leaders felt that the children's book reinforced negative stereotypes of African Americans, and the NAACP lobbied the school board until the book was removed from circulation.[20]

The NAACP was reluctant to engage in public direct-action protests during the 1950s out of fear of being labeled "subversive." The moderate civil rights activists argued that they were not trying to undermine the American system, but they were attempting to secure African Americans' place within it. Distancing themselves from leftist organizations and avowed Communists, the moderate black reformers pursued a middle course and eschewed any hint of radicalism. In light of the history of labor militancy and Communist activity in the Bay Area, NAACP leaders quickly distanced themselves from Communist groups following the Second World War. In 1947, panic struck NAACP officials when they learned that the Richmond Branch "has been completely under the control and domination of a small Communist group who practically run the branch in such a way that every move and action of the branch has been the avowed intention of the party." Many black leaders feared that such infiltration by Communists would alienate supporters of the NAACP and would jeopardize the group's program for racial reform. M. W. Griffin warned his colleagues that the Richmond case would "bring discredit in the eyes of many people who otherwise would be supporters of the Association, but who are pulling away from it because of the tactics that are being used." Their fears were somewhat justified, for two years later, a group of black ministers in Richmond notified the NAACP Board of Directors that they would no longer cooperate with the leaders of the Richmond branch "because of their definite Communistic affiliations and inclinations." Cautious that they might also be stained with the taint of

Communism, the CFCU announced in 1949 that the civic unity movement "is strictly non-partisan and works only with non-Communist groups for such objectives as equal employment opportunity, non-discrimination in public places, etc. We aim to make our local groups as broadly representative as possible, with a cross-section of business, professional and labor people involved, as well as representatives of the various racial, national and religious groups."[21]

The West Coast Branch of the NAACP hardened its anti-Communist stance in the early 1950s, offering several public announcements that it was not allied with or influenced by the Communist Party. After the grisly murders of two African American activists in Groveland, Florida, the NAACP announced that it would not participate in a Communist-organized public demonstration in Oakland. "Information has come to our office that certain groups consisting of Communists and Communist-sympathizers are holding such a demonstration and parade...," the Association explained. "While we are calling on organizations interested in action against the terrorist murders of Mr. Moore, we cannot afford to have linked with our protest left-wing organizations which seek to use this issue for purposes contrary to those of [the] NAACP. We are working only with organizations approved by the NAACP." In another instance, Franklin H. Williams, secretary-counsel for the West Coast Branch, asked Nat Yanish of the *Daily People's World* to leave the press table at a speech by black labor activist A. Philip Randolph in 1954, because he did not want members of "the Communist press" associated with the NAACP. The NAACP also abandoned a potentially fruitful political alliance with the labor-based Congress of Industrial Organizations (CIO) because of its ties to the American Communist Party (CPUSA). In 1954, the moderate civil rights organization proclaimed that the International Longshoremen's and Warehousemen's Union (ILWU) "does not have their support, and furthermore authorizes no one from the ILWU to use their organization as a front for the Communist Party." In the midst of a bitter election fight between rival AFL and CIO unions, the NAACP was torn between supporting the AFL affiliate that discriminated openly against African Americans and the CIO affiliate that was aligned with the Communist Party. The black reformers decided to stay clear of the fray, and they concluded that "the essence of our position is what it has always been, namely, that the NAACP does not endorse or cooperate with any union that is dominated by left wingers, nor does it endorse and cooperate with any union which either operates under a Jim Crow policy or practices Jim Crow in its business." Rejecting the unrespectable nature of white American radicalism, the black elite in the San Francisco Bay Area allowed the paranoid politics of the McCarthy era to foul the waters of left-wing interracial reform.[22]

During the 1950s, the NAACP worked mainly through the courts and city hall. Using the legal expertise of men like Terry Francois, president of the San Francisco chapter and eventually a member of the city's Board of Supervisors, the NAACP waged a legal war against segregation and discrimination by testing laws in court and by lobbying for reforms such as the Fair Employment Practices Act of 1959 or the Rumford Fair Housing Act of 1963. Many moderate leaders were skeptical about the benefits of sensational public demonstrations, and William Byron Rumford blamed protesters for almost derailing his Fair Housing Act after they staged a sit-in at the California Assembly:

> I might mention to you that after the bill went to the senate, the CORE organization attempted to assist us by occupying the rotunda of the Capitol as protesters and petitioners. I had felt that we were able to get the legislation that far without this kind of assistance and I had asked them to please leave. But they did not. They remained there throughout with their children. They occupied the rotunda and many of the senators were upset about it, saying this was an attempt to threaten them and that type of thing. Of course I wasn't sure that CORE was really trying to 'help me.' If they were trying to help me, as far as I was concerned, this was a poor way to do it!

Most of the NAACP's victories took place behind the scenes instead of on the streets, and although the black press heralded the group's successes, the moderate reformers lacked the intense passion of radical activists. NAACP leaders shied away from embracing direct-action tactics and hoped that by cultivating a respectable image they could win more victories and counter the traditional stereo-types of black Americans.  At its 1956 national convention, for example, the NAACP declared that it was "not yet ready to take a position" on the matter of nonviolent direct-action tactics used in the Montgomery Bus Boycott, and it affirmed its commitment to "press on the legal, legislative and educational fronts to carry through their determination for full civil rights by 1963."  These legal campaigns would pay off in the FEP and open-public-housing ordinances, but they would not solve all, or perhaps most, of the problems that African Americans in the Bay Area faced in the post-war era.[23]

Occasionally, the NAACP would encourage black residents to boycott an employer who refused to hire African American workers, and the Association did organize pickets if white businessmen proved completely unresponsive to their demands.  The NAACP's most visible effort to unite public opinion behind their civil rights initiatives, however, came in the form of the Freedom Rallies of the late 1950s and early 1960s.  In one of the earliest such mass public meetings, more than ten thousand people jammed into the Oakland Auditorium in March 1956, to join a prayer-protest meeting in support of the Montgomery Bus Boycott and to condemn segregation in the Jim Crow South.  The NAACP helped organize two large rallies the following year, each of which drew more than nine thousand participants.  In January, Jackie Robinson visited the Bay Area to support the NAACP's Freedom Fund Campaign, and the baseball hero helped raise more than $12,900 for the Association's northern California branches.  Several months later, the NAACP and the East Bay Ministers' Alliance welcomed the Rev. Dr. Martin Luther King, Jr., to the Oakland Auditorium, and a large and enthusiastic crowd demonstrated their solidarity with the southern civil rights leader.  The NAACP continued to capitalize on its ability to bring black celebrities to the Bay Area, and over the course of the next several years, the Association drew large crowds to rallies featuring civil rights leaders like Martin Luther King, Jr., sports stars like Olympic decathlete Rafer Johnson, and other figures including Ernest Green, the first black graduate of Central High School in Little Rock, Arkansas.  The enthusiasm surrounding such large rallies was difficult to sustain, however, and in the mid-1960s, some members of the NAACP encouraged the organization to embrace direct action in order to fight segregation and discrimination in the Bay Area. In 1964, several NAACP leaders and student organizers became more aggressive and sat-in at a Cadillac dealership on Van Ness Avenue. San Francisco Chapter President Dr. Thomas N. Burbridge and Tracy Simms were arrested along with 110 other protesters after the group entered the dealership and refused to leave. When Burbridge was arrested during a mass demonstration against Barry Goldwater and the Republican National Convention at the Cow Palace in San Francisco later that same year, Judge David D. French sentenced Burbridge to nine months in jail, three years probation, and gave him a $900.00 fine. After a lengthy appeals process and several more public rallies, Burbridge served his jail term in 1966. The experiment with direct action proved less fruitful than the NAACP leaders had hoped, and the San Francisco chapter announced that it would "only engage in demonstrative activities as a last resort measure when all other avenues of negotiation have failed."[24]

The failure of the NAACP and other moderate civil rights groups to end employment discrimination, to solve the problems of housing and school segregation, and to curb police brutality allowed an increasingly vocal minority of black militants to be heard. Despite the overwhelming odds that groups like the NAACP faced in the Bay Area, two decades of what seemed like little progress on the racial front to thousands of African Americans locked out of decent jobs and into inferior schools and overcrowded slums fed an increasing black frustration and rage. When months-old issues of employment, housing, and educational discrimination turned into decades-old crises, more and more blacks in the Bay Area would seek other alternatives than the middle-class legalism offered by the NAACP. As the Civil Rights Movement in the South picked up momentum and pictures of Montgomery and Selma were broadcast on television sets in the Bay Area, more African Americans in the urban West began to question the appropriateness of legal tactics and polite protest in the struggle for racial equality. Young radicals began to take to the streets to demand immediate reforms, and they tapped a reservoir of energy that had been building in black communities since the Second World War.

## CORE AND THE RISE OF THE MILITANTS

In sharp contrast to the moderate reform offered by the NAACP, the Congress of Racial Equality (CORE) embraced the free use of direct-action tactics from its earliest days in the Bay Area. CORE agitated in the streets and at the site of injustice instead of working through the legal system, and the organization focused on immediate goals and issues rather than on larger systems of segregation and discrimination. CORE chapters in San Francisco and the East Bay struggled to gain a foothold in African American communities throughout the 1940s and 1950s, and they toiled largely in the shadow of the popular and relatively well-funded NAACP. Rising to prominence during the early 1960s, however, CORE would become a major factor in the development of the Civil Rights Movement in the San Francisco Bay Area, and the organization would leave a legacy of militant direct-action protest that other radicals would draw upon later in the decade.

Black San Franciscans first established a CORE chapter in that city during the early 1940s, but the group folded after many of its leaders were drafted during the Second World War. In January 1948, another group of African Americans reorganized the chapter and applied to the national headquarters for official recognition. The new local chapter had three co-chairmen, Charles Johnson, Jr., Allen Willis, and Asher Harer, who held bi-weekly meetings with the thirty-seven other members. In their application to the national office, the members of the San Francisco CORE chapter reported a successful campaign to end discrimination in a local launderette. In the spring, the chapter began a boycott of Lucky Stores in Hunter's Point to protest employment discrimination, and it forced the chain to hire at least three black workers by the end of that summer. Controversy soon gripped the San Francisco chapter, however, when Abraham Lincoln Fletcher charged that Communists had infiltrated the group and had taken over. Fletcher appealed to CORE national headquarters, which sent representative George Houser to investigate. After a trip to the Bay Area in August 1948, Houser concluded that although there were some Trotskyites among the local CORE leadership, the national office should support the chapter in light of its recent success against Lucky Stores in Hunter's Point. Unlike his counterparts in the NAACP, Houser notified the local San Francisco leadership that he would overlook their ties to Communist groups, and he concluded that "I might say that I don't take Abraham Lincoln Fletcher seriously. He button-holed me for a talk before I left San Francisco, and he quite obviously is away off the beam. He even implied that I had sympathy with the CP [Community Party] when I didn't think he was doing right in publicizing the kind of stories he was." The leadership of both the local chapter and national office of CORE did not back away from radicalism if it served their ends, and they would hold onto this pragmatic militancy throughout the next two decades.[25]

In the East Bay, CORE chapters emerged in Berkeley and Oakland in the late 1940s, and like their counterpart in San Francisco, these chapters quickly adopted direct-action tactics in the struggle for racial equality. Fourteen activists, including Chairman James Clark, organized the Berkeley chapter in December 1948. Consisting largely of whites from the University of California and the race relations departments of the local YMCA and YWCA, the Berkeley membership held weekly meetings and agitated to stop landlords from discriminating in student boarding houses. In 1949, the Berkeley chapter organized a sit-in at the Teacup Restaurant in Oakland to protest the owner's refusal to serve black patrons. The proprietor of the Chinese restaurant feared that serving African Americans would drive away his white customers. Twenty-five CORE activists held a dine-in at the restaurant on February 26, after which the owner agreed to change his policy and start serving blacks. By 1950, the Berkeley chapter had joined with CORE members in Oakland to launch an aggressive campaign against Oakland's Sears store to protest the retail giant's unfair hiring practices. CORE objected to the fact that Sears had not hired blacks in any position other than as cleaning staff in its twenty-year history, with the exception of one light-skinned tailor. The organization called for a change in the store's employment practices and demanded that it immediately hire qualified African Americans and other minorities in positions that involved considerable responsibility and that yielded considerable financial reward. Despite six weeks of constant picketing outside of the store, Sears management seemed unmoved by the protesters. A local newspaper reported that the store's manager, Mr. Ridener, argued that "he had a right to refuse to hire Negroes and Orientals as sales and office help on the grounds that certain groups naturally go into certain occupations. He argued that there are no Jewish farmers since they all go into business and banking, and that in a like manner, Negroes become janitors and maids." Although there was obviously great need for the efforts of the East Bay chapters of CORE, the groups won only limited victories in the late 1940s and early 1950s in their campaigns against racial discrimination.[26]

Following their initial activism, CORE chapters throughout the Bay Area sank into decline in the 1950s, and most had closed their doors by 1955. As with the NAACP, the years from 1951-1958 represented a low point for CORE. The civil rights group had few significant victories, and the activists struggled unsuccessfully to keep their chapters afloat. By the end of the decade, however, a new group of civil rights leaders had reorganized CORE chapters in San Francisco and the East Bay, and the Congress of Racial Equality began anew the war against racism in northern California. In the spring of 1959, Gordon R. Carey, a field representative from the CORE national office, encouraged activists in the Bay Area to create new CORE chapters. Ellen Fisk, of San Francisco State College, became chairperson of the reincarnated San Francisco chapter, and Bob Walter headed the new group in Berkeley. The Berkeley chapter was again predominantly white, and it had some difficulty inspiring activity among East Bay African Americans. In the summer of 1959, CORE made its first successful foray into Richmond, and a chapter of the civil rights group was organized there in late July. The small chapter had only eight key members, and it struggled to solidify its base for the rest of that year. The CORE national office suggested a merger between the Richmond group and the Berkeley chapter, but the Richmond activists were finally able to establish themselves by June 1960.[27]

Like much of the rest of the nation, the Bay Area CORE activists found their attention focused on the southern Civil Rights Movement during 1960 and 1961. African Americans in northern California felt that their struggles for racial equality in the urban West were fundamentally connected to their brethren's efforts in the rural South. The newly founded CORE chapters in San Francisco and the East Bay boycotted and picketed area Woolworth's and Kress stores to show their support for the sit-ins and other civil rights demonstrations that were occurring across the South. The Woolworth's and Kress protests were followed by rallies to show solidarity with southern African Americans and to raise funds for the Freedom Riders and other southern blacks in need. The Richmond chapter's greatest early contribution was a $25.00 check to the CORE fund that aided black farmers in Fayette and Haywood, Tennessee, who faced eviction from their farms for registering to vote. CORE chapters throughout the Bay Area supported many similar projects and programs, and they tried to use the cause of southern civil rights to spur reforms in northern California.[28]

After a brief outpouring of community sentiment and support for southern blacks, however, the Bay Area CORE chapters again faced grave difficulties. In San Francisco, interest in the chapter quickly faded in the early 1960s, and yet another set of activists reestablished the group in June 1961. The new leadership consisted of Bob Slattery and six other officers, three of whom were female. Thirty-two active members completed the chapter, and although they had frequent bi-weekly meetings, the group lacked a clear sense of direction. The San Francisco chapter joined a picket campaign against the Washington Redskins during a San Francisco 49ers home game because the visiting team refused to hire black players, but the group was largely inactive for the rest of the year. Although a field agent, Genevieve Hughes, judged in late 1961 that the San Francisco chapter did have potential, she noted that it did not have a large black membership and it had failed to build a strong base of support in the city's African American communities. Hughes later took over leadership of the chapter in the summer of 1962, after she concluded that "San Francisco CORE is probably only exceeded in weakness on the West Coast by Richmond-El Cerrito, Oakland, and San Fernando Valley," all of which were notoriously feeble chapters. She was distressed at the largely white membership of the chapter, and she felt that Wilfred Ussery was the only active and effective black member. Hughes herself would not last long as head of the San Francisco group, and she was replaced by

Fredricka Teer in the fall of 1962. Teer informed the CORE central office that the San Francisco chapter was disorganized and wracked with internal divisions. Aside from its challenge to the San Francisco School Board over segregation in the city's schools, the group had failed to mount an impressive civil rights campaign in more than a year.[29]

Across the bay, conditions for CORE were not much better. In the spring of 1961, the Oakland chapter was reorganized and James Lee became its new chairman. Although Lee was perhaps most responsible for reestablishing the chapter in Oakland, he caused a major disagreement within the group after sending a letter to the governor of California urging him to end discrimination at the Moler Barber College in Oakland. Apparently, the other members of the chapter felt that the strongly worded letter was inappropriate, or at the very least that it should have been brought up for discussion by the entire group. Soon after this flap, Lee was charged with being a Communist, and several members wrote to the national headquarters asking for his dismissal. Wracked by inner turmoil, the group voted to dissolve itself on November 2, 1961. Soon thereafter, Tom Roland, a white veteran Freedom Rider, helped to rebuild the Oakland chapter, but even he would abandon the organization after it failed to gain much community support. The Richmond chapter was likewise mired in inactivity. A CORE field agent concluded in the fall of 1962 that the chapter consisted mainly of "middle-aged school teachers who formed during the Woolworth's campaign and have done very little since then." Although the chapter had raised funds for the Civil Rights Movement in the South, they were unable to do much to improve conditions in Richmond. The chapter disbanded in September.[30]

It was not until local CORE chapters turned their attention back to conditions in the Bay Area that they were able to use their direct-action techniques to build a strong base of support among African American communities in northern California. Although the Berkeley chapter remained largely white and consisted mainly of students from the University of California, it led the direct-action charge in the winter of 1961 with protests outside of Hink's Department Store in Berkeley. Beginning December 2, the Berkeley CORE chapter picketed the store for its failure to hire a single

African American salesperson in its fifty-seven year history. The group won a quick victory, as Hink's capitulated to the organization's demands and hired two blacks for its sales staff. Following their success against Berkeley retailers, the CORE chapter began a more ambitious campaign against the city's realtors in the spring of 1962. The group picketed the office of realtor Joseph C. Eyring "after one of his saleswomen refused to show a house to a Negro, but agreed to show the same house to a white member of CORE who was testing [for discrimination]." After a half-hour sit-in in Eyring's office, the realtor agreed to show the home to the black customer, Robert Jefferson. A meeting between CORE and the Berkeley Realty Board resulted in another firm agreeing to stop discriminating against African Americans in rental property. The civil rights organization then staged several mass rallies against housing discrimination in the East Bay, and a successful four-day picket campaign against Nakamura Realty ended when that agency also promised not to discriminate against black customers. San Francisco's CORE chapter responded to the new wave of direct-action protests with a sit-in at a city School Board meeting in August 1962. African American parents denounced the board's plan to fill a new temporary Central Junior High School with sixty percent black students and forty percent white students, and they called for more integration in the city's schools.[31]

These demonstrations sparked other protests during the next several years. In January and February 1963, the Berkeley and Oakland chapters of CORE pressed Montgomery Ward in the East Bay for better hiring practices. At the Oakland store, twelve of thirteen janitors were black, all of the cafeteria staff was black, and only four of 200 to 250 salespeople were African American. The civil rights groups called for a large public campaign against the retailer, which lasted through the spring of that year. The Berkeley CORE continued its vigorous assaults on East Bay employers the following year, and in November 1964, the organization planned a boycott of ten businesses on Shattuck Avenue in Berkeley that discriminated against African Americans. In December 1963, the San Francisco chapter began similar protests against the J. C. Penney's and Macy's stores in that city. At the Westlake Penney's, only one of 180 employees was black, and he worked as a janitor. At the downtown store, only five percent of the 405 employees were African American, and they were concentrated in the janitorial services as well. Similar trends were found at Macy's. CORE joined with the San Francisco Ministers Union in a boycott until the stores revised their hiring policies. The following spring, the San Francisco CORE began a more daring offensive against Lucky stores with their use of the "shop-in." To denounce the stores' abysmal minority hiring record, protesters filled shopping carts with groceries, went through the check-out lanes, and then announced that they had forgotten their money and were unable to pay for the goods. The NAACP objected to this particular tactic and announced that they supported direct-action public protest only when other methods of persuasion had failed. Wilfred Ussery of CORE then shot back that Lucky store management had acted in bad faith after agreeing with CORE on a plan to increase the numbers of minority workers on their payroll.[32]

The civil rights demonstrations of the early 1960s led to the creation of the United San Francisco Freedom Movement (USFFM), which was organized by Wilfred Ussery in the spring of 1963. The USFFM consisted of groups like CORE, the NAACP, the Ad Hoc Committee to End Discrimination, and the Student Nonviolent Coordinating Committee (SNCC). Although some of the members disagreed over the appropriate use of direct-action protest, the USFFM began a furious campaign of sit-ins and other demonstrations in San Francisco during 1964. Large protests at the Sheraton-Palace Hotel in January, along Auto Row in February, and at the Bank of America in April resulted in the arrest of hundreds of demonstrators. Consternation over these mass arrests among some of the leaders of the USFFM led to a split among civil rights groups in San Francisco, with CORE leading the militant wing and the NAACP heading up the moderates. The USFFM's greatest achievement came in December 1963, when it signed an agreement with the Retailers Community Relations Group (RCRG), which promised an end to discrimination against minorities and which stated that stores must comply with the agreement or they would be dropped from the RCRG. CORE and the RCRG revised the agreement in January 1965 to grant the Human Relations Commission the power to "investigate specific complaints of discrimination."

The leading black newspaper in the Bay Area, the San Francisco *Sun-Reporter*, hailed the agreement as an endorsement for the direct-action approach: "In forcing the Retailers Community Relations Group to install a complete program of fair hiring, the USFFM has won an important victory. This victory can solely be attributed to the direct action and boycott engaged in by members of the movement."[33]

In 1965, the members of CORE redoubled their efforts to use direct-action to bring the Bay Area's racist system of discrimination and segregation to its knees. In March, CORE and the Civic Committee of the Baptist Ministers Union started a boycott of Sears Roebuck stores in San Francisco. The black leaders announced that they would boycott the stores until Sears agreed to change its discriminatory hiring practices and abide by the agreement between the USFFM and the RCRG. Unlike the earlier campaign against Sears in the East Bay, this time CORE came out on top, and the store, along with Macy's and J. Magnin, capitulated to the protesters' demands to give CORE and the Baptist Ministers Union reports on their hiring policies. Across the bay, CORE began its restaurant project in the spring of 1965. Eugene A. Drew, chairman of the Oakland chapter, announced that "only *direct action* will bring the restaurant industry of the East Bay up-to-date with our era of civil rights and equal opportunity for all." The civil rights group targeted eateries in Oakland and Berkeley that refused to hire African Americans or kept them segregated into the lowest-skill, lowest-paying jobs. In Oakland alone, CORE reported that 245 of 283 waiters and waitresses in the city were white, twenty-seven were Oriental or Mexican-American, and eleven were black. The blacks worked in the back room of Sambo's Restaurant or at Kwik-Way Shops. Most African Americans worked as busboys or cooks, and none were bartenders. The East Bay Restaurant Association stonewalled CORE, and so the civil rights group began a picket campaign in early February. Protests were centered in Oakland's upscale Jack London Square, and CORE reported frequent cases of police brutality and false arrests that were used to try to break the demonstrations. Through dine-ins and a boycott that lasted more than a year, CORE influenced several restaurants to reform their hiring policies. In April 1966, one of the last holdouts, Goodman's in Jack London Square, finally agreed to become an equal opportunity employer and CORE called off its boycott of the restaurant.[34]

The increased use of direct-action tactics by Bay Area CORE chapters paralleled the rise of black militancy in the organization. African American activists became significantly more vocal in their objections to white dominance in the civil rights group, and more blacks demanded leadership positions in the Bay Area chapters. Echoing the trend in CORE's national headquarters, black nationalism became an increasingly important and divisive issue in San Francisco and the East Bay. The San Francisco chapter was particularly affected by the growing radicalism, and the group's black chairman, Bill Bradley, alienated many members with his increasing militancy in the mid-1960s. Walter Riley wrote to James Farmer and Floyd McKissick at the national office in New York to protest the direction of the San Francisco chapter, and he complained that "S.F. C.O.R.E. is adopting a policy of racism and the leadership expresses many black nationalist views." Riley reported that a recent project by CORE to organize blacks in Hunter's Point was changed from having integrated units to having all-black units to work in the predominantly African American community. Bill Bradley argued that such a change was necessary because "unity between black people is the most important thing," and he told white members that "it doesn't make any difference who your ancestors are, you are still white." Bradley concluded that "the civil rights movement as we know it is going backwards," and he argued that the San Francisco chapter needed to become more militant and more nationalist to create any lasting changes for African Americans in northern California. Other black members at the meeting agreed with Bradley, and Lucille Jones told one moderate member that "integration is a dirty word. You are twenty years behind the movement. I can't even sit here and listen to this. I don't have time." Another irate black member demanded "Would you die for me?" Riley warned the national office that such militancy was becoming the norm in the San Francisco chapter, and he worried that some members were considering arming themselves for the unavoidable future conflicts with such white supremacist groups as the Minute Men. Much to the moderates' horror, the San

Francisco chapter would become even more militant under the next chairman, Wilfred Ussery. During 1965 and 1966, the San Francisco chapter of CORE would become the center of African American radicalism in the Bay Area, and the group's use of direct-action protest and their manipulation of the federal anti-poverty program would set the stage for the rise of Black Power radicals like Huey Newton and Bobby Seale in the late 1960s.[35]

By the mid-1960s, a younger and more militant civil rights leadership had emerged in the Bay Area and begun using nonviolent direct-action tactics in their campaigns against discrimination and segregation. Young activists in the Congress of Racial Equality held rallies and raised money in support of southern civil rights demonstrators, including the Freedom Riders, and they picketed stores and events in the Bay Area to protest discrimination and racial inequality. Although initial participation in CORE demonstrations was disappointingly low and their tactics did not gain immediate wide-spread approval from black residents of the Bay Area, the younger, more militant wing of the Civil Rights Movement would pick up steam in the 1960s and would dramatically accelerate in the decade's later years. By 1965, CORE's public protests would upstage the traditional middle-class black leadership ensconced in the NAACP and the Urban League, and African American youths in San Francisco, Oakland, Berkeley, and Richmond would gain a greater role in civil rights demonstrations and the policy making of black protest.

# Notes

1.     Mrs. Scott is quoted in Gretchen Lemke-Santangelo, *Abiding Courage: African American Migrant Women and the East Bay Community* (Chapel Hill: University of North Carolina Press, 1996), 150; Mr. Shelbon's story is in Samantha H. Lee, "East Bay Chatter," *Sun-Reporter*, 7 July 1951, 7.

2.   "Negro History Week Observed Here," *Sun-Reporter*, 2 February 1957, 9; "The Challenge of Negro History Week," *Sun-Reporter*, 8 February 1958, 12; "Downes Methodist Sponsors Seminar on Negro History," *Sun-Reporter*, 17 January 1959, 5; "The Meaning of Negro History Week," *Sun-Reporter*, 6 February 1960, 12; "Negro History Classes Started," *Sun-Reporter*, 15 August 1964, 4; "Negro History Program at Beth Eden Baptist," *Sun-Reporter*, 6 February 1965, 9.

3.   "Parents of Seven Children Killed in Auto Accident," *Sun-Reporter*, 3 January 1953, 1; "$60 Check to Aid 7 Orphans," *Sun-Reporter*, 24 January 1953, 1; "Form Unity Club to Aid Children," *Sun-Reporter*, 7 April 1951, 4; "New Club Formed for East Bay Jrs.," *Sun-Reporter*, 29 December 1951, 2; Samantha H. Lee, "East Bay Chatter," *Sun-Reporter*, 23 June 1951, 7; Linda Grant and Maureen Mundorff, "The Sutter St. YWCA Story," *Sun-Reporter*, 24 February 1962, 4–5; Linda Grant and Maureen Mundorff, "C. J. Walker Home Story," *Sun-Reporter*, 13 January 1962, 4.

4.   "'Youth City' Elects Its City Officials," *Sun-Reporter*, 5 January 1957, 1; "Youth City Becomes a Real Live Project: Charter Next," *Sun-Reporter*, 5 January 1957, 3; "Youngsters to Give Views on Convention," *Sun-Reporter*, 30 March 1957, 1; Dr. Arthur H. Coleman, letter to the editor, *Sun-Reporter*, 10 May 1958, 10; Linda Grant and Maureen Mundorff, "Bayview Neighborhood Community Center: 'We Have to Turn Away Children Due to the Lack of Funds,'" *Sun-Reporter*, 30 December 1961; Linda Grant and Maureen Mundorff, "The Booker T. Washington Community Center Story," *Sun-Reporter*, 17 February 1962, 4–5; "De Fremery Offers Children's Arts and Crafts Workshop," *Sun-Reporter*, 23 January 1954, 7; "Teen-Age Problems Target of Discussion at deFremery [sic] Youth Workshop," *Sun-Reporter*, 26 March 1955, 2; "How Dope-Drink Affect Youngsters Subject of de Fremery [sic] Workshop," *Sun-Reporter*, 27 April 1957, 3.

5.   Flyer, "Do You Want a Fair Employment Practices Law?" 26 April 1953, Tarea Hall Pittman Papers, Bancroft Library, University of California, Berkeley [Hereafter cited as Pittman Papers]; "Dr. King to Speak at Third Baptist Sunday Morning," *Sun-Reporter*, 22 February 1958, 13; "Dr. Du Bois at Third Baptist," *Sun-Reporter*, 12 April 1958, 1; J. Alfred Smith, *Thus Far by Faith: A Study of Historical Backgrounds and the First Fifty Years of the Allen Temple Baptist Church* (Oakland: Color Art Press, 1973), 51–52, 58–59; Taylor Memorial Methodist Church, *Yesterday-Today, Tomorrow and Forever: Through Faith with Work* (Oakland: Taylor Memorial Methodist Church, 1954); Memo, "Donations from Churches: 'Civil Rights Rally,'" n.d., Carton 38, NAACP

West Coast Region Papers, Bancroft Library, University of California, Berkeley, |Hereafter cited as NAACP Papers|; William L. Nicholls, II, Esther S. Hochstim, and Sheila Babbie, *The Castlemont Survey: A Handbook of Survey Results* (Berkeley: Survey Research Center, June 1966), 192–93.

6 .     "Fall and Winter Program Announced by Oakland's De Fremery Youth Center," *Sun-Reporter*, 8 November 1952, 3; Harry and Marguerite Williams, "Reflections of a Longtime Black Family in Richmond," an oral history conducted in 1985 by Judith K. Dunning, Regional Oral History Office, The Bancroft Library, University of California, Berkeley, 1990, 127–31; Lemke-Santangelo, *Abiding Courage*, 155–62, 170–74; "Negro Leaders Undertake Self-Help Project," *Sun-Reporter*, 20 February 1965, 4; Smith, *Thus Far by Faith*, 58–59.

7.     The best account of the early history of the NAACP in northern California is in Albert S. Broussard, *Black San Francisco: The Struggle for Racial Equality in the West*, 1900–1954 (Lawrence: University Press of Kansas, 1993), 76, 84–85, 193, 221–26 passim. Survey, NAACP Regional Office to Alameda County Branch, 25 September 1945, Carton 26, NAACP Papers; Alameda County Branch, NAACP, "Report of Election of Officers," 24 November 1946, Carton 26, NAACP Papers; Richmond Branch, NAACP, "Report of Election of Officers," 4 January 1948, Carton 26, NAACP Papers.

8.     Membership information was collected from Memo, "Comparative Study of West Coast Branches," n.d., Carton 7, NAACP Papers. For an illustrative membership campaign, see Samantha H. Lee, "East Bay Chatter," *Sun-Reporter*, 24 March 1951, 7; and "NAACP Battlefront: Alameda County Starts Drive for 5,000 Members," *Sun-Reporter*, 31 March 1951, 3.

9.     Alameda County Branch, NAACP, "Annual Report of Branch Activities, 1949," Carton 26, NAACP Papers; "NAACP Holds Grievance Hearing; Supervisor Wins Reinstatement," *Sun-Reporter*, 3 October 1953, 1; "NAACP Head Joins Picket Line," *Sun-Reporter*, 27 August 1955, 2. See also the editorial, "What About Yellow Cab?" *Sun-Reporter*, 3 March 1956, 8; "NAACP Threatens to Picket the New Jack Tar Hotel: 437 People Hired, 40 Negro," *Sun-Reporter*, 26 March 1960, 1; "Jack Tar Pickets Halted," *Sun-Reporter*, 23 April 1960, 2; "Francois Gives Jack Tar OK Sign," *Sun-Reporter*, 7 May 1960, 3; Letter, Leonard H. Carter to Joseph Wellington, 6 May 1966, Carton 17, NAACP Papers. See also the attached flyer, "Here We Go Again!", that chronicles the maids' story.

10.    Lee Soto, "Negroes Last Hired, First Fired Revealed in Civic Unity Survey," *Sun-Reporter*, 2 August 1958, 1, 6; Broussard, *Black San Francisco*, 216–20; "Picket Line Formed, Bayview Merchant Agrees to Hire Negroes," *Sun-Reporter*, 27 January 1962, 5.

11.    Linda Grant and Maureen Mundorff, "The Urban League Story," *Sun-Reporter*, 6 January 1962, 3, 13; Seaton W. Manning, "The Urban League Story in San Francisco and Oakland," *Sun-Reporter*, 6 October 1956, 3; D. Donald Glover, "Review of a Decade of Progress on the Job Front," *Sun-Reporter*, 6 October 1956, 6; Kenneth F. Smith, "Response to Needs in East Bay," *Sun-Reporter*, 6 October 1956, 9.

12.    "Brown Asks State FEPC," *Sun-Reporter*, 10 January 1959, 1; "No Amended State FEPC," *Sun-Reporter*, 28 February 1959, 10; "Senate Passes F.E.P.C.," *Sun-Reporter*, 11 April 1959, 1; "Brown Signs FEPC," *Sun-Reporter*, 18 April 1959, 1; "A Long Tough Fight...Victory at Last," *Sun-Reporter*, 18 April 1959, 2; Franklin H. Williams, "Analysis of California Fair Employment Law," *Sun-Reporter*, 18 April 1959, 3; Letter, Tarea Hall Pittman to Frank [Williams], 16 March 1953, Pittman Papers.

13.    Commission on Equal Employment Opportunity, "CEEO Illustrative Case History," 17 July 1959, Carton 3, William Byron Rumford Papers, Bancroft Library, University of California, Berkeley [Hereafter cited as Rumford Papers]; William Byron Rumford, "Legislator for Fair Employment, Fair Housing, and Public Health," an oral history conducted by Joyce A. Henderson, Amelia Fry, and Edward France, Earl Warren Oral History Project, Regional Oral History Office, The Bancroft Library, University of California, Berkeley, 1973, 52.

14.    Letter, Everett P. Brandon to George Christopher, 23 September 1958, Carton 7, NAACP Papers; Letter, Everett P. Brandon to Richard E. Doyle, 3 July 1958, Carton 7, NAACP Papers. See also, Broussard, *Black San Francisco*, 221–26.

15.    "Segregation Ended in S. F. Public Projects: NAACP Asks 3 Officials to Resign," *Sun-Reporter*, 29 May 1954, 1; "Gov. Signs Housing Bill: Hawkins Bill Prohibits Discrimination in Housing," *Sun-Reporter*, 18 July 1959, 1.

16.    For a fuller discussion of the Rumford Fair Housing Act and Proposition 14, see Chapter 2; the various documents in Carton 3, NAACP Papers; Rumford, "Legislator for Fair Employment, Fair Housing, and Public Health," 116–117 passim; and "Fair Housing Office Opened in Richmond to Back Rumford Act," *Sun-Reporter*, 11 July 1964, 2. Rev. Ellis H.

Casson, "Oakland Branch NAACP Housing Report," n.d., Carton 38, NAACP Papers; Tom Thompson, Rev. H. Solomon Hill, and Dr. J. B. Jackson, "Statement on Public Housing to the Oakland City Council," 22 December 1959, Carton 38, NAACP Papers.

17.    "SF NAACP Sues in School Case," *Sun-Reporter*, 6 October 1962, 4; Linda Grant, "De Facto Segregation Aired: Background of School Situation in San Francisco," *Sun-Reporter*, 22 September 1962, 2; "NAACP Chief Raps S.F. School System," San Francisco *Chronicle*, 2 December 1965, 4. See also Chapter 2 for a fuller discussion of educational segregation in the Bay Area.

18.    Letter, Dorothy E. Handy to Mayor Z. S. Leymel, 16 April 1946, Box 1, California Federation for Civic Unity Records, 1945–1956, Bancroft Library, University of California, Berkeley [Hereafter cited as CFCU Records]; Letter, Dorothy E. Handy to Palmer Van Gundy, 16 April 1946, Box 1, CFCU Records; Letter, Josephine W. Duveneck to Vernon Kilpartick, 19 January 1950, Box 3, CFCU Records; Alameda County Branch, NAACP, "Annual Report of Branch Activities, 1949" 1949, Carton 26, NAACP Papers; "Teenage Row at Theatre," *Sun-Reporter*, 21 July 1956, 1.

19.    "San Francisco NAACP Story," *Sun-Reporter*, 3 February 1962, 5; "Bradley Calls for Review Board," *Sun-Reporter*, 13 March 1965, 3, 13; "NAACP Mass Rally Here Sunday," *Sun-Reporter*, 13 March 1965, 3, 13; Letter, Everett P. Brandon to John O'Connell, 26 June 1968, Carton 7, NAACP Papers; "Call for Investigation: TAC Squad Blasted by NAACP Leader," *Sun-Reporter*, 31 August 1968, 2.

20.    Letter, Laurence I. Hewes, Jr., to William C. Robinson, 1 April 1946, Box 1, CFCU Records; Letter, Stanley S. Jacobs to Harris Rickseeker, 9 March 1953, Box 3, CFCU Records; Letter, Tarea Hall Pittman to Annie L. Barnett, 20 November 1956, Carton 7, NAACP Papers.

21.    Broussard, *Black San Francisco*, 227–30; Letter, M. W. Griffin to Gloster B. Current, 19 November 1947, Carton 16, NAACP Papers; Memo, M. W. Griffin to Roy Wilkins, 7 August 1947, Carton 16, NAACP Papers; Clipping from *Richmond Independent*, 3 February 1949, Carton 16, NAACP Papers; Letter, The People of Richmond to the NAACP Board of Directors, 28 February 1949, Carton 16, NAACP Papers; Letter, Richard W. Dettering to J. R. Vanghan, 14 December 1949, Box 3, CFCU Records.

22.    "NAACP Not Involved in Saturday Protest Parade in Oakland," *Sun-Reporter*, 9 February 1952, 3; "6000 Hear A. Philip Randolph Launch 'Fight for Freedom,'" *Sun-Reporter*, 3 April 1954, 1; Clipping from *The Stewards News*, 11 February 1954, Carton 37, NAACP Papers; Letter, Roy Wilkins to

Justin W. Day, 24 February 1955, Carton 37, NAACP Papers; Memo, Franklin H. Williams to Walter White, Roy Wilkins, Gloster Current, Herbert Hill, and Clarence Mitchell, 31 January 1955, Carton 37, NAACP Papers; Max Silverman, "Urban Redevelopment and Community Response: African Americans in San Francisco's Western Addition" (M.A. Thesis, San Francisco State University, 1994), 35–41.

23.    Rumford, "Legislator for Fair Employment, Fair Housing, and Public Health," 116–17; "Full Equality in All Phases of American Life by 1963: NAACP," *Sun-Reporter*, 16 January 1954, 1; "NAACP Lists Assets & Liabilities for 1955," *Sun-Reporter*, 7 January 1956, 8; "NAACP Convention Reports," *Sun-Reporter*, 7 July 1956, 8; "San Francisco NAACP Story," *Sun-Reporter*, 3 February 1963, 5.

24.    "Thousands Jam Auditorium at Prayer-Protest Meet," *Sun-Reporter*, 31 March 1956, 1; Edith Austin, "10,000 Hear Jackie at Freedom Fund Rally," *Sun-Reporter*, 2 February 1957, 2; Pamphlet, "Fight for Freedom Rally," 27 January 1957, Carton 42, NAACP Papers; "East Bay Ministers Expect Thousands to Hear Dr. King," *Sun-Reporter*, 22 June 1957, 1; Front-page Photograph, *Sun-Reporter*, 29 June 1957; Folders, "NAACP Freedom Rally, Oakland, Oct. 19, 1958," Carton 42, NAACP Papers; "King...Negroes' Dixie Fight Just Beginning," *Sun-Reporter*, 1 April 1961, 2; "King Predicts Favorable ICC Ruling on August 15," *Sun-Reporter*, 29 July 1961, 3, 4; Thomas Fleming, "Police Arrest 110 Cadillac Pickets," *Sun-Reporter*, 21 March 1964, 4; Quintard Taylor, *In Search of the Racial Frontier: African Americans in the American West, 1528–1990* (New York: W. W. Norton and Company, 1998), 290–91; "Sunday's March to Draw 70,000 for Human Rts.," *Sun-Reporter*, 11 July 1964, 3; "Thousands Picket GOP," *Sun-Reporter*, 18 July 1964, 2; "Dr. Burbridge: Unfair Jail Term Shocks People," *Sun-Reporter*, 18 July 1964, 5; Ella Leffland, "Burbridge's Term Begins," *Sun-Reporter*, 23 July 1966, 4; "Two Thousand Attend Sit-In Rally," *Sun-Reporter*, 23 July 1966, 3; "Local NAACP for Demonstrations when Necessary," *Sun-Reporter*, 8 August 1964, 2.

25.    Letter, George M. Houser to Abraham Lincoln Fletcher, 11 December 1947, Reel 14, Series 3, File 73, The Papers of the Congress of Racial Equality, 1941–1967, Microfilm, Sanford, NC: Microfilming Corporation of America, 1980 [Hereafter cited as CORE Papers]; Congress of Racial Equality, Affiliation Blank, San Francisco Chapter, Reel 14, Series 3, File 73, CORE Papers; "Boycott Lucky Stores: CORE Spurs Action in Hunter's Point District," *San Francisco Reporter*, 30 April 1948, 1, Reel 14, Series 3, File 73, CORE Papers; Letter, George Houser to Orval Etter, 12 May

1948, Reel 14, Series 3, File 73, CORE Papers; Letter, Dixon Adams to George Houser, 31 May 1948, Reel 14, Series 3, File 73, CORE Papers; Letter, Abraham Lincoln Fletcher to George Houser, 15 June 1948, Reel 14, Series 3, File 73, CORE Papers; Letter, Orval Etter to George Houser, 12 July 1948, Reel 14, Series 3, File 73, CORE Papers; Letter, Orval Etter to George Houser, 14 July 1948, Reel 14, Series 3, File 73, CORE Papers; Letter, George Houser to Allen Willis, 18 August 1948, Reel 14, Series 3, File 73, CORE Papers; Letter, Dixon Adams to George Houser, 14 September 1948, Reel 14, Series 3, File 73, CORE Papers; Letter, George Houser to Dixon Adams, 12 October 1948, Reel 14, Series 3, File 73, CORE Papers.

26.    Congress of Racial Equality, Affiliation Blank, Berkeley Chapter, Reel 8, Series 3, File 7, CORE Papers; Memo, "Tea Cup Project," n.d., Reel 8, Series 3, File 7, CORE Papers; News Release and CORElator Report Sheet, 6 May 1949, Reel 8, Series 3, File 7, CORE Papers; Clipping, unknown newspaper, "CORE Continues Picketing Drive," 18 March 1950, Reel 8, Series 3, File 7 CORE Papers; Memo, "Facts on the Sears Project," n.d., Reel 8, Series 3, File 7, CORE Papers.

27.    Letter, Gordon R. Carey to Orval Etter, 20 March 1959, Reel 18, Series 5, File 14, CORE Papers; Letter, Gordon R. Carey to Frank L. Allard, Jr., 20 March 1959, Reel 18, Series 5, File 14, CORE Papers; Letter, Gordon R. Carey to Hank G. Maiden, 20 March 1959, Reel 18, Series 5, File 14, CORE Papers; Letter, Frank L. Allard, Jr., to Gordon R. Carey, 2 April 1959, Reel 18, Series 5, File 14, CORE Papers; Letter, Gordon R. Carey to Frank L. Allard, Jr., 8 April 1959, Reel 18, Series 5, File 14, CORE Papers; Letter, Gordon R. Carey to Hank G. Maiden, 28 April 1959, Reel 18, Series 5, File 14, CORE Papers; Letter, Gordon R. Carey to Frank L. Allard, Jr., 28 April 1959, Reel 18, Series 5, File 14, CORE Papers; Letter, Frank L. Allard, Jr., to Gordon R. Carey, 30 April 1959, Reel 18, Series 5, File 14, CORE Papers; Letter, Ellen Fisk to Gordon R. Carey, 28 July 1959, Reel 18, Series 5, File 18, CORE Papers; Letter, Phil Roos to James R. Robinson, 20 July 1959, Reel 18, Series 5, File 14, CORE Papers; Letter, Robert H. K. Walter to Gordon R. Carey, 25 January 1960, Reel 18, Series 5, File 14, CORE Papers; Letter, Robert B. Haldane to James R. Robinson, 25 July 1959, Reel 18, Series 5, File 16, CORE Papers; Letter, Gordon R. Carey to Robert B. Haldane, 28 December 1959, Reel 18, Series 5, File 16, CORE Papers; Letter, Gordon R. Carey to Gay Cox, 28 June 1960, Reel 18, Series 5, File 16, CORE Papers; Letter, Gordon R. Carey to Gay Cox, 19 July 1960, Reel 18, Series 5, File 16, CORE

Papers; Congress of Racial Equality, Application for Affiliation, Richmond Chapter, n.d., Reel 18, Series 5, File 16, CORE Papers.

28.     Clipping, from *The Berkeley Review*, 14 April 1960, Reel 18 Series 5, File 14, CORE Papers; Clipping, from the *Oakland Tribune*, 13 April 1960, Reel 18, Series 5, File 14, CORE Papers; Memo, "Freedom Writers: Sign and Give a Dime," n.d., Reel 18, Series 5, File 14, CORE Papers; Poster, "CORE Freedom Ride Meeting," 9 June 1961, Reel 18, Series 5, File 14, CORE Papers; Form letter to appeal for funds, 2 June 1961, Reel 18, Series 5, File 14, CORE Papers; Letter, Richard Haley to Gay Cox, 2 February 1961, Reel 24, Series 5, File 99, CORE Papers; Memo, Richard Haley to CORE National Council, 11–12 February 1961, Reel 24, Series 5, File 99, CORE Papers.

29.     Letter, Sherina K. Friedlander to Gordon R. Carey, 1 June 1961, Reel 18, Series 5, File 18, CORE Papers; Congress of Racial Equality, Application for Affiliation, San Francisco Chapter, n.d., Reel 18, Series 5, File 18, CORE Papers; Flyer, "Why Picket the Redskins?" n.d., Reel 18, Series 5, File 18, CORE Papers; Genevieve Hughes, "Field Report," December 1961, Reel 18, Series 5, File 18, CORE Papers; Genevieve Hughes, "Field Report: San Francisco CORE," 11 June 1962, Reel 39, Series 5, File 322, CORE Papers; Letter, Fredricka Teer [?] to Jim McCain [?], 1 September 1962, Reel 37, Series 5, File 269, CORE Papers.

30.     Letter, James Lee to Gov. Edmund Brown, 20 April 1961, Reel 39, Series 5, File 319, CORE Papers; Letter, Theodore R. Alpen to Gordon R. Carey, 3 May 1961, Reel 39, Series 5, File 319, CORE Papers; Letter, Gordon R. Carey to Theodore R. Alpen, 16 May 1961, Reel 39, Series 5, File 319, CORE Papers; Letter, Gordon R. Carey to James Lee, 16 May 1961, Reel 39, Series 5, File 319, CORE Papers; Letter, Gordon R. Carey to James Lee, 19 July 1961, Reel 39, Series 5, File 319, CORE Papers; Letter, Gordon R. Carey to Theodore R. Alpen, 28 July 1961, Reel 39, Series 5, File 319, CORE Papers; Letter, Gordon R. Carey to Theodore R. Alpen, 1 November 1961, Reel 39, Series 5, File 319, CORE Papers; Letter, Gordon R. Carey to Theodore R. Alpen, 6 December 1961, Reel 39, Series 5, File 319, CORE Papers; Genevieve Hughes, "Field Report: Oakland, Calif.," 18 June 1962, Reel 39, Series 5, File 319, CORE Papers; Fredricka Teer, "Field Report: Bay Area Chapters," 24 September 1962, Reel 37, Series 5, File 269, CORE Papers; Letter, Barbara Thollaug to James Farmer, 13 October 1962, Reel 18, Series 5, File 16, CORE Papers; Letter, James Farmer to Barbara Thollaug, 7 December 1962, Reel 18, Series 5, File 16, CORE Papers.

31.    Press releases, "Hink's Picketed after 57 Years in Berkeley," and "Hink's Takes Step towards Fair Employment," n.d. [December 1961], Reel 18, Series 5, File 14, CORE Papers; Press releases, "CORE Sits-In on a Realtor," 14 May 1962, and "Berkeley CORE Warns Realty Board of Action; Large Realtor Ends Rental Discrimination," n.d., and an untitled release from 30 May 1962, all in Reel 18, Series 5, File 14, CORE Papers; "Nakamura Yields to CORE's Request," *The Berkeley CORE-spondent*, July 1962, 1–2, Reel 18, Series 5, File 14, CORE Papers; "CORE Stages Sit-In on S.F. School Segregation," *Sun-Reporter*, 11 August 1962, 2; Fredricka Teer, "Field Report: San Francisco CORE," 24 September 1962, Reel 37, Series 5, File 269, CORE Papers.

32.    Berkeley and Oakland Chapters of CORE, "Discrimination in Employment: The Case of Montgomery Ward," 4 May 1963, Reel 39, Series 5, File 316, CORE Papers; Flyer, "140 Jobs Are at Stake: Join Our Picket Line," 18 May 1963, Reel 39, Series 5, File 316, CORE Papers; Flyer, "Let's Finish the Job!!", 24 November 1964, Box 1, Newell Hart Ephemera, 1961–1969 Papers, Bancroft Library, University of California, Berkeley [Hereafter cited as Hart Papers]; Press releases, 3 December 1963 and 26 February 1964, Reel 18, Series 5, File 18, CORE Papers; "CORE Explains Shop-In Tactics," *Sun-Reporter*, 21 March 1964, 3.

33.    Natalie Becker and Marjorie Myhill, *Power and Participation in the San Francisco Community Action Program* (Berkeley: Institute of Urban and Regional Development, 1967), 5–10; "CORE at Peace with RCRG," *Sun-Reporter*, 9 January 1965, 3.

34.    "Over 40,000 Boycott Sears," *Sun-Reporter*, 6 March 1965, 4; "CORE, BMU, RCRG Continue Talks," *Sun-Reporter*, 27 March 1965, 3; "3 RCRG Stores Come to Terms with CORE," *Sun-Reporter*, 24 April 1965, 10; San Francisco CORE, "Freedom Now," 1965, Carton 3, Social Protest Collection, Bancroft Library, University of California, Berkeley [Hereafter cited as Social Protest Collection]; Berkeley Campus CORE, "The CORE Restaurant Project: What It's About, Where It's Going," 21 April 1965, Carton 3, Social Protest Collection; Letter, Eugene Drew to the public, 28 June 1965, Carton 3, Social Protest Collection; Flyer, 23 April 1965, Box 1, Hart Papers; "Oakland CORE Introduces Eat-In," *Sun-Reporter*, 27 March 1965, 36; M. C. Stallings, "Goodman Reaches Settlement with CORE," *Sun-Reporter*, 9 April 1965, 3; Gene Drew, "Discriminatory Hiring," *Flatlands*, 21 May to 4 June 1966, 2, 6; W. J. Rorabaugh, *Berkeley at War: The 1960s* (New York: Oxford University Press, 1989), 70–74.

35. Letter, Walter Riley to James Farmer and Floyd McKissick, 30 May 1965, Reel 17, Subgroup F, Series II, File 23, The Papers of the Congress of Racial Equality, Addendum: 1944–1968, Microfilm, Sanford, NC: Microfilming Corporation of America, 1980. For the national radicalization of CORE, see August Meier and Elliot Rudwick, CORE: A *Study of the Civil Rights Movement*, 1942–1968 (New York: Oxford University Press, 1973).

Workers Leaving the Richmond Shipyard, Selections from the Henry J. Kaiser Pictorial Collection, 1941–1946, Item 23, Group 1, 1983.017–019, 027, *Courtesy of the Bancroft Library, University of California, Berkeley*

Clarence Smith, Yard 3, January 1, 1946, Selections from the Henry J. Kaiser Pictorial Collection, 1941–1946, item 445, group 21, 1983.017–019, 027, *Courtesy of the Bancroft Library, University of California, Berkeley*

C.L. Dellums, Spencer Jordan, and Ben Watkins at the Kaiser Shipyards, 1943, California Faces: Selections from the Bancroft Library Portrait Collection, Item 5, *Courtesy of the Bancroft Library, University of California, Berkeley*

William Byron Rumford, California Faces: Selections from the Bancroft Library Portrait Collection, Item 1, No. 42542-3, Photography by E.F. Joseph, *Courtesy of the Bancroft Library*, *University of California*, *Berkeley*

Terry Francois and William Chester, 1968, African Americans in the San
Francisco Bay Area, 1963–1974, Item 78, Series 5, 1985.079—AX,
Photography by Greg Peterson, *Courtesy of the Bancroft Library, University of
California, Berkeley*

CORE Pickets at Penney's, 1963, African Americans in the San Francisco Bay Area, 1963–1974, Item 1, Series 1, 1985.079—AX, Photography by Peter Breinig, *Courtesy of the Bancroft Library, University of California, Berkeley*

Matthew Johnson Shot by Police at Hunter's Point, 1996, African Americans in the San Francisco Bay Area, 1963–1974, Item 83, Series 5, 1985.079—AX, Photography by Peter Brienig, *Courtesy of the Bancroft Library, University of California, Berkeley*

Huey P. Newton, California Faces: Selections from the Bancroft Library Portrait Collection, Item 1, Photography by Jeffrey Blankfort, *Courtesy of the Bancroft Library, University of California, Berkeley*

"Free Huey" Rally, July 16, 1968. African Americans in the San Francisco Bay Area, 1963–1974, Item 31, Series 3, 1985.079—AX. Photography by Barney Peterson, *Courtesy of the Bancroft Library, University of California, Berkeley*

# CHAPTER 4

# Liberalism

As the debates over unemployment, poor housing, segregated schools, and police brutality approached their zenith in the early 1960s, the hand of federalism once again stuck its fingers into the socio-economic pie of the San Francisco Bay Area. Local forces representing the white establishment and the black minority continued to spar over the race question, and Uncle Sam entered the ring to counsel a truce between them. He had with him a bold, new plan to undo the problems in the urban centers of the North and West created during or amplified by the Second World War. Washington's best and brightest had designed a comprehensive plan to eliminate America's underclass and pull the poor into the mainstream. Community action was the center-piece of the program, and it encouraged the return of power to communities and local municipalities and represented a shift away from the centralizing legacy of the New Deal state. Launched with great fanfare and rhetoric, the anti-poverty crusade would yield many unexpected results and create massive confusion and controversy. The War on Poverty would be the greatest failure of President Lyndon B. Johnson's Great Society.

In the San Francisco Bay Area, the federal anti-poverty program bore the fruit of black radicalism. Previously overshadowed by moderate, middle-class African American civil rights organizations, black radicals and militants would come into their own in the 1960s, aided by the influx of federal anti-poverty funds. To placate southern Democrats and Republican critics, Washington's poverty planners agreed to channel money away from civil rights groups and religious organizations. In San Francisco, these policies meant that the leading community organizations, the black churches and the National Association for the Advancement of Colored People (NAACP), were left out of the initial grab for much-needed programs and financial support. Militant black leaders, such as Wilfred Ussery and Bobby Seale, stepped into the void and claimed control of the local poverty programs. The federal funds translated into instant status for the enfranchised militants, and they used their newfound legitimacy to spread the doctrines of black nationalism and Black Power throughout the ghettos of Berkeley, Oakland, Richmond, and San Francisco. This new leadership reached out to the disaffected black youth and found in them a responsive audience. By the end of the decade, another African American movement was afoot in the Bay Area, and its rallying cry was not non-violence and integration but violent revolution.

## POVERTY IN THE BAY AREA

As the nation looked forward to increasing prosperity in the 1960s, many African Americans in the San Francisco Bay Area faced hard times. The arrival of hundreds of thousands of wartime migrants had recast life in northern California, and the long-term effects of the war years began to become fully apparent by the early 1960s. High rates of black unemployment troubled community leaders and government officials alike, and concerned voices raised the alarm about disturbing changes in the urban cores of the Golden State. The dramatic demographic shift that occurred during the 1940s and 1950s affected not only political, economic, social, and cultural relations in the Bay Area, but it also put serious strains on municipal budgets. In 1959, for example, the City of Berkeley reported that its Community Welfare Commission depended more heavily upon public tax dollars to support charitable organizations and causes than it had prior to the 1940s. In 1914 and 1915, for example, only 64% of the city's budget for welfare and public charity came from tax revenue, while private giving comprised the other 36%. By 1957 and 1958, however, public taxes accounted for 90% of Berkeley's charity and welfare resources, and private giving had fallen to only 10% of the city's needs. As welfare expenditures siphoned more from city budgets throughout the Bay Area, elected officials struggled to find ways to avert the emerging urban crisis. The limitations of their reforms left thousands of alienated and frustrated African Americans on the fringes of society, and by the middle of the decade, a host of militant leaders came forward to speak out for the poor.[1]

By the early 1960s, poverty was entrenched in the East Bay. The deindustrialization of Oakland and Richmond after the Second World War left large numbers of black residents unemployed, chronically underemployed, or trapped in low-skill, low-wage jobs. Whites fled to surrounding suburbs, black in-migration continued, and by mid-decade, African Americans accounted for nearly a third of Oakland's total population. About one in five families in Oakland lived in poverty, although nearly a quarter of black families were poor. North Oakland alone contained nearly half of the city's substandard housing, and a third of its residents received welfare. Four of ten families in North Oakland earned less than $4,000 in 1966, which placed them below the poverty line. In the predominantly African American neighborhood of West Oakland, conditions were remarkably worse. By 1965, nearly half of West Oakland's black population was poor, and the neighborhood contained about one-quarter of the total poverty population of the entire city. Unemployment for blacks in Oakland was staggering. Black men suffered jobless rates that were double those of their white counterparts, and by mid-decade, the black male unemployment rate for Oakland stood at nearly ten percent. In West Oakland, the jobless rates for black men and women were even higher, as 13.8% of men and 15.2% of women were without employment. The burdens were heaviest for young black men throughout the city. Forty-one percent of African American male teenagers were unemployed, as compared to only seventeen percent of white male teens. Furthermore, those black men fortunate enough to secure employment were often laborers, while their white counterparts held more lucrative and high-status positions as white-collar workers or craftsmen and foremen. The raw employment numbers, however, do not tell the whole tale.[2]

## Table 4
### Black Unemployment in West Oakland

| Gender | 1960 | 1966 |
|--------|------|------|
| Men    | 18.4% | 13.8% |
| Women  | 17.1% | 15.2% |

SOURCE: William L. Nicholls, II, *Tables on Employment and Unemployment from the* 701 *Household Survey of Oakland* (Berkeley: Survey Research Center, 1968), 19.

## Table 5
### Male Unemployment in Oakland, 1966

| Age | Whites | Blacks |
|-----|--------|--------|
| 14-19 | 17% | 41% |
| 20-24 | 9% | 10% |
| 25-34 | 4% | 8% |
| 35-44 | 3% | 9% |
| 45-64 | 3% | 6% |

SOURCE: William L. Nicholls, II, *Tables on Employment and Unemployment from the* 701 *Household Survey of Oakland* (Berkeley: Survey Research Center, 1968), 21.

High unemployment in black neighborhoods throughout the East Bay was compounded by poor housing, inadequate education, police brutality, inefficient social services, and political isolation. In West Oakland, over one-quarter of the housing was unsound, yet ninety percent of the buildings were occupied. The conditions in East Oakland, where the housing market was even tighter, were not much better, yet the number of acceptable dwellings was not significantly greater. Segregation in schools continued to be a major problem. Officials reported apathy, frustration, and low self-esteem among black children in the ghetto schools, and few observers were optimistic about the future. The sub-par schools produced a vastly inferior product, as nearly a third of the adult population in West and East Oakland had less than an eighth-grade education. Oakland's police force employed only nineteen black officers out of a total force of more than six hundred men, and complaints of police brutality continued unabated throughout the 1960s. Black residents in the East Bay also complained of lax garbage collection and deficient welfare services, which were dispensed by condescending and hostile public service officials. In September 1964, for example, the Welfare Rights Organization held a sleep-in at the Alameda County Welfare Department to protest the city's policy of making welfare recipients engage in agricultural labor for which they were not well suited. African American leaders often had to resort to such direct-action tactics, for when they appealed to Oakland's city hall, black citizens were haughtily dismissed by the white establishment controlled by former Senator William Knowland's conservative clan. The economic, social, and political alienation of African Americans in Oakland led one visiting white official to conclude, "Oakland is a powder keg."[3]

In the face of mounting social problems and white official indifference, East Bay African Americans organized to fight back. In the summer of 1966, the Committee for Low-Cost Housing led a tenants' camp-in to protest the decision to demolish Alameda's Estuary Housing Project. The city had agreed to give the navy control over the land on which the housing projects had been built, and the federal government's plans did not include low-cost housing for African Americans. For several years, the residents of the Estuary Housing Project and Alameda's mayor, William Godfrey, had wrangled over the fate of the project, and on June 20, 1966, the Committee for Low-Cost Housing led twenty of the evicted tenants to camp-in at Franklin Park, along the posh Gold Coast section of Alameda and only one block from the mayor's home. Dorothy Reed, a 28 year-old mother of five, feared that her family would not be able to find decent, affordable housing in Alameda after the Estuary Project was torn down. A native of Beaumont, Texas, Reed had migrated to the East Bay in 1943, when her father found carpentry work in the wartime industries. Her family had moved from one housing project to another after the war, and she was determined not to lose the only accessible housing she could find.

"Three years ago we decided to fight this phasing out the project without relocating the people," she said. "Lot of the people really couldn't afford to move out.... Some was able to buy. Some moved out with four or five kids and tried to find a place to rent—two or three bedrooms. How many found places in Alameda? Very few, if any. Most went to East Oakland or Hayward." Many other wartime migrants supported and led the Committee for Low-Cost Housing, including Mabel Tatum and Eliza Coleman. At the height of the camp-in, Tatum vowed that "we are down to the hard core now; we will stay in the park until Hell freezes over." After five long days, the mayor finally capitulated and agreed to help relocate all of the families displaced from the Estuary Project.[4]

Across the bay, African Americans in the ghettos of San Francisco struggled under similar circumstances. The city's five poorest neighborhoods contained more than half of San Francisco's population, 85% of the city's Aid to Families with Dependent Children recipients, 62% of its old-age assistance cases, 50% of its unemployed, and 59% of the people who did not finish grade school. The neighborhoods, which contained four-fifths of the city's minority population, also had the highest incidences of venereal disease, tuberculosis, and pre-natal mortality. Three other predominantly black neighborhoods also suffered high levels of economic distress, with unemployment rates ranging from 9% to 18% and poverty rates from 18% to 37%. The worsening crisis in San Francisco's black neighborhoods compelled some African Americans to turn to extralegal methods to survive. On December 29, 1959, Paul Bullock, a 26 year-old part-time night clerk, stole $2,400 from Walgreens Drug Store on Powell Street to purchase Christmas gifts for his children and "a lot of poor kids in the Fillmore District." Bullock's wife refused the stolen money, however, and he turned himself in to the San Francisco Police Department. "I don't know why I did it," Bullock told reporters. "I was making $36 a week, and I had a wife and four little kids. I was so tired of seeing them go around with worn out shoes. They needed decent things.... Neither my wife nor I had been able to give them anything for Christmas." The *Sun-Reporter* noted that "in the couple's sparsely furnished Hunters Point [sic] home, police noticed a colored picture entitled 'Christ Is Our Hope.'"[5]

Two black neighborhoods in San Francisco, Hunter's Point and the Western Addition, stand out as particularly poignant examples of the growth of poverty on the peninsula. Hunter's Point was home to more than 50,000 people, of whom ninety-five percent were black. About four in ten families were single-parent units, and nearly forty percent of Hunter's Point residents toiled below the poverty line. Twenty-three hundred families lived in public housing in Hunter's Point, and their incidence of poverty was higher than that of the rest of the area's inhabitants. In the Western Addition, blacks made up about two-fifths of the population, and the total poverty rate for the area was slightly over one person out of four. Unemployment among blacks in both neighborhoods was high, especially among teenage males, and about one in five adults in the Western Addition had less than an eighth-grade education. Black residents lived in cramped, rodent-infested housing, and while over ninety percent of the available dwellings were occupied, officials estimated that about one in four were in serious disrepair. Mae Gray, a mother of six who lived in a public housing project in Hunter's Point, told the *Sun-Reporter* that rats infested the units in her complex. "Some mornings when I get up about seven and look out on my steps there are rats as large as cats that sit there," she noted. "If I open the door, they may leave. They don't even run from us anymore. The maintenance men give us powder to put down to kill the rats in the apartments, but it only makes the rats mad. I had to get a private exterminator to kill the rats in my place. There aren't many now, but they'll be back soon. They're everywhere." African Americans of the Western Addition or Hunter's Point complained of inadequate police protection, police brutality, poorly lighted and unsafe streets, ineffective welfare services, poor garbage collection, and a complete feeling of alienation from the city government. The crises and policies of the 1950s had by the 1960s produced isolated ghettos in San Francisco, and the poverty populations they contained grew more restless as conditions worsened and the rest of the city seemed to leave them further behind.[6]

## WASHINGTON BUREAUCRATS PLAN THE OFFENSIVE

As federal action had inspired the mass migration to northern and western industrial centers during the Second World War, so too did federal agents attempt to deal with the aftermath of that major demographic shift. Although the connection between federal spending during the war and the urban crises of the 1960s was perhaps not consciously recognized by all of Washington's social policy bureaucrats, the need for reform and anti-poverty measures was definitely understood by the early 1960s. Concern over the cities began during the Eisenhower Administration with attempts to curb mounting juvenile delinquency rates. As private organizations, especially the Ford Foundation, began to create programs for the problem of juvenile crime, federal planners soon moved into the field, and by the mid-1960s, a massive government-funded program was underway to eradicate poverty in the United States. The relocation of hundreds of thousands of white and black migrants during the 1940s left ripples that could still be seen in national policy making two decades later.[7]

The first coordinated federal attempt to deal with the problems of urban America in the 1960s began with John F. Kennedy's appointment of the President's Committee on Juvenile Delinquency on May 11, 1961. Headed by Attorney General Robert F. Kennedy and his former college roommate, David Hackett, the President's Committee became a culmination of the reform attempts of the previous decade. Influenced mainly by the Ford Foundation's Grey Areas Projects and the community action theories of Columbia University social scientists Lloyd Ohlin and Richard Cloward, Hackett pulled the President's Committee together and began attracting former Ford Foundation stars like Richard Boone and Paul Ylvisaker. Hackett's "Guerrillas" wholeheartedly embraced the concept of "community action" and they drew from past experiences in urban reform movements that included Grey Areas Projects in cities like Oakland and Ohlin and Cloward's Mobilization for Youth program in New York. Federal planners desired to attack the national problem of poverty at its local source, and in so doing, they believed it was possible to undo the structural causes of poverty, democratize local power relationships, and uplift the poor. The main theories behind the most innovative anti-poverty projects of the late 1950s and early 1960s were that local communities needed to be in control of the programs that served their area and that there should be a more "comprehensive" approach that coordinated the actions of many social service agencies at the local, state, and federal level, under what one planner labeled the "umbrella thesis." These ideals of community action and coordination would greatly influence the formation of the War on Poverty's main agency, the Office of Economic Opportunity.[8]

After the assassination of John F. Kennedy in November 1963 and during the early planning stages for the legislation that would become the Economic Opportunity Act of 1964, the architects of the anti-poverty program, including some Kennedy holdovers like Richard Boone, scrambled to mount a comprehensive campaign against poverty in America. The nation's new president, Lyndon B. Johnson, appointed R. Sargent Shriver, director of the Peace Corps and brother-in-law of Robert Kennedy, to head the anti-poverty task force. After six months of frantic activity, LBJ's poverty warriors offered up a plan that contained both a community action segment and the Office of Economic Opportunity, which was responsible for coordinating federal anti-poverty efforts already underway in other government agencies, including the Department of Labor and the Department of Health, Education, and Welfare. This new assault on poverty drew much of its inspiration from the concerns over juvenile delinquency in the 1950s and the alarm at the emerging urban crisis, which had become all too apparent by 1964. Many of the planners most responsible for drafting Johnson's War on Poverty legislation had extensive experience fighting urban poverty, and much of their attention was captured by the growing numbers of desperate blacks trapped in America's inner cities. To counter the fears of southern Democrats and conservative Republicans that the poverty program was designed solely for African Americans, however, Shriver and others included projects for low-income whites in Appalachia and vigorously tried to discount any insinuations that the federal government was secretly using the poverty program as a way to further the cause of the Civil Rights Movement or stir up racial tensions in the country.[9]

With their sights set firmly on the problems of the major urban centers of the North and West, most of the planners targeted what they thought were the multiple causes of poverty, and they sought to create more than just a jobs program. Despite the influence of bureaucrats in the Department of Labor, including Labor Secretary Willard Wirtz and Daniel P. Moynihan, who argued that what was most needed was a massive job-creation program, the architects of the 1964 EOA balanced between job training, political mobilization, social services, and low-income resident rehabilitation. Testifying before Congress in 1964, Sargent Shriver explained that "because poverty has many interrelated causes, financial assistance under Title II will be made available to organizations to assist in the development and operation of *action* programs which are of sufficient size and scope to show promise of concrete progress toward the elimination of poverty and a cause or causes of poverty." In a similar vein, William P. Kelly, Jr., who served as director of the Job Corps in the late 1960s, argued that a job was not a sufficient answer to the problem of poverty in urban ghettos. Numerous factors, including discrimination, segregated education, political disfranchisement, and social disorganization, plagued black communities across the nation, and Kelly felt that providing jobs to every ghetto resident was not only unfeasible, but it would be ultimately ineffective:

> A job doesn't provide an exit to the suburb. A job doesn't allow you to buy a house in Prince Georges County or Montgomery County, where Negroes can't go. A job doesn't provide your child with a good school. It's no exit for a lousy school that your kid has still got to go to in Woodlawn or Harlem. A job doesn't teach you anything about nutrition. A job doesn't get your teeth fixed. A job doesn't teach you a darned thing about installment buying, or about how to avoid a usurer. The notion that a job is an answer to these people is crazy! It is naive!

Kelly concluded that the only way to pull people out of poverty was to counter the years of social neglect they had suffered and to instill them with new attitudes about work, their personal health and appearance, the value of education, and the importance of being involved in politics. Despite the condescension inherent in their "fix the poor" approach, the poverty planners had begun to recognize the complexity of urban poverty and formulate new approaches to an ages-old problem.[10]

In order to put their community action-oriented plans into effect, the poverty warriors sought to use the coordinating powers of the federal Office of Economic Opportunity to not only tie together national poverty programs but also to provide a new bureaucracy that could circumvent the authority of local and state welfare agencies and help community groups work together to solve their collective problems. Many of the federal activists felt that established anti-poverty organizations at the local level had stagnated, had failed to reach low-income people, and were afflicted with bureaucratic rigor mortis. To avoid having federal moneys lost in city and state welfare labyrinths, the Office of Economic Opportunity (OEO) designers hoped to create a "fourth branch of government" that would allow them to coordinate effective grassroots organizations and actually communicate with the low-income ghetto residents. Strategists like Richard Boone wanted the OEO to sponsor the development of new local anti-poverty organizations led and operated by the poor themselves and supported with federal grants. OEO dollars would empower a new leadership among low-income people, who would in turn create anti-poverty programs that were applicable to the particular circumstances and needs of each local community. This approach would result in considerable friction between Washington and powerful big-city mayors like Richard Daley of Chicago and Jerome P. Cavanagh of Detroit, and many of LBJ's anti-poverty warriors would later question the wisdom behind such efforts. Christopher Weeks, deputy director of the Job Corps, agreed that the idea of circumventing stagnant local welfare bureaucracies had a certain appeal, but he criticized the idealistic notion that local groups could work together without conflict. "That's like saying that all you have to do to solve the problems of integration and civil rights in Mississippi is to get the NAACP and the Ku Klux Klan together in a room and establish a common set of goals and objectives and programs and everything will work out hunky-dory thereafter," he noted. "It just doesn't work that way." Indeed, the anti-poverty program did not produce the results that the planners intended, and the creation of a new grass-roots leadership would be one of the greatest mixed legacies of the War on Poverty.[11]

The kind of conflict and controversy created by the planners' desire to involve the poor was unintentional and unexpected. The turmoil was a consequence of the Washington bureaucrats' naiveté and idealism, and it did not reflect a "radical" desire to turn the world upside down and foment class struggle and racial strife. The OEO has frequently been misperceived as a den of insurrectionaries, but in reality many of the planners themselves did not realize some of the complexities and paradoxes that were inherent in the community action model. Several staffers expected trouble from local welfare officials and other federal agencies when the OEO tried to flex its coordinating muscles, but few people foresaw the kind of attacks that Shriver and his crew would face from both below and above. Rarely did the members of the task force embrace the more radical community action and confrontation theories of Saul Alinsky, and most of the theoretically oriented planners were driven more by romanticism than by revolutionary zeal. The planners who supported community action were very cautious with the organization and implementation of the new strategy, and they only originally scheduled to fund about fifty demonstration projects that would each require nearly a year's planning before they would be implemented. LBJ had called for an "unconditional war on poverty," however, and the president pressured Shriver and the OEO to fund projects across the nation and to cut the planning time down so that funds could start flowing to local agencies in early 1965. The explosion of community action projects across the country, and the enormous amount of confusion and controversy they caused, was more the result of Johnson's wish to get the ball rolling in his War on Poverty rather than a concerted effort from a few radical poverty planners who sought to overturn power relationships in America's cities. The main aim of the champions of community action was to change how poverty programs in the United States operated and to redefine the relationship between the federal government and local agencies in order to return power to citizens and bypass existing bureaucracies that were bound in red tape and unresponsive to the needs of the people.[12]

The turmoil surrounding the Office of Economic Opportunity's Community Action Programs (CAPs) swirled around the meaning of the rather innocuous phrase, "maximum feasible participation." Few of the poverty planners had reasoned out the exact meaning, or even the range of acceptable meanings, for the phrase before they sent the draft legislation to Congress. The words gained little notice during the legislative hearings on Capitol Hill, and they quietly became part of Title II of the Economic Opportunity Act of 1964. According to bureaucratic legend, Richard Boone had used the phrase several times during a meeting, and when Sargent Shriver expressed some interest, Boone wondered aloud how many more times he needed to say it for it to be included in the antipoverty program. After a few more hints, the phrase was incorporated into the community action component of the legislation. Harold Horowitz, a member of the War on Poverty Task Force, confessed that the planners had intentionally left the meaning of "maximum feasible participation" ambiguous in part because they themselves could not come to a consensus, in part because it would give them some flexibility in selling the program to a potentially antagonistic Congress, and in part because they felt it should imply an "operational meaning" that could be determined by local officials on a case-by-case basis. "That's the glorious thing about statutory drafting or writing contracts or things like that," he noted; "you can fall back on words like maximum and reasonable and feasible and what have you and fend off questions about what that means specifically."[13]

Most of the task force members agreed that "maximum feasible participation" meant that local officials should make a sincere effort to include target-area residents in the planning and implementation of Community Action Programs. How much low-income resident participation constituted a "sincere" effort, however, remained clouded in real ideological difference and a wait-and-see attitude that assumed great variation from one CAP to the next. On the one hand, activists like Richard Boone hoped that the poor could control the CAPs and use them to challenge unresponsive local governments and social service agencies. On the other hand, more cautious planners like Bertrand Harding were skeptical that poor people could effectively run Community Action Programs because they did not have the necessary training or education to handle them. Harding felt that low-income people should be consulted about the needs of their community and their ideas for solving problems should be incorporated into the final program, but they were simply not capable of running the CAPs. Ultimately, the consensus at OEO over "maximum feasible participation" boiled down to a rough "three-cornered stool" approach, where local government, private welfare agencies, and low-income residents would each have equal representation on CAP boards and equal say in the planning process.[14]

Perhaps because of their uncertainty of the meaning of the phrase "maximum feasible participation," almost no one involved in the drafting stages of the Economic Opportunity Act anticipated the radical interpretations that many low-income groups would make of its language. Adam Yarmolinsky, reflecting on his failure to foresee the attempts by many low-income groups to take control of the CAPs, wryly noted that "in a community as sensitive to the problems of the distribution and transmission of power as Washington, the power potential—constructive and destructive— of the poor themselves was largely overlooked." President Johnson remained wary of possible political booby traps in the community action concept, and he ordered Sargent Shriver and others to "make sure that no crooks, Communists, or cocksuckers get into this program." When Bureau of the Budget Director Charles Schultze wrote the president and warned him that mayors were grumbling about attempts of the poor to take over CAPs and create independent political power bases in big cities throughout the United States, LBJ agreed that low-income residents should be involved in the operation of the program, but that they should not run them. The OEO's official CAP *Guide* also contained the ominous caveat that "each applicant and delegate agency will be expected to employ only capable and responsible personnel who are of good character and reputation, are sympathetic with the objectives of the Economic Opportunity Act and the administrative policies promulgated thereunder, and are not members of subversive organizations." Despite the president's caution and the official acceptance of the "three-cornered stool" concept, however, the phrase "maximum feasible participation" opened the door to challenges for power from below, and armies of the poor would lay siege to numerous CAPs across the country.[15]

## THE POOR DEMAND CONTROL

Some of the greatest challenges to the politicians' and bureaucrats' control over the Community Action Programs came in the San Francisco Bay Area. Low-income groups in San Francisco and Oakland demanded majority representation on area poverty boards, placement in the high-salaried positions in the poverty program, and authority over the day-to-day operations of local CAPs. Black ghetto residents had long been familiar with the community action concept by the time the OEO began planning its foray into the area, and many low-income blacks had grown tired of long planning phases, empty promises, and ambiguous results. In May 1960, the San Francisco Board of Supervisors used funds totaling more than $400,000 from the Ford Foundation, the President's Committee on Juvenile Delinquency, and the Department of Labor to set up a Committee on Youth to combat the problem of juvenile delinquency, but it took over three years before the newly created Youth Opportunities Center attempted to place at-risk youth into jobs. The Ford Foundation also poured another $2,000,000 into Oakland in 1961 when it created the first Grey Areas Project in the country. Wayne Thompson, the city manager, and Evillio Grillo, the "juvenile control co-ordinator," won the grant for Oakland and began to assemble an anti-juvenile delinquency program, but its effects were at best inconclusive. In 1963, residents from the Hunter's Point-Bayview Citizens Committee planned a protest after being left out of the planning process of another Ford Foundation project with a $400,000 price tag, and they concluded that "we can no longer stand idly by and watch members of the white community plan projects to solve our problems. We feel that there is a great deal at stake and are constantly developing ways and means of solving our problems. [W]e are of the opinion that [any white-planned project] is doomed to failure because of the initial exclusion of our group." Despite the growing frustration in black communities in the Bay Area, federal planners at the Office of Economic Opportunity failed to anticipate the coming struggle between low-income residents and the local political leadership over control of the Community Action Programs. When they announced a $55,080 planning grant for the city of San Francisco in November 1964, Washington's poverty warriors were completely oblivious to the storms gathering on the horizon.[16]

Calls for low-income residents' control over local CAPs echoed throughout the Bay Area during the mid-1960s. In January 1965, several residents of Hunter's Point hoped that they would get a better understanding of how the War on Poverty worked after attending the National Conference on Poverty in the Southwest, but they left Phoenix feeling frustrated and certain that the latest attempt to uplift the poor would be no different than its predecessors. Mrs. George M. Washington summarized the feelings of many representatives of low-income neighborhoods when she concluded that "history is going to repeat itself, and the money that is supposed to be for the poor people will be paid out for research for problems of which we are already aware, and in high salaries, and by the time it gets to the people who are really in need there won't be enough left to do any good." Similar feelings prevailed in Oakland the following year during the First Statewide Convention of the Poor. While discussing the course of the War on Poverty, over one hundred delegates called for more local control by the poor, majority representation on all local, state, and national poverty boards, discretion over the employment of all bureaucrats and professionals associated with the poverty program, drastic changes in how welfare and public housing systems were operated, increased funding for the poor, and more political venues for low-income people to discuss their grievances. Critics charged that the poverty program was "phony" if it failed to live up to the ideal of "maximum feasible participation." One observer recorded that a woman from Hunter's Point proclaimed "that we are fed up with *everyone* from the outside and are going to do this job ourselves!" Another black man from Oakland argued that the poor "had no reason to trust anyone, in or out of government, liberal or do-gooder conservative, affluent white or middle-class educated black." Low-income residents of the Bay Area were tired of the stale rhetoric from politicians and welfare reformers, and they resented the condescension and prejudice that came from government bureaucrats. One black community leader from Hunter's Point noted that:

> Now the administration level needs to change the way they view poor people.... [T]he person at the top level always feels that he knows what he's doing; he can't understand why you're poor in the first place, if you had enough sense you wouldn't be poor.... I think Washington feels that people should pick themselves up by their own bootstraps, and, frankly, I don't think there are any shoelaces left to even tie the knots, let alone pick yourself up, you know.

Her sentiments were shared by many low-income blacks of the Bay Area, and the calls for resident control over the War on Poverty would continue to reverberate off of ghetto walls and city halls for the rest of the decade.[17]

The conflict over control of the poverty program in San Francisco was waged between the city's mayor and its black, low-income population. Some of the OEO planners had expected tensions between local welfare agencies on the one hand and the poor and local government leaders on the other, but few of them had foreseen the possibility of conflict between city mayors and urban slum dwellers. In San Francisco, the battle raged between Mayor John F. Shelley, a liberal white Democrat, and low-income residents, often represented by the organization Citizens United Against Poverty (CUAP). First known as the "Macedonia Group" and rising out of citizens' meetings at the Macedonia Baptist Church in January 1965, CUAP drew up a list of demands that outlined their view of resident participation and presented them to Mayor Shelley in February. CUAP's leaders were troubled with Shelley's appointment of his political cronies to leadership positions in the San Francisco Economic Opportunity Council (EOC), and they demanded that poor people, instead of white professionals, be placed in the high-salary jobs and that low-income people have majority representation in the poverty program. Shelley rejected the early demands of CUAP, and cries rose up from low-income groups that Shelley was "in a most awkward and unpolished fashion [fighting] his own war—not against poverty, but a war against the poor."[18]

Frustrated and surprised by the low-income residents' charges, Shelley backpedaled quickly and offered several compromise measures that would have divided the power of the Executive Council between the poor, the mayor, and the San Francisco Board of Supervisors. Draping themselves in the banner of "maximum feasible participation," however, CUAP and the low-income residents rejected the offers and instead demanded control of the poverty program. Shelley then pulled his offers off the table, held an emergency meeting of the EOC's Executive Council in May 1965, and railroaded his program through. CUAP and other low-income residents appealed to Washington, and funding for the San Francisco CAPs was frozen until a compromise could be reached. Shelley and CUAP continued to wrangle throughout the summer, and Shelley complained of his troubles at the United States Conference of Mayors in St. Louis in early June. The following month, over fifty speakers gathered at a San Francisco City Hall meeting and demanded majority representation of the poor, and Shelley finally capitulated to the pressure. The mayor agreed to restructure the poverty board's membership so that a majority of the thirty-one members would be elected from the target areas. The new Executive Board would include eight representatives of the low-income groups and seven other members, and it would screen proposals and have veto power over them. The mayor and the low-income residents continued to wrestle for control over the poverty program, but after the summer of 1965, the balance had shifted in favor of the poor, and San Francisco's City Hall had learned the potential of the phrase "maximum feasible participation."[19]

## THE POOR IN CONTROL

The victory of low-income groups in the battle for control over the poverty program also marked the rise of a more militant strain of black liberation ideology in the Bay Area. Many poor people did indeed win positions in the San Francisco Community Action Projects, and they were joined by a radical new leadership that rejected the ideals of nonviolent integration and instead espoused black self-determination, a separatist black nationalism, and confrontation as ways to fight racism in San Francisco and the East

Bay. The new leaders of San Francisco's CAPs reached out to previously disfranchised groups and sought to involve all of the poor
in the poverty program. Poverty organizers targeted schools and
churches as well as pool halls and street corners in an effort to
organize the disparate elements of San Francisco's ghetto community, the "deserving poor" and, as one Washington insider put it,
"the cream of the crap."[20]

Both by design and by choice, the moderate, middle-class leaders of the NAACP were left out of the initial grab for leadership
positions in Bay Area Community Action Programs. Although the
Office of Economic Opportunity apparently wanted to use the
NAACP's regional branches as barometers of black sentiment about
the War on Poverty, the federal government kept the civil rights
organization at a safe distance from its CAPs during the first year of
their implementation. Wary of complaints from conservative con-
gressmen, the OEO did not desire that NAACP representatives
would take control of projects in low-income black communities.
Similarly, the NAACP did not initially become involved in Bay Area
CAPs because the organization's leaders were not comfortable with
the nature of the reforms offered by the War on Poverty. The West
Coast branches of the NAACP remained firmly committed to their
moderate approach to racial reform, and Bay Area leaders were
slow to embrace the community action concepts embodied in the
Economic Opportunity Act of 1964. The NAACP only saw CAPs as
one potential vehicle for civil rights reform in northern California,
and the organization continued to focus upon polite reform and
legislative lobbying. In 1966, the OEO actually rejected a NAACP-
sponsored proposal to use CAPs to organize a voter education and
registration drive in Bay Area African American communities
because the agency felt the project went beyond the boundaries
authorized by the anti-poverty legislation. The NAACP's hesitancy
might be explained in part by the Association's ill-fated attempts to
create youth work groups across California during the mid-1960s.
The group's foray into anti-poverty activism was fraught with confusion, contention, and failure, and the NAACP quickly abandoned
the idea of youth mobilization after their youth work project fell
apart under the strains of miscommunication, ignorance, and
infighting. Although some leading black municipal officials

appealed to the NAACP to "stimulate a more active role in these target areas among many of the middle-class members of your organization who are not as supportive of the program as they could be," the Association only mildly encouraged its members to take leadership positions in Bay Area CAPs. San Francisco's more militant civil rights groups did not share the NAACP's reticence to become involved in the War on Poverty programs, however, and the advocates of direct-action quickly became champions of community action.[21]

The most radical of the Bay Area CAPs was located in the Western Addition. Headed by Director Wilfred Ussery, who was by then also national chairman of the Congress of Racial Equality (CORE), the Western Addition poverty program embraced the full implications of the "maximum feasible participation" clause of the 1964 Equal Opportunity Act. Ussery and his co-workers organized a series of "Grits and Gripes" conferences where target area residents were to voice their opinions about the poverty program, state their needs, and offer their solutions to problems affecting their community. The poverty workers hoped to lure low-income residents to the conferences with the promise of a free breakfast and lunch, and over two thousand residents attended the sessions and gave the representatives a list of demands that included rent controls, better housing, job training, improved recreation facilities, better schools, child day care for working mothers, a general information agency for the Western Addition, more representation for youth in the poverty program, and improved social and welfare services. The Western Addition poverty workers canvassed all types of places in the target area from bars to missions to shoeshine parlors to get poor people to come to the "Grits and Gripes" meetings. Ussery noted that "a lot of people will probably raise their eyebrows at our efforts to recruit such people as pool hall rack boys and prostitutes along with the rest. But these people are poor, too, and they have relatives and friends who are poor and we intend to reach them all." Ussery realized that the first step in organizing low-income residents through the poverty program was to get them to identify with the projects and develop a sense of connection with them.[22]

Reaching out to the roughest elements of the ghetto society was dangerous and controversial, not just to white politicians in city hall and the OEO, but also to moderate African American activists who objected to the more militant attitudes and radical actions of Ussery and his staff. The most outspoken black critic of the Western Addition Target Area leadership was Rev. Robert Gardley, a middle-aged African American clergyman who embraced the nonviolent integrationist philosophy of Martin Luther King, Jr., and the Southern Christian Leadership Conference (SCLC). Gardley, a graduate of Langston University and the Conroe Industrial, Normal and Theological Seminary, taught in Oklahoma black schools before he migrated to California to work as an insurance agent and then as a salesman. He joined Dr. King and other civil rights demonstrators in the Selma to Montgomery march, and he embodied the ideals of the moderate southern Civil Rights Movement. Gardley was aghast at the way Wilfred Ussery ran the Western Addition poverty program, and he wrote letters to Sargent Shriver, the president, and the attorney general informing them that Ussery was using the CAP to preach Black Power and white hatred, and that the poverty program was filled with members of the Black Muslim "cult" and Ussery's cronies. Charging Ussery with illegally using the War on Poverty moneys to fund his version of the black freedom movement, Gardley complained that such radicals tainted the image of sincere advocates of the African American community. He told Sargent Shriver that he was "sad that a few hoodlums and pseudo-intellectual Negroes are allowed, as per usual, to stigmatize the decent element of the Negro community and create a stereotype image which is insulting and offensive to the better class of Negroes." Proclaiming that Ussery "and his associates are enemies to their country," Gardley warned that "Mr. Will Ussery continues to flout the law, and advocate Black Power, and court Black Nationalists on staff. God forbid such an anathema."[23]

Throughout the summer of 1966, Gardley continued to charge Ussery and the Western Addition staff with mismanagement of anti-poverty funds and illegally using money to bankroll militant civil rights efforts. He forwarded a flyer made in the Western Addition office that announced a "Rally for Justice" on the steps of city hall to denounce the convictions and sentences of demonstrators who had been jailed in a series of 1964 CORE-led protests against job discrimination. Gardley accused Ussery of using approximately $9,500 of the Community Action Program's budget to finance the flyers, and he noted that "this is not relative to the Poverty Program, but 'Black Power.'" He also claimed that Ussery, Tomastra Scott, and Nasser Shabazz held secret meetings to teach people how to make Molotov Cocktails and discuss the "strategic" areas of San Francisco. The reverend denounced the radicals' control over the poverty program, and he pleaded with Shriver and other government officials to intervene and return the Western Addition Target Area back to the hands of responsible, moderate black leaders.[24]

Gardley's complaints raised eyebrows at OEO headquarters, and after a series of investigations, Edgar May, the chief of the Inspection Division, informed Shriver that most of Gardley's accusations were true. May's agents confirmed that Ussery had used CAP funds to print and distribute flyers for the "Rally for Justice," and he even compensated workers who attended the rally with four hours of overtime pay. When the agents contacted Ussery and the Western Addition staff, most of them admitted to using the funds to support their civil rights agenda, and they argued that such a use was totally justified. The staff concluded that they were the last line of defense against potentially deadly riots in the Western Addition, and they warned that if they were removed, then the city could expect a "long, hot summer." Unmoved by their warnings, Shriver ordered OEO officials to inform Ussery that such expenditures were unacceptable, and he agreed that an audit of the San Francisco Economic Opportunity Council was in order. May warned Shriver that "this has more the makings of a major national poverty war news story, Congressional inquiry and 'Black Arts'-type cause celebre than anything we've seen for some time." The director concurred, and he scribbled on the memo: "I assume that we have not and will not refinance this group. If I'm wrong then this can be considered an instruction not to refinance it without my personal approval."[25]

Ussery's opponents on the Western Addition Area Board acted quickly in the wake of Washington's complaints, and in a hastily called meeting on September 15, the board voted to dismiss one of

Ussery's supporters, Nasser Shabazz, without a full hearing or complete investigation into charges made against him by other poverty program workers that he was unreasonable to work with and that he had advocated armed conflicts with the police and the U.S. military and the violent overthrow of the San Francisco establishment. Several female staff members had been insulted by Shabazz's claim that if any black woman was caught with a white man "we'll whip her and strip her and throw her in the street," and his insistence that women should learn how to shoot guns and dress bullet wounds for the upcoming revolution. The board also voted to look into charges of financial mismanagement by Ussery and others. When Edgar May informed Shriver of the board's actions, the director responded: "Finally! They're moving."[26]

The insurgency among the Western Addition CAP was not quelled so easily, however, and when, during the height of the 1966 San Francisco riots, Ussery announced that he had discovered Gardley's letters to Shriver and President Johnson, the militant CORE leader was able to regain his position within the poverty program. During the tense meeting, Ussery confronted Gardley and proclaimed "old whitey's got to go. We're going to raise hell tonight.... We're going to raise hell in Fillmore tonight and then we're going to go on to Oakland." Gardley, who had been feeding information to the OEO and the FBI, went into hysterics after the meeting and begged for protection from Ussery and his gang. "The troops are here. Lives are being lost," Gardley reported during the height of the rioting. "Civil insurrection [h]as [s]tymied our city and the Black Moslem [sic] are in power. The good people are helpless to resist.... The Black Moslems are now in power and the files of the OEO are open to their disposal...." Fortunately for the reverend, Ussery did nothing worse than suspend him from the poverty program for libel, and the radicals continued to claim that their use of anti-poverty funds was well within the guidelines of the 1964 Economic Opportunity Act. Ussery then pressured the Western Addition Area Board into granting him full authority over the hiring and firing of personnel.[27]

In another about-face, however, the Area Board voted several days later to dismiss Ussery and keep Gardley in his job. A bitter period of infighting and power struggle followed, and Ussery claimed that his firing had been inappropriate since a quorum had not been present to vote on the matter. The Area Board chairman, Jeff Andrews, was besieged by the Ussery faction, and he was temporarily removed from power, but the board supported him at another tumultuous meeting on the first of November. Ussery was reappointed to his job several days later, and all sides agreed to meet in the middle of November to try and work out a compromise. Hanging on to his position to make a political statement about the operation of the poverty program, Ussery eventually resigned in early 1967 and he channeled his energies back into CORE. The controversy surrounding Ussery led to sensational press coverage, and the added publicity helped the radicals to spread their message and build a widening base of support among the ghetto community. Even Dr. Carlton B. Goodlett, publisher of the *Sun-Reporter*, came to Ussery's defense and argued that he was a true champion of the poor: "the enemy is trying to destroy CORE and SNCC. The enemy is outside the Negro community. I would hope the Western Addition would not repudiate this man. He has been to jail for us.... The white power structure who don't like what you are doing (in the poverty program) would like to see you commit suicide."[28]

The Gardley and Ussery factions continued to snipe at each other throughout 1967, and the reverend sent another batch of correspondence to Washington when Ussery's old ally Nasser Shabazz ran unsuccessfully for reelection to the Western Addition Area Board. Gardley charged Shabazz with violating election rules and illegally using a CAP sound truck to broadcast propaganda throughout the Western Addition, and he admonished the FBI that "this is a crucial time, and the Federal Government is feeding a dangerous religious cult which, if left alone, will soon attack the white community and all-hell will break out." He claimed that Shabazz's actions had alienated decent blacks who no longer wanted to participate in the poverty program, and most of the candidates for the board elections were "Black Muslims disguised as just common Negroes." Washington continued to keep a close eye on the situation in the Western Addition, but a Price-Waterhouse audit completed in 1967 found little evidence of intentional fraud, although some funds had been used in civil rights activities. The San Francisco EOC responded that they could account for most of the discrepancies in funds and they argued that no provision in the 1964 EOA specifically prohibited the use of anti-poverty moneys for civil rights programs.[29]

The belief that the War on Poverty was a part of the black struggle for civil rights was widely held among low-income residents throughout the Bay Area. Few poor blacks disagreed with the notion that the CAPs should serve as vehicles for protest against segregation and discrimination, and many ghetto dwellers believed that the poverty programs should be on the front lines in the battle against racism. In March 1966, for example, anti-poverty program employees led over one hundred people in an "invasion" of the San Francisco Housing Authority to stop the eviction of poor families from public housing units in Hunter's Point. A spokesman for the Hunter's Point-Bayview project argued that the protest was "part of our anti-poverty program of helping people," and he noted that "we take orders from the residents out here. They hired us to do a job—and that was part of the job." Similar attitudes prevailed in the East Bay, and the Oakland Economic Development Council, Inc. (OEDCI) declared that its basic commitment "was for jobs for the poor residing in Oakland and at decent wages.... This basic concern with who worked and for how much...often placed the OEDCI in conflict with the public and private attitudes of business as usual. It was a conflict which added strength to the OEDCI because it made the OEDCI credible within the low income communities of Oakland." The OEDCI advocated confrontation as a way of solving the problems of ghetto residents, and the executive director of the program, Percy Moore, admitted that "he saw in the poverty program a mandate to organize the poor." Many of Oakland's anti-poverty organizers expressed militant attitudes about using direct-action tactics to confront the Establishment and gain "real change" for the city's poor. One poverty program supervisor stated that "most of the aides I have hired have been militant civil rights workers because I thought that they would be good at C.O. [Community Organization] work." Other low-income blacks, including Ruth Williams of Hunter's Point, told the Senate's Subcommittee on Employment, Manpower, and Poverty that they should ease restrictions that kept poverty program workers from joining civil rights demonstrations against employers who discriminated against

African Americans. Clearly, most low-income blacks realized that fighting poverty necessarily meant fighting racism.[30]

Community Action Programs throughout the Bay Area also provided militant and radical blacks with funds and an audience. Earl Anthony, a young black employee of the San Francisco Housing Authority (SFHA) and a future Black Panther, organized a tenants' rent strike in the Western Addition with the help of Audrey Smith, common-law wife of Nasser Shabazz and a pro-Ussery staffer at the Western Addition poverty office. Anthony's militant Independent Action Movement (I AM) grew out of the rent strike, and when he was fired by the SFHA, he went to work as a director of "a government funded anti-poverty program with twenty-five employees working for me." Other future Black Panther Party members, including Bobby Seale, Huey P. Newton, and Bobby Hutton, also got their starts in the anti-poverty program in North Oakland, and Seale even visited the Hunter's Point CAP in the summer of 1967 to give a speech before some two hundred black youths. Although he was apparently not paid to speak before the group, Seale did gain the opportunity to preach his gospel of revolutionary black nationalism, and he told the crowd that:

> we have been miseducated about what politics really is.... [P]olitics is war without bloodshed and war is politics with bloodshed.... [P]olitics starts with hungry stomachs; dilapidated houses; murder and brutal treatment by racist cops; unfair treatment received in the courts; the way black men are drafted into the military forces and are forced to fight other colored people of the world.... [Black youths] must develop a tactic and unite around something practical, and...the only practical thing that a people can unite around to win their liberation is the gun.... If we organize and use gun power in a strategic fashion against a racist power structure, the power structure then becomes aware of the facts that we are correctly educated on the true understanding of politics.... The only thing we can do now, brothers and sisters, is get our guns organized, forget the sit-ins, and shoot it out.

Troubled by Seale's comments and afraid that this story would turn into another public relations nightmare for the OEO, Sargent

Shriver ordered his Inspection Division to "nip in the bud any connection between this guy with any of our programs & publicize the facts in S.F. [San Francisco]." Shriver's concern was warranted by the numbers of black militants who had infiltrated the Bay Area's Community Action Programs, and although the Inspection Division was eventually successful in driving many of them out of the poverty program, the damage had been done and black militancy had sunk deep roots in the northern California soil.[31]

## WHO BENEFITS?

The War on Poverty has long been criticized for stirring up militants, raising false hopes among the poor, failing to commit enough resources to adequately attack the problem of poverty, and providing the opportunity for graft and corruption among inner-city welfare agents, politicians, and local community leaders. Indeed, there is little doubt that the Johnson Administration's grand assault failed to live up to the bold assertions and audacious rhetoric of Washington planners who claimed that they could wipe out poverty in America. The elderly benefited the most from such programs as Medicare and Medicaid, yet the majority of the urban poor, and especially minority children, remained trapped beneath the poverty line. Complaints of high staff salaries, low target-area resident participation, and inadequate and irrelevant programs arose around the country, and they were only weakly countered with talk of "empowerment" and scant proof of real progress. The paradox of poverty amidst plenty continued to plague the nation despite the energies of the OEO staff, and as the United States rolled into 1966, the prospect of ever successfully addressing the problem of poverty seemed increasingly remote. The poverty programs in the San Francisco Bay Area typified the confusion over the War on Poverty, and the questions surrounding the concept of community action echoed throughout the ghettos of Hunter's Point, the Western Addition, and West Oakland.

High staff salaries were a constant bone of contention in Bay Area anti-poverty projects. Federal guidelines stated that CAP workers' salaries could be no more than twenty percent higher than their earnings in their previous job, but local board members throughout the Bay Area argued that this unfairly discriminated against people who had been unemployed or stuck in low-skill, low-wage work because of employer bias.  Complaints frequently arose from the low-income residents when target area boards submitted budgets that were almost totally exhausted by staff salaries, and many people scoffed that the money was never going to get to the poorest people who most needed it.  When Wilfred Ussery proposed that $450,000 of a $609,000 budget for the Western Addition Target Area be spent on salaries for the more than one hundred workers in the program, some local residents claimed that he was milking the poverty program for his own benefit.  Ussery argued that the Community Action Program should be a way to create jobs for local black people, and he noted that the Western Addition needed a solid bureaucratic infrastructure to secure more poverty funds from Washington in the future.  The San Francisco Economic Opportunity Council also had its share of salary boosts.  Its executive director, Everett P. Brandon, enjoyed a considerable jump in salary from $12,000 in his former job to $18,000 in his new position, an increase of well over the twenty percent mandated by the OEO.  In 1967, Earl Anthony received a $5,000,000 grant to set up the Potrero Hill Manpower Program, yet most of the money was eaten up in fat staff salaries, and Anthony himself enjoyed a $20,000-a-year position.  One cynical community organizer and CAP employee in Oakland complained that the only people really aided by the poverty program were the ones on its payroll: "the program has at least done some little good and it has taken one family out of poverty—mine."[32]

The benefits of generous staff salaries in Bay Area War on Poverty programs fell almost exclusively to men.  Although black women participated in Community Action Programs and they represented their communities on planning boards in San Francisco and the East Bay, African American men dominated leadership positions in the local CAPs.  After low-income advocates wrested control of the War on Poverty away from Mayor Jack Shelley, women comprised more than half of San Francisco's poverty board.  No women, however, were listed as Program Coordinators or other high-ranking CAP officers on a report from the San Francisco Economic Opportunity Council.  African American women served on planning boards in Oakland as well, but they were not well represented in salaried positions in East Bay CAPs. Despite the low monetary benefits of working in the poverty program, black women organized many important community projects, oversaw the day-to-day operations of many CAPs, and engineered many of the successes enjoyed by Bay Area anti-poverty activists. A partial explanation for black women's low status in the War on Poverty programs was that most federal planners and local community organizers were focused upon black male employment as a means to protect and strengthen black families. Influenced by the findings of the infamous *Moynihan Report*, most male organizers apparently believed that urban poverty could in large part be traced to the supposed weaknesses in black families and could be explained by the predominance of female-headed, single-parent families. To counter this alarming trend, male planners subordinated African American women into supporting roles in the War on Poverty and they reserved the most lucrative jobs for men. In Hunter's Point, for example, African American women were kept almost exclusively in secondary positions. In 1965, several women working for the Hunter's Point CAP complained to federal officials at OEO headquarters that they were passed over for promotion in favor of men who had more education but considerably less experience. The complainants told of how Mrs. Osceola Washington, who had more than a decade community organizing experience in Hunter's Point, was denied a job that was eventually offered to Harold Brooks, a college graduate who had been the unpaid executive director of the Bayview Community Center for six years. Although the women protested that "Mrs. Washington was the one who took all the college graduate social workers...by the hand when they came to Hunter's Point to get experience," the bureaucrats in Washington agreed that Brooks, a 40 year-old unemployed man, was the more qualified candidate for the job. For many War on Poverty planners, "maximum feasible participation" did not mean maximum feasible equality for black women.[33]

Even if poverty program funds had not been tied up in staff salaries, much of them probably would not have reached those most in need because so many low-income people were poorly informed about the programs and skeptical that they offered substantial help. While more than seven out of ten poor people favored the War on Poverty in an Oakland survey taken during the mid-1960s, almost twenty percent of those polled had no opinion on the subject. Fewer low-income residents felt that the poverty programs in their area were effective, and many respondents stated that officials were "going about it wrong" or that they were not "doing what's needed." Although a majority of low-income residents in Oakland voiced some opinion of the War on Poverty for the survey, only twenty-one percent were aware of anti-poverty service centers in the city, only sixteen percent of West Oakland residents knew where their anti-poverty office was located, and only three percent of those surveyed in West Oakland had ever visited a center. Anthropologist Arthur Hippler found a similar situation in Hunter's Point in the mid-1960s, and he noted that one unemployed 29 year-old African American mother of five children was "only vaguely aware of the existence of a food stamp program" and that she "profess[ed] not really to understand how 'the welfare' works or to have even the sketchiest knowledge of her obligations and rights." Despite federal outlays of $6,579,000 in 1966, San Francisco's poverty program could still not guarantee that its youth job-training program would result in full-time employment for the graduates, and the five neighborhood centers; job development program with 2,500 beneficiaries; health program; upward bound and compensatory education projects; legal aid and bail system; summer Head Start classes for 1,530 children; performing arts workshop; and a total CAP payroll for 255 people of whom 219 were poor did relatively little to end poverty in San Francisco's ghettos or bring thousands of low-income black residents into the American mainstream.[34]

Despite the limitations of the War on Poverty and the CAPs' shortcomings, many target-area representatives and community organizers insisted that community action was the key component in combating poverty. Many low-income people argued that the community action component of the poverty program helped to "empower" the poor by giving them a sense of purpose and control over their destinies. In an eloquent plea in defense of the Hunter's Point CAP, Mrs. Osceola Washington declared that the concept of "maximum feasible participation" was "the one outstanding aspect of the total War on Poverty.  It presents a chance for the first time in this nation's history for the poor to become a participant in developing meaningful approaches to their problems.   This involvement of the poor in the policy making process allows ideas from the residents to become realities."  Percy Moore, executive director of the San Francisco Council for Civic Unity, agreed, noting that "community organization develops a specific result: It gives people power and dignity to make decisions that affect their own lives."  Such noble sentiments were cold comfort to thousands of Bay Area low-income residents, however.  No matter how accurate the assertion was that the poor needed to develop this sense of empowerment, the decades old crises of unemployment, segregated schools, poor housing, and deteriorating community-police relations had fouled the air and people began to desperately look in new directions for answers to the racial problems that plagued Berkeley, Richmond, San Francisco, and Oakland.  For thousands of low-income African Americans, those answers were found not in a government-sponsored welfare system, but in a small office on Grove Street in the heart of West Oakland's black ghetto, and their new rallying cry would not be "maximum feasible participation," but "All Power to the People!"[35]

## WASHINGTON'S COUNTER REVOLUTION

By the summer of 1966, Johnson and the OEO warriors were wondering what had happened to their War on Poverty.  Plagued by Republican criticism, sensational press coverage, and waning public enthusiasm, the anti-poverty program limped into its second year desperately trying to protect its budget, maintain its direction, and hold onto its most promising programs.  The president was becoming increasingly frustrated with Sargent Shriver and the OEO, and as the quagmire of Vietnam began to suck away more of his attention, Johnson distanced himself from the crown jewel of his Great Society.  Many of the main proponents of community action had left the OEO for greener pastures, and as bureaucratic conservatism set in, other programs began to take precedence over the Community Action Programs.  Head Start and Job Corps programs began springing up in almost every grant application to the

OEO, and local communities were encouraged to replicate projects that had been successful, or at least non-controversial, elsewhere. As radicalism among the poor increased and calls to end poverty began to mix with anti-war rhetoric and chants of "Black Power," many white Americans began to turn against the War on Poverty. The collapse of the OEO signaled the beginning of the end of the Johnson Administration, and as the walls around LBJ began to crumble, a host of critics from the right and left picked up the rubble and hurled it at the president.

The American public had never been staunch supporters of the War on Poverty. A March 1964 Gallup Poll reported that a third of Americans felt that people were poor because they were lazy, and more than eight out of ten thought it impossible to eliminate poverty in America. Two years later, in the spring of 1966, nearly half of the public had a favorable impression of the poverty program, but only a third felt that its funds were well spent. By September of the same year, however, public sentiment had shifted strongly against the OEO, and although urban blacks backed the office by a margin of five to one, the majority of Americans felt the OEO was failing. Only three in ten poor whites thought the War on Poverty was working, and more than half of the respondents complained that the anti-poverty program was too tainted by politics. Critical of giving "handouts" to millions of people unable to realize their version of the American Dream, many Americans argued that what was needed was not more welfare spending, but a tough-love policy that forced people to go out and get jobs. James Lopez of Inglewood, California, expressed this widely held sentiment in his terse and cynical letter to the editor of the San Francisco *Chronicle*: "I'm fighting poverty. I'm working."[36]

Opponents of the War on Poverty also stepped up their complaints against the OEO. The Bay Area continued to witness its own saga of poverty program scandals, and the OEO scrambled to put out a series of brush fires in the spring of 1966. In January, the Bay Area Neighborhood Development (BAND) announced its plan to create three new co-ops in Hunter's Point, the Mission District, and North Oakland, with the help of anti-poverty grants. The co-op organizers complained that low-income shoppers were susceptible to the "brand name trap" and sly sales tactics of large companies, and they passed out pamphlets urging consumers to buy generic and off-brand products that were of similar quality but lacked the price inflation caused by advertising. The pro-business San Francisco *Chronicle* denounced the plan as un-American and editorialized that:

> the keen competition among brand name manufacturers is a mainstay of our free enterprise economy.... It is wickedly ironic that a few of our far-out dreamers would try to shut off the golden flow of the American cornucopia through such slogans as 'beware of the brand name trap' at the very time that Soviet Russia's rulers are recognizing the need for competition to eliminate the drab, inferior, high priced merchandise of their controlled economy.... [A]ny program that appears to attack the very source of American strength—using federal dollars to do so—is utterly out of place.

The Brand Name Foundation, the National Federation of Independent Businesses, and the Better Business Bureau all agreed with the *Chronicle*, and the OEO ordered BAND to stop circulating its pamphlets and reform its consumer education project. Similar protests were raised when the Oakland Economic Development Council announced that it would seek funding from the OEO or the Ford Foundation for a community police review board. The OEO refused the proposed $23,225 grant, however, and Oakland Mayor John H. Reading announced that he would veto any Ford Foundation grant that would be used to establish such a project. Royce L. Givens, executive director of the International Conference of Police Associations, wrote a letter to LBJ later that summer announcing the resolution by the ICPA that denounced the use of federal funds for a police practices review board in Oakland. During their July 1966 meeting in San Francisco, the association opposed the use of anti-poverty funds to establish community review boards "in any...city within these United States." By the end of the year, many critics in the Bay Area wondered aloud if the poverty program was doing more harm than good, and some respected public figures, like the Pulitzer Prize-winning reporter Edward Montgomery, claimed that the poverty program threatened the basic values of most Americans.[37]

At the national level, the OEO also faced a constant barrage of complaint from Republicans and southern Democrats in Congress. The White House kept a close eye on unrest in the Capitol Building, and the congressional relations staff reported increasing attacks on the OEO in the mid-1960s.  From 1964 to 1968, for example, Republicans offered one hundred forty amendments and motions to legislation authorizing the OEO and its budgets.  The peak of congressional resistance came in 1967, when Republicans offered fifty-one amendments to change or stall Democratic initiatives. The *Christian Science Monitor* reported in August 1967 that southern Democrats and Republicans who opposed the Great Society reforms claimed that the War on Poverty programs had caused riots in Newark, Detroit, and elsewhere.  The critics argued that the reforms challenged the basic tenets of American society. "They see a Communist conspiracy behind much of the arson, sniping, and looting of this long, hot summer," the paper reported.  A siege mentality was setting in at OEO headquarters, and as rhetorical bombs dropped on the Community Action Program concept, the staff complained of increasing "political harassment" from their opponents in Congress.  Blistering critiques from Republicans and conservative Democrats were entered into the *Congressional Quarterly*, and CAPs were charged with everything from gross mismanagement to "fiscal irresponsibility and chicanery."  The OEO countered the charges as best it could, and its defenders shot back that politicians who criticized the program were afraid of losing their reelection bids once the public realized they had sold out to the Establishment: "In some localities, CAP officials and affiliates, engaged in the reorientation of the political structure, were critical of their representatives in the Congress; some community action programs actually threatened to build counter-political power bases, pitting their own choices against the incumbents, who found it more necessary to accommodate the established local political machinery."  The OEO was fighting a losing battle, however, and the forces of their political opposition had broken through the front lines and scored damaging victories against Johnson's Great Society programs. [38]

The president himself had always been skeptical of the community action concept, and he envisioned the War on Poverty as a way to help people break out of the lower class and end the cycle of dependency that kept them on the public dole. At the signing ceremony of the Economic Opportunity Act of 1964, LBJ proclaimed: "This [measure] is not in any sense a cynical proposal to exploit the poor with a promise of a handout or a dole. We know—we learned long ago—that answer is no answer.... [T]he purpose of the Economic Opportunity Act of 1964 is to offer opportunity, not an opiate...." His staff members recalled that the president had a "Populist attitude" concerning the poor, and he saw his Great Society programs as a way to help people help themselves by training and educating them and providing for their basic physical needs. Johnson favored programs like the Job Corps and Head Start, and he visualized the War on Poverty as a reincarnation of the New Deal programs of the Franklin D. Roosevelt Administration. During a conversation with Johnson after his appointment as deputy director of the OEO in 1966, Bertrand Harding recalled that "it became clear to me that his view of the poverty program was pretty much an extension of his earlier experience with the New Deal—the early days of the New Deal and the National Youth Administration; that he was very cool, if not opposed, to some of the more way-out activities that had characterized OEO."[39]

The seemingly endless parade of scandals that marched out of the OEO's offices convinced Johnson that his initial skepticism had been well founded. Confused by the outburst of rioting in northern cities in 1967 and angered by liberal critiques that the government was spending too much money on Vietnam and shortchanging the poor, LBJ was becoming quickly alienated from the central agency of his Great Society. The problems had begun as early as the summer of 1965, when Johnson heard from a long-time friend who complained that the OEO was funding a group in Syracuse, New York, to train low-income people in the methods of direct-action protest. "The *political implications* of using public funds contributed by the tax payers to *instruct* people how to protest are quite obvious to me,..." he warned. "When neighborhood workers are organizing groups in the poorest neighborhoods to 'protest' and take 'direct action' which is not in behalf of any program or anything constructive, I am sure the tax payer and voter will not be happy!" Outraged, Johnson scribbled a quick note to his press secretary, Bill Moyers, "Bill—For

God's sake get on top of this & put a stop to it at once." Other flaps occurred in Chicago when the OEO funded a youth gang, the Blackstone Rangers, through a local CAP and raised the ire of Mayor Richard Daley; in Nashville where poverty funds supported a black nationalist, "Hate Whitey" school; in New York as War on Poverty dollars were used to help bankroll revolutionary playwright LeRoy Jones's controversial Black Arts Theater; in Los Angeles where OEO grants were tied up in a "clear goof" as the Community Alert Patrol used them to monitor the LA police in black neighborhoods; and in San Francisco where Mayor John F. Shelley was besieged by the poor who demanded control over the local poverty program. Johnson fumed as reports of theft, corruption, and local political upheaval poured into the White House, and as one observer put it, "he just had the strongest kind of reaction to it. I mean it would be accompanied by a certain amount of profanity and, 'By God, we're not here to run that kind of thing.' It really got to him."[40]

In reaction to these scandals, Johnson began to pull hard on the reins in 1967. The OEO staff felt they were not getting any support from the LBJ during that summer, and Shriver himself was "persona non grata in the White House." Other staff members reported "that by 1967 [the White House] would just as soon have us go down the drain." Cursing the "kooks and sociologists" who ran the OEO, Johnson withdrew his support and canceled public appearances with any OEO-sponsored programs. He required Shriver to send him bi-weekly reports on OEO activities throughout the summer of 1967, and although Shriver used them to counter charges that CAP workers were involved in inciting riots, embezzling funds, or stirring up radicalism, the OEO slipped further out of favor with the president. In August, Joe Califano, the president's chief of staff, encouraged Johnson to allow him and Attorney General Ramsey Clark to set up an investigative body to start looking into the charges against the CAPs. Both he and Clark thought an independent and secret body would be better than people from the Budget Bureau or OEO because both "are too 'milktoast' on the problem to investigate effectively." It is unclear whether such a body actually did begin to scrutinize the OEO, but by the late summer of 1967, the agency was already dying on the vine, and Johnson insisted that they be left out in the cold.[41]

Uncle Sam's return to the Bay Area in the 1960s caused nearly as much turmoil and left as many mixed legacies as had his previous visit during the Second World War. The arrival of millions of federal dollars set off another "gold rush" that was reminiscent of the 1940s, and the problems the funds produced were similarly disturbing. Both eras witnessed a social revolution of sorts, and black Americans were key actors in both dramas. In the 1960s, low-income African Americans challenged the hegemony of the white establishment, and for a brief moment their voices echoed outside of the ghetto walls. Demanding control of local poverty programs and rejecting the paternalism of white bureaucrats and poverty warriors, low-income residents throughout the Bay Area struggled to attain their place in the American democratic order. As economic and social conditions grew worse in northern California's black communities throughout the 1960s, African American leaders and ordinary citizens embraced the opportunities provided by the War on Poverty and transformed them into dramatic new approaches to combat the persistent problems that they had faced for more than two decades.

The federal anti-poverty program also encouraged the growth of radical black nationalist groups in the Bay Area. By providing non-traditional black leaders with funds and publicity through its Community Action Programs, the OEO unwittingly supported and trained a new generation of black radicals that included the co-founders of the Black Panther Party. As the Panthers solidified and grew in the decade's later years, they drew upon their experiences in the poverty program to develop their Community Survival Programs and to establish a firm base of support among low-income residents in Berkeley, Oakland, Richmond, and San Francisco. As black radicalism arose from the ashes of community action, it soared to the heavens and left a burning path across the sky. Its glowing trail was both a ray of hope and a signal of doom.

# Notes

1.   City of Berkeley, "The First Fifty Years of the Community Welfare Commission," (Berkeley, February 1959), 34.

2.   "State Report: The Trouble with Oakland," San Francisco *Chronicle*, 25 May 1966, 2; Gene Bernardi, *Oakland's Poverty Population*, 1965 (Oakland: n.p., 1967), 1. The definition of "poverty" of course varies depending upon the study consulted for this period, but a rough poverty line for this work is $4,000 for a family of four. "Model City Plan for Oakland," *Sun-Reporter*, 25 February 1967, 2, 7; William L. Nicholls, II, *Poverty and Poverty Programs in Oakland* (Berkeley: n.p., 1966); 18–19; Gene Bernardi, *Income Needs in West Oakland: A Preliminary Report* (Oakland: Oakland Economic Development Council, 1967), 1; William L. Nicholls, II, *Tables on Employment and Unemployment from the 701 Household Survey of Oakland* (Berkeley: Survey Research Center, 1968), 11, 18–21; Tom Roland, "Oakland: Crisis Next Door," *The Campus Core-Lator: Magazine of the Berkeley Campus Chapter of the Congress of Racial Equality* (January 1965), 26, Carton 3, Social Protest Collection, Bancroft Library, University of California, Berkeley; Memo, Sherwin J. Markman to the President, 14 March 1967, Office Files of James C. Gaither, Box 352, Lyndon Baines Johnson Presidential Library, Austin, Texas [hereafter cited as LBJL].

3.   Memo, Roche, Howden, Keffer, Locher, Parker, Watts to Hugo Fisher, 24 September 1965, Human Rights Collection, Ex HU 2/St 2–12, Box 25, LBJL; Memo, Markman to the President, 1–6; Roland, "Oakland: Crisis Next Door," 26–27; Warren Hinckle, "Metropoly: The Story of Oakland, California," 4 *Ramparts* (February 1966), passim; "Major Victory Won by Oakland Welfare Pickets," *Sun-Reporter*, 12 September 1964, 2; William L. Nicholls, II, Esther S. Hochstim, and Sheila Babbie, *The Castlemont Survey: A Handbook of Survey Results* (Berkeley: Survey Research Center, 1966), Appendix C.

4.   "Tight Little Island Cracks: The CAMPING-IN Tactic," *Flatlands*, 2 July to 15 July 1966, 1, 2; "Estuary Project Evictees' 'Camp-In,'" *Sun-Reporter*, 2 July 1966, 10.

5.   Economic Opportunity Council, *Progress* (San Francisco: Economic Opportunity Council, 1966), Record Group 381, Office of Economic Opportunity, Inspection Division, Inspection Reports, 1964–1967, National

Archives, College Park, Maryland [Hereafter cited as OEO Inspection Files]; "Poverty Report Offered on S.F. Neighborhoods," San Francisco *Chronicle*, 3 March 1966, 5; "Turns Self In: Janitor Robs for Family, But Wife Refuses Money," *Sun-Reporter*, 24 January 1959, 1.

6. Arthur E. Hippler, *Hunter's Point: A Black Ghetto* (New York: Basic Books, 1974), 13–20; Memo, Roche, et. al. to Fisher; Lee Soto, "What Is There Left for Hunter's Point," *Sun-Reporter*, 18 January 1964, 27, and 25 January 1964, 20, 26; R. J. Sye, "Rats, Roaches and Rain in the Plaza," *Sun-Reporter*, 2 December 1967, 1; "Freedom House: Area-2 Residents Working to Beat Redevelopment," *Sun-Reporter*, 13 June 1964, 3; Donovan Bess, "Charge by UC Anthropologist: A 'Plantation in S.F.," San Francisco *Chronicle*, 1 August 1966, 4; "No Rent for Rats: Richmond Tenants Battle Landlords," *Flatlands*, 27 August to 10 September 1966, 1, 3; Memo, Dick Fullmer through C. B. Patrick to Edgar May, 3 August 1966, OEO Inspection Files; Walterene Jackson, "*San Francisco Housing Authority*: Can Kane Improve Its Image?" *Sun-Reporter*, 6 November 1965, 2; "Hunters Point [sic] Residents March on S.F. Housing Authority—Rent Strike Threatened," *Sun-Reporter*, 12 March 1966, 3.

7. See Henry Cohen's comments from the transcript of the Brandeis University Conference on Poverty and Urban Policy, 16–17 June 1973, p. 48–53, John F. Kennedy Presidential Library, Boston, Massachusetts [hereafter cited as JFKL]; Nicholas Lemann, *The Promised Land: The Great Black Migration and How It Changed America* (New York: Alfred A. Knopf, 1991), 125; and Thomas J. Sugrue, *The Origins of the Urban Crisis: Race and Inequality in Postwar Detroit* (Princeton: Princeton University Press, 1996), 10.

8. Peter Marris and Martin Rein, *Dilemmas of Social Reform: Poverty and Community Action in the United States*, 2nd. ed. (Chicago: Aldine Publishing Co., 1973), 14–21; James L. Sundquist, ed., *On Fighting Poverty: Perspectives from Experience* (New York: Basic Books, 1969), passim; the "umbrella thesis" is from Transcript, Christopher Weeks Oral History Interview, 10 December 1980, by Michael L. Gillette, p. 11–14, LBJL; Transcript, David L. Hackett Oral History Interview, 22 July 1970 and 21 October 1970, by John W. Douglas, p. 69, 71, 73, 83, JFKL; Transcript, Robert Lampman Oral History Interview, 24 May 1983, by Michael L. Gillette, p. 10–12, LBJL; Lemann, *The Promised Land*, 149–52 passim.

9. Anti-poverty planner Adam Yarmolinsky, Shriver's second-in-command, and historian Gareth Davies have argued that the War on Poverty began with its focus firmly centered on poor whites rather than on African

Americans in northern inner cities. They both point to President Kennedy's revelation about American poverty during his campaign trip through West Virginia and the influence of books like Harry Caudill's *Night Comes to the Cumberlands* as key evidence for their assertions that Appalachia was the first target of the Economic Opportunity Act of 1964. Both Yarmolinsky and Davies argue that it was only after the riots of 1965 and thereafter that poverty planning in Washington swung its focus to urban blacks. While there is some validity to their conclusions, the majority of evidence I have found weighs in on the side of an urban, black focus from the outset. The legacy of private poverty planning and social scientific thought from the 1950s and early 1960s as well as the structure and goals of JFK's President's Committee on Juvenile Delinquency provided the base for the Office of Economic Opportunity. Political expediency in getting the Economic Opportunity Act passed in 1964 accounts for the temporary focus on low-income whites in Appalachia, and Yarmolinsky's late entry in the planning for the EOA explains his unfamiliarity with the community action theories of other planners like Richard Boone. See Adam Yarmolinsky, "The Beginnings of OEO," in Sundquist, *On Fighting Poverty*; Yarmolinsky's comments in the transcript of the Brandeis Conference on Poverty, 162–63, JFKL; and Gareth Davies, *From Opportunity to Entitlement: The Transformation and Decline of Great Society Liberalism* (Lawrence: University Press of Kansas, 1996), 45–47. For the opinion of a poverty planner who was present during the early days of the task force and who argues that the planners had an overwhelmingly urban bias to their thinking on poverty, see Transcript of James L. Sundquist Oral History Interview, 7 April 1969, by Stephen Goodell, p. 8–9, 13–14, LBJL.

   10.   The Shriver quotation is from Advisory Commission on Intergovernmental Relations, *Intergovernmental Relations in the Poverty Program: A Commission Report* (Washington, D. C.: United States Government Printing Office, 1966), 24–25; Statement, Sargent Shriver to the President, 17 March 1964, Ex FG 11–15, WHCF, Box 124, LBJL; Transcript, William P. Kelly, Jr., Oral History Interview, 11 April 1969, by Stephen Goodell, p. 47, LBJL; Marris and Rein, *Dilemmas of Social Reform*, Chp. 2 passim. In his important work on the black migration to Chicago, Nicholas Lemann criticizes the "culture of poverty" perspective of many of Johnson's poverty warriors, and he concludes that "almost all of the programs that Shriver's group was considering fit under the rubric of acculturating poor people into the folkways of the middle class." While I agree that most Washington bureaucrats did

subscribe to the "culture of poverty" interpretation, I think the more important aspect of the early planning behind the War on Poverty was the recognition that poverty does indeed have multiple causes. Therefore, I disagree with Lemann that the only and most effective way to move people out of poverty is to create a large, federally sponsored jobs program. While such a program would be useful and is certainly necessary, it would be ultimately ineffective if it was not coupled with other programs to undo the tangle of poverty in America. See, Lemann, *The Promised Land*, 120 passim, 150–51, 345–53.

11.    Transcript, Harold W. Horowitz Oral History Interview, 23 February 1983, by Michael L. Gillette, p. 17–18, LBJL; Lampman Oral History, 19–20; Transcript, Jerome P. Cavanagh Oral History Interview, 22 March 1971, by Joe B. Frantz, p. 5–6, LBJL; Weeks Oral History, 57.

12.    For the unintended consequences of community action, see Transcript, Donald M. Baker Oral History Interview, 24 February 1969, by Stephen Goodell, p. 13, LBJL; and Adam Yarmolinsky's comments in the transcript of the Brandeis Conference on Poverty, 247–48, JFKL. Richard Boone and Paul Ylvisaker were among the most ardent supporters of community action as a way to challenge the political status quo in America, but their influence in the planning stages of the War on Poverty was always tempered by Sargent Shriver's firm hand and by the more staid voices of James Sundquist and others. Boone and Ylvisaker also left the government to continue their careers in the private sector (Boone founded the Citizens Crusade Against Poverty) before the OEO actually got off the ground, and their enthusiasm for community action was not always shared by their successors. For a critique of Boone and Ylvisaker as "radicals," see Transcript, John A. Baker Oral History Interview, 21 April 1981, by Michael L. Gillette, p. 6–7, 10, LBJL. Jack T. Conway, who headed the Community Action Program division of the OEO and whose background was in organized labor, noted that he was never as smitten with the Alinsky or the Ohlin and Cloward approaches to community organization as Boone. See, Transcript, Jack T. Conway Oral History Interview, 13 August 1980, by Michael L. Gillette, p. 1–5, LBJL. Harold Horowitz admitted that he was attracted to the poverty program by the romantic idea that Sargent Shriver was actually getting things done and was involved in a new project that might actually be able to put an end to poverty. See, Horowitz Oral History, 34–35. For Johnson's desire to speed-up poverty funding, see Sundquist Oral History, 31–32. Daniel P. Moynihan, in his *Maximum Feasible*

*Misunderstanding: Community Action in the War on Poverty* (New York: Free Press, 1969), argues that a small cadre of "social scientists" had surreptitiously included the community action aspect of the EOA of 1964, and that they irresponsibly tested their theories about community organization on unsuspecting cities. The evidence, however, does not support such conclusions. A sharp critique of Moynihan's work is in Transcript, Eric Tolmach Oral History Interview, 19 March 1969, by Stephen Goodell, p. 13–16, 21, 26, LBJL. For a criticism of local poverty bureaucracies, see Sanford Kravitz's comments in the transcript of the Brandeis Conference on Poverty, 57, JFKL.

13.   Adam Yarmolinsky tells the tale of "maximum feasible participation" in the transcript of the Brandeis Conference on Poverty, 255, JFKL; Horowitz Oral History, 24–25; Advisory Committee on Intergovernmental Relations, *Intergovernmental Relations in the Poverty Program*, 53; Office of Economic Opportunity, *Community Action Program Guide, Vol. I: Instructions for Applicants* (Washington, D. C.: Office of Economic Opportunity, 1965), 7, 16.

14.   Weeks Oral History, 12–14; Brian Henry Smith, "The Role of the Poor in the Poverty Program: The Origin and Development of 'Maximum Feasible Participation'" (Master's Thesis, Columbia University, 1966), 16–21 passim; Transcript, Bertrand M. Harding Oral History Interview, 20 November 1968, by Stephen Goodell, p. 18–20, LBJL; Conway Oral History, 29–30; "The War as He Sees It: Shriver—Man on the Anti-Poverty Hot Spot," San Francisco *Chronicle*, 12 December 1965, 1, 3; John G. Wofford, "The Politics of Local Responsibility: Administration of the Community Action Program—1964–1966," in *On Fighting Poverty*, 77.

15.   Yarmolinsky, "The Beginnings of OEO," 50; Johnson is quoted in Transcript, Herbert Kramer Oral History Interview, 10 March 1969, by Stephen Goodell, p. 21, LBJL; Memo, Charles L. Schultze to the President, 18 September 1965, Ex WE 9, WHCF, Box 26, LBJL; Office of Economic Opportunity, *Community Action Program Guide*, 18–19.

16.   Lee Soto, "What Is There Left for Hunter's Point?" *Sun-Reporter*, 11 January 1964, 7; Marris and Rein, *Dilemmas in Social Reform*, 18; "Proposal to the Ford Foundation for a Program of Community Development with Special Reference to Assimilation of the Newcomer Population," 1961, Carton 44, NAACP West Coast Region Papers, Bancroft Library, University of California, Berkeley [Hereafter cited as NAACP Papers]; Nicholls, et. at., *The Castlemont Survey*, passim; Citizens Committee quoted in "Plan Protest on Hunter's Point Project," *Sun-Reporter*, 11 May 1963, 2, 23; Press release

by the OEO public affairs office, 25 November 1964, Ex FG 11–15, WHCF, Box 124, LBJL.

17.    Washington    quoted    in    "Poverty    Conference    Proves Disappointing," *Sun-Reporter*, 6 February 1965, 13; "Proceedings and Summary: First Statewide Con[v]ention of the Poor, Held February 26 and February 27, 1966, in Oakland, California," Carton 10, NAACP Papers; Resolution from the Poor People's Convention, 26–27 February 1966, Carton 10, NAACP Papers; Jerome N. Sampson, "The Poor Unite in California: A First Statewide Convention," Carton 10, NAACP Papers; Hunter's Point community leader quoted in Neil Arthur Eddington, "The Urban Plantation: The Ethnography of an Oral Tradition in a Negro Community" (Ph.D. diss., University of California, Berkeley, 1967), 34-36.

18.    Willie Thompson, *Enemy of the Poor: A Report of the Struggle of the War on Poverty in San Francisco* (n.p., n.d.), 2, 4–7; "S.F. Poverty Program Under Fire," *Sun-Reporter*, 17 April 1965, 2; Reginald Wood, "Sabotage of Poverty Program," *Sun-Reporter*, 24 April 1965, 3 and 1 May 1965, 3; Willie Thompson, "Shelley Fails to Convince CUAP," *Sun-Reporter*, 8 May 1965, 2. See also, Ralph Kramer, *Participation of the Poor: Comparative Case Studies in the War on Poverty* (Englewood Cliffs, NJ: Prentice-Hall, Inc., 1969), esp. Chps. 2 and 4.

19.    Memo, Bill Haddad to Sargent Shriver, 21 May 1965, OEO Inspection Files; Memo, Tom Kelly to Bill Haddad, n.d., OEO Inspection Files; Memo, Bill Haddad to Sargent Shriver, 17 June 1965, OEO Inspection Files; Memo Jack Williams to Bill Haddad, 23 July 1965, OEO Inspection Files; Memo, C. B. Patrick to Bill Haddad and Bob Clampitt, 27 July 1965, OEO Inspection Files; Memo, C. B. Patrick to Bill Haddad and Bob Clampitt, 31 July 1965, OEO Inspection Files; Thompson, *Enemy of the Poor*, 13–16 passim; Reginald Wood, "Sabotage of Poverty Program," *Sun-Reporter*, 8 May 1965, 3; "So Little Wisdom," *Sun-Reporter*, 5 June 1965, 8; Everett Brandon, "Inside the Poverty Program," *Sun-Reporter*, 12 June 1965, 5 and 3 July 1965, 3.

20.    Horowitz Oral History, 9.  See also Natalie Becker and Marjorie Myhill, *Power and Participation in the San Francisco Community Action Program, 1964–1967* (Berkeley: Institute of Urban and Regional Development, 1967), 89–91.

21.    Memo, John A. Morsell to NAACP Regional and Field Directors, 15 March 1965, Carton 12, NAACP Papers; Political Action Committee Report, 1966, Carton 9, NAACP Papers; Letter, Arnold W. Leonard to Leonard

Carter, 7 February 1966, Carton 9, NAACP Papers; Memo, "Youth Work Committee," n.d., Carton 9, NAACP Papers; Letter, Norvel Smith to Leonard Carter, 8 February 1966, Carton 9, NAACP Papers.

22.    Ussery quoted in "Grits & Gripes: Anti-Poverty Program, Western Addition Community Planning Get Togethers, Saturday, April 2, 1966," *Sun-Reporter*, 2 April 1966, 4-page special insert.  See also, "Underprivileged Frame Their Needs," *Sun-Reporter*, 30 April 1966, 1, 3; "5 Rallies in Anti-Poverty Program," San Francisco *Chronicle*, 25 March 1966, 2; Jonathan Root, "A Reluctance in S.F. Poverty War," San Francisco *Chronicle*, 31 March 1966, 2; "Grits and Gripes: The Poor Talk About Their War," San Francisco *Chronicle*, 3 April 1966, 10.  An audio-recording of some of the meetings was made and aired by Berkeley's public radio station, KPFA, and is available to researchers; see, "Voices of Poverty," cassette E2BB1337, Pacifica Radio Archive, North Hollywood, California, 1966.

23.    Letter, Rev. Robert Gardley to Sargent Shriver, 15 June 1966, OEO Inspection Files; Letter, Rev. Robert Gardley to the President, 17 June 1966, OEO Inspection Files; Letter, Rev. Robert Gardley to Nicholas Katzenbach, 20 June 1966, OEO Inspection Files.  Ussery's militancy in other areas, including his comments about white participation in CORE, is document-ed in August Meier and Elliott Rudwick, CORE: A *Study of the Civil Rights Movement*, 1942–1968 (New York: Oxford University Press, 1973), esp. 293, 336, 393, 402–03, 407.  Letter, Rev. Robert Gardley to Sargent Shriver, 7 July 1966, OEO Inspection Files; Memo, Rev. Robert Gardley to Sargent Shriver, 7 July 1966, OEO Inspection Files.

24.    Memo, Rev. Robert Gardley to Sargent Shriver, 11 July 1966, OEO Inspection Files; Letter, Rev. Robert Gardley to Sargent Shriver, 24 August 1966, OEO Inspection Files.

25.    Memo, Edgar May to Ted Berry, 29 July 1966, OEO Inspection Files; Memo, Edgar May to Sargent Shriver, 10 August 1966, OEO Inspection Files; Memo, Dick Fullmer through C. B. Patrick to Edgar May, 3 August 1966, OEO Inspection Files.

26.    Memo, Paul Weeks through Dick Fullmer and C. B. Patrick to Edgar May, 21 September 1966, OEO Inspection Files; Memo, Edgar May to Sargent Shriver, 23 September 1966, OEO Inspection Files.

27.    Edgar May, Memorandum for the Record, 28 September 1966, OEO Inspection Files; Telegram, Rev. Robert Gardley to Richard Fullmer, 29 September 1966, OEO Inspection Files; Telegram, Rev. Robert Gardley to Sargent Shriver, 30 September 1966, OEO Inspection Files; Letter, Rev.

Robert Gardley to the President, 11 September 1966, OEO Inspection Files; Memo, Dick Fullmer through C. B. Patrick to Edgar May, 3 October 1966, OEO Inspection Files; Telegram, Rev. Robert Gardley to the President, 6 October 1966, OEO Inspection Files; Memo, Dick Fullmer through C. B. Patrick to Edgar May, 26 October 1966, OEO Inspection Files.

28.    Memo, Paul Weeks through C. B. Patrick and Dick Fullmer to Edgar May, 31 October 1966, OEO Inspection Files; "S.F. Poverty Aid Ussery is Fired," San Francisco *Chronicle*, 29 October 1966, 1; Memo, Paul Weeks through Dick Fullmer and C. B. Patrick to Edgar May, 2 November 1966, OEO Inspection Files; Goodlett quoted in Memo, Paul Weeks through Dick Fullmer and C. B. Patrick to Edgar May, 4 November 1966, OEO Inspection Files; Memo, Paul Weeks through C. B. Patrick and Dick Fullmer to Edgar May, 16 November 1966, OEO Inspection Files; Memo, Paul Weeks through C. B. Patrick and Dick Fullmer to Edgar May, 21 December 1966, OEO Inspection Files; Memo, Dick Fullmer through C. B. Patrick to Edgar May, 5 January 1967, OEO Inspection Files.

29.    Letter, Rev. Robert Gardley to Richard Fullmer, 15 February 1967, OEO Inspection Files; Memo, Owen O'Donnell through C. B. Patrick and Dick Fullmer to Edgar May, 23 February 1967, OEO Inspection Files; Memo, Dick Fullmer through C. B. Patrick to Edgar May, 23 February 1967, OEO Inspection Files; Memo, Everett P. Brandon and Arthur Coleman to Daniel M. Luevano, 20 January 1967, OEO Inspection Files, is the San Francisco EOC's official response to the Price-Waterhouse audit.

30.    Michael Grleg, "Hunter's Pt. Sit-in Halts All Evictions," San Francisco *Chronicle*, 9 March 1966, 1, 8; J. Campbell Bruce, "Hunter's Point: Angry Uproar by Crowd at Housing Session," San Francisco *Chronicle*, 10 March 1966, 1, 18; Oakland Economic Development Council, Inc., *The Press and the O.E.D.C.I., 1969–1971: How the Press Reported Oakland's Controversial Anti-Poverty Program which Governor Reagan Vetoed Because It Gave too Much Power to the City's Poor* (Oakland: OEDCI, 1971), I–XII; Harold Nawy and Martin Thimel, *The East Bay Community Action Program; Part Two: Strategy or Stratagem* (Berkeley: University of California, 1966 (?)), 6, 22–25; United States Senate, Subcommittee on Employment, Manpower, and Poverty, *Examination of the War on Poverty*, Part 11: May 10–11, 1967 (Washington, D. C.: United States Government Printing Office, 1967), 3441–43.

31.    Earl Anthony, *Spitting in the Wind: The True Story Behind the Violent Legacy of the Black Panther Party* (Malibu, CA: Roundtable Publishing, Inc., 1990), 14–15.    Audrey Smith's background is in Memo, Dick Fullmer

through C. B. Patrick to Edgar May, 3 August 1966, OEO Inspection Files; and in the statement she made before the U.S. Senate's Subcommittee on Employment, Manpower, and Poverty when it visited the Bay Area in 1967. See, U.S. Senate, *Examination of the War on Poverty*, 3444–45; Memo, Eric Biddle to C. B. Patrick, 21 July 1967, Personal Papers of Bertrand M. Harding, Box 59, LBJL. Patrick passed this memo on to Shriver, who then sent it to Harding with the instructions to cut off the Panthers' connection with the Hunter's Point CAP.

32.    "S.F. Battleground: Slashing Attack in Poverty War," San Francisco *Chronicle*, 17 March 1966, 2; Don Warman, "S.F. Poverty War—Crisis Talks Set," San Francisco *Chronicle*, 23 July 1966, 1, 6; Don Warman, "Washington Wins: Local Poverty Fighters Yield," San Francisco *Chronicle*, 28 July 1966, 4; "S.F. Poverty Fighters Beat a Retreat," San Francisco *Chronicle*, 5 August 1966, 1, 10; "Western Addition: Deadline Row on Poverty Budget," San Francisco *Chronicle*, 20 April 1966, 34; List of San Francisco CAP Officers, no date, OEO Inspection Files; Anthony, *Spitting in the Wind*, 26–27; CAP employee quoted in Nawy and Thimel, *The East Bay Community Action Program*, 35.

33.    Becker and Myhill, *Power and Participation in the San Francisco Community Action Program*, 47; List of San Francisco CAP Officers, n.d.; Amory Bradford, *Oakland's Not for Burning* (New York: David McKay Company, Inc., 1968), 50; Council of Social Planning—Berkeley Area, "Community Action under 'Economic Opportunity Act of 1964'" (Berkeley, 1965); Telegram, Gloria Dean Jones to Sargent Shriver, 15 November 1965, OEO Inspection Files; Letter, Gloria Dean Jones to Sargent Shriver, 15 November 1965, OEO Inspection Files; Letter, Bernard L. Boutin to Gloria Dean Jones, 26 November 1965, OEO Inspection Files; Letter, Everett P. Brandon to Gloria Dean Jones, 29 November 1965, OEO Inspection Files; Letter, John Dukes to Bob Westgate, 9 December 1965, OEO Inspection Files; Memo, Bob Westgate to Edgar May, T. C. Hasser, and Bob Anthony, 10 December 1965, OEO Inspection Files; Memo, Bob Westgate to T. C. Hasser, 10 December 1965, OEO Inspection Files; Letter, Edgar May to John Dukes, 15 December 1965, OEO Inspection Files.

34.    Nicholls, *Poverty and Poverty Programs in Oakland*, 79, 82, 91, 121–125; Hippler, *Hunter's Point*, 89; Memo, Joe Califano to Alex Greene, n.d., Ex HU 2/ST 2–12, WHCF, Box 25, LBJL; George Draper, "A Job Ends: S.F. Youth with a Big Problem," San Francisco *Chronicle*, 8 January 1966, 1, 12; Elmont Waite, "Who Called It?: Furor over Meeting on Poverty War

Programs," San Francisco *Chronicle*, 12 January 1966, 2; "Legal Aid for Poor All Set," San Francisco *Chronicle*, 12 June 1966, 28; "New Fronts in the S.F. Poverty War," San Francisco *Chronicle*, 22 June 1966, 5. For similar problems in the East Bay, see Council of Social Planning—Berkeley Area, "Community Action under "Economic Opportunity Act of 1964," 24 passim; Gene Bernardi, *Evaluation Analysis of the Council of Social Planning's Neighborhood Organization Program* (Oakland: Department of Human Resources, 1966), 50–58 passim.

35.     U.S. Senate, *Examination of the War on Poverty*, 3441, 3522–23.

36.     Gallup Poll, 21 March 1964; American Institute of Public Opinion, "Local Opinion Split on Poverty Program," *Washington Post*, 7 May 1966; and Harris Survey, 5 September 1966, all in Office Files of Fred Panzer, Box 181, LBJL; James Lopez, letter to the editor, San Francisco *Chronicle*, 20 March 1966, II, 2.

37.     Charles Cruttenden, "Co-ops for Bay Poor: $500,000 Experiment," San Francisco *Chronicle*, 9 January 1966, 1, 25; Editorial, San Francisco *Chronicle*, 16 January 1966, II, 2; Charles Cruttenden, "Surgery in the War on Poverty," San Francisco *Chronicle*, 6 March 1966, 2; "Police Review Board for Oakland," San Francisco *Chronicle*, 26 February 1966, 5; "Brushoff for Oakland Cop Review Unit," San Francisco *Chronicle*, 26 May 1966, 4; Letter, Royce L. Givens to the President, 15 August 1966, Gen WE 9, WHCF, Box 40, LBJL; "Examiner Reporter Says EOC Aids Communists," *Sun-Reporter*, 6 July 1968, 2.

38.     Memo, Richard S. Franzen to Bertrand M. Harding, 3 October 1968, Office Files of James C. Gaither, Box 31, LBJL; William C. Sellover and Lyn Shepard, "Opposition to Great Society Hardens," *Christian Science Monitor*, 5 August 1967, Office Files of Fred Panzer, Box 364, LBJL; Administrative History of the Office of Economic Opportunity, vol. I, p. 546–48, 565, 608, LBJL.

39.     Johnson quoted in Davies, *From Opportunity to Entitlement*, 40–41; Transcript, Samuel V. Merrick Oral History Interview, 28 September 1981, by Michael L. Gillette, p. 22, LBJL; Transcript, C. Robert Perrin Oral History Interview, 10 March 1969, by Stephen Goodell, p. 11, LBJL; Kelly Oral History, 36–37, LBJL; Harding Oral History, 5–6, LBJL; Adam Yarmolinsky's comments in the transcript of the Brandeis Conference on Poverty, 249–50, JFKL.

40.     Memo, James Rowe to the President, 29 June 1965, Office Files of Bill Moyers, Box 56, LBJL.  For a history of the Syracuse imbroglio, see

Allan J. Matusow, *The Unraveling of America: A History of Liberalism in the* 1960s (New York: Harper & Row, 1984), 248–252. Harding Oral History, 21–22, LBJL; Kramer Oral History, 17–18, LBJL; Memo, Harry C. McPherson to the President, 3 September 1968, Confidential File, Ex FG 11–11, Box 21, LBJL; Memo, Joe Califano to the President, 2 June 1967, Ex FG 11–15, WHCF, Box 125, LBJL; Matusow, *Unraveling of America*, Chp. 9 passim; Lemann, *The Promised Land*, 188–89; Transcript, Harold Barefoot Sanders, Jr., Oral History Interview, n.d., by Joe B. Frantz, p. 17, LBJL.

41.    Kramer Oral History, 19, LBJL; Donald M. Baker Oral History, 9, LBJL; Transcript, Robert A. Levine Oral History Interview, 26 February 1969, by Stephen Goodell, p. 28, LBJL.  Shriver's reports actually started in February 1967, and most of them are in Confidential File, Agency Reports, Office of Economic Opportunity, Box 129, LBJL.  Of particular note are memos that Shriver sent to Johnson on the following dates: 27 July 1967, 14 August 1967, 15 September 1967, and 21 September 1967.  Memo, Joe Califano to the President, 19 August 1967, Ex FG 11–15, WHCF, Box 125, LBJL.

# Chapter 5

# Revolution

By 1966, the San Francisco Bay Area teetered at the brink of Armageddon. A large population of low-income, jobless, and disaffected African Americans stood opposite a paranoid white power structure, and observers feared that at any moment one of the ghetto cores of San Francisco or the East Bay would erupt into another Watts. City leaders, civil rights workers, and anti-poverty officials scrambled to ameliorate the worst conditions of the inner-city slums, but more than two decades of neglect could not be undone overnight. Hunter's Point in San Francisco would actually see racial unrest that summer, and although there was only one death connected with the riots, tensions between whites and blacks throughout the region remained high for the rest of the decade. Sporadic disturbances flared up in Richmond, Oakland, and San Francisco, but no massive riots took place in the Bay Area on the scale of those in Watts, Newark, and Detroit. These brief periods of interracial conflict, however, were coupled with the rise of a growing militancy among young, low-income African Americans, and together racial violence and black rage created a Black Revolution that was in full swing by the long, hot summer of 1968.

At the pinnacle of that revolution was the Black Panther Party. Organized in the fall of 1966, the Black Panther Party (BPP) would become an international sensation by the end of the decade, but its roots stretched back far into the history of African Americans in the Bay Area. The migration of blacks from the Old Southwest during the Second World War provided not only the population for the new ghettos in Berkeley, Richmond, San Francisco, and Oakland, but it also deposited there a group of young blacks who would form the central leadership of the BPP during the late 1960s. Likewise, the social crises of the 1950s and early 1960s would become the main targets of the militants' rage, and the Panthers' Ten Point Platform and Program was designed to confront the problems of unemployment, poor housing, segregated education, and police brutality that had remained tenaciously entrenched in northern California life. Finally, the federal moneys that returned to the Bay Area under the auspices of the War on Poverty often ended up lining the pockets of an emerging radical leadership, who used the funds to support more aggressive civil rights campaigns and who benefited from the organizational knowledge they gained as employees of the Community Action Programs. The origins of the Black Revolution were sown in this history of struggle and discord; its harvest would be a bitter one.

## THE AFTERMATH OF MIGRATION: THE SECOND GENERATION EXPLODES

Since many of the black wartime migrants remained in the Bay Area after the end of international hostilities in 1945, the population boom of the 1940s and 1950s became a permanent feature of Bay Area society. In the postwar years, African Americans constituted a substantial minority of the population in the cities of Berkeley, Oakland, Richmond, and San Francisco, and by the 1960s, blacks were the largest racial minority group in the Bay Area. In Oakland and San Francisco, for example, African Americans accounted for eleven percent of the total population by 1970, while the white majority had shrunk to only eighty-three percent. California's black population had been overwhelmingly urban since the 1940s, and it remained so for the next three decades. Only a tiny fraction of the state's black population lived in rural areas in 1960, and their number actually decreased by 1970. Increasingly concentrated in crumbling urban centers, black Californians became the Golden State's new "minority problem" in the postwar years.[1]

One of the most dramatic features of the increase in the Bay Area's black population, and a factor that worried white social planners and politicians, was the meteoric rise in the number of African American teenagers. The children of the migrant generation, black teens in the 1960s became the base of that decade's Black Revolution. Between 1960 and 1970, Oakland and San Francisco's population of male and female African Americans between the ages of fifteen and nineteen nearly doubled. Due to the large numbers of African Americans under the age of twenty-five, the median age of blacks dropped to 23.3 years for males and 24.4 years for females, which was about six years younger than their white counterparts. This growth mirrored a similar increase among white teenagers, whose numbers swelled to include over one-fifth of the total population of the two cities, yet it was the black teens who posed the greatest social crisis for the Bay Area. Black teens had a higher incidence of unemployment and a greater percentage of high-school dropouts than any other racial or demographic group in northern California's urban areas. African American teenagers suffered under high rates of poverty, and they were often crowded into ghettos with inferior housing and social services. By the mid-1960s, they were ripe for revolution.

The leaders of this radical awakening were largely drawn from the ranks of the second generation of black migrant families to the Bay Area. The prominent members of the Black Panther Party (BPP) came from this group, and they tapped into the large ranks of younger alienated African Americans to build an insurrectionary movement that would shock the entire nation. Bobby Seale, cofounder and chairman of the BPP, hailed from Dallas, Texas, and his family relocated to Berkeley when his father went to work as a carpenter for the war industries. Seale grew up in the Codornices Village public housing project, attended Berkeley schools, and served a short stint in the Air Force before receiving a bad conduct discharge for arguing with an officer. He returned to the Bay Area and entered Merritt College, where he met Huey Newton and began circulating among militant black nationalist groups. Huey P. Newton, co-founder and minister of defense of the BPP, was originally from Oak Grove, Louisiana, and his family moved to Oakland during the war so that his father could work in the Naval Supply Depot located there. Newton attended school in Berkeley, but he transferred and graduated from high school in Oakland. He

## Table 6
### White and Black Population of
### Oakland and San Francisco, 1960 and 1970

| Year | Total | White | Percent of Total | Black | Percent of Total |
|------|-------|-------|-----------------|-------|-----------------|
| 1960 | 2,783,359 | 2,436,665 | 88% | 237,428 | 9% |
| 1970 | 3,109,519 | 2,574,802 | 83% | 330,107 | 11% |

SOURCE:     United States Department of Commerce, *The Eighteenth Decennial Census of the United States, Census of the Population:* 1960, Vol. 1, Part 6 (Washington, D. C.: United States Government Printing Office, 1961), 58, 475; United States Department of Commerce, 1970 *Census of Population,* Part 6, Section 1 (Washington, D. C.: United States Government Printing Office, 1973), 86, 127.

## Table 7
### Median Age of White and Black Population,
### Oakland and San Francisco, 1960 and 1970

| Year | White Males | White Females | Black Males | Black Females |
|------|-------------|---------------|-------------|---------------|
| 1960 | 31.6 | 33.7 | 24.1 | 25.0 |
| 1970 | 29.6 | 32.0 | 23.3 | 24.4 |

SOURCE:     United States Department of Commerce, *The Eighteenth DecennialCensus of the United States, Census of the Population:* 1960, Vol. 1, Part 6 (Washington, D. C.: United States Government Printing Office, 1961), 58, 475; United States Department of Commerce, 1970 *Census of Population,* Part 6, Section 1 (Washington, D. C.: United States Government Printing Office, 1973), 86, 127.

**Table 8**
**White and Black Population, Age 15-19,**
**Oakland and San Francisco, 1960 and 1970**

| Year | White Males | White Females | Black Males | Black Females |
|------|------|------|------|------|
| 1960 | 232,050 | 224,872 | 22,829 | 24,314 |
| 1970 | 322,192 | 324,836 | 42,612 | 45,278 |

SOURCE:   United States Department of Commerce, *The Eighteenth Decennial Census of the United States, Census of the Population:* 1960, Vol. 1, Part 6 (Washington, D. C.: United States Government Printing Office, 1961), 58, 475; United States Department of Commerce, 1970 *Census of Population*, Part 6, Section 1 (Washington, D. C.: United States Government Printing Office, 1973), 86, 127.

**Table 9**
**White and Black Population, Age 15-19,**
**As Percent of Total Population, Oakland and**
**San Francisco, 1960 and 1970**

| Year | Total City | White Teen | White Teen Percent of City | Black Teen | Black Teen Percent of City |
|------|------|------|------|------|------|
| 1960 | 2,783,359 | 456,922 | 16.4% | 47,143 | 1.7% |
| 1970 | 3,109,519 | 647,028 | 20.8% | 87,890 | 2.8% |

SOURCE:   United States Department of Commerce, *The Eighteenth Decennial Census of the United States, Census of the Population:* 1960, Vol. 1, Part 6 (Washington, D. C.: United States Government Printing Office, 1961), 58, 475; United States Department of Commerce, 1970 *Census of Population*, Part 6, Section 1 (Washington, D. C.: United States Government Printing Office, 1973), 86, 127.

attended Merritt College, briefly studied law, and eventually settled in with Seale to form the Panthers in 1966. Bobby Hutton, the first member that Seale and Newton inducted into the BPP, was born in Pine Bluff, Arkansas, and moved to the Bay Area with his parents in 1953. He dropped out of school after the tenth grade, and he went to work for Bobby Seale in the poverty program in Oakland. Hutton was killed by police during a shoot-out in April 1968, when he was seventeen. Finally, David Hilliard, future chief of staff of the BPP, grew up in Rockville, Alabama, and settled in Oakland after his older brothers had found steady, high-paying jobs in the wartime factories. Hilliard later noted that the southern backgrounds of many Panther leaders had a profound influence on the party's operations in California's ghettos: "[We]...were imbued with the moral and spiritual values of [our] parents; and the work that went into the Party, our dignity as an independent people, the communal ideal and practice that informed our programs, all stem in part from the civilization of which my mother and father were so representative a part."[2]

Most observers thought that the explosion would occur in Oakland. In January 1965, the Berkeley Campus Chapter of the Congress of Racial Equality (CORE) prophesied that racial unrest was inevitable, and they urged their members to begin organizing low-income African Americans to strike out against the Establishment. "Negro protest in Oakland may take the form of fruitless, undirected rioting or, on the other hand, it may be captured, smothered, and misdirected by Democratic politicians and conservative Negro leaders," the CORE activists argued. "Another course, that of militant, uncompromising struggle by a well organized Negro community is [also] possible." The following year, the radical Bay Area magazine, *Ramparts*, joined in the leftist chorus of doomsayers, and in an exposé of the city, Warren Hinckle complained of the police brutality, slum housing, high unemployment, and corrupt political system that oppressed blacks. Like the CORE leaders, Hinckle argued that the only solution to the city's crises was a violent upheaval from below. Oakland "desperately, essentially requires a revitalization, a redefinition of itself as an heterogeneous community. And this rebirth can only come, as the Phoenix, from the ashes of the ghetto. Only such a revolutionary

awakening, stirring in the slums...can save Oakland from the deep-
ening and eventually disastrous war between its two worlds." Even
the city's conservative leaders feared an outbreak of racial violence
in Oakland's black neighborhoods, and in the spring of 1966, Mayor
John Reading desperately sought to alleviate the worst conditions
and improve relations between the city's poor and the police
department.[3]

The mayor's actions did little to calm the waters, however, and
young black leaders throughout the Bay Area abandoned non-violence for more militant approaches. In the East Bay, young black
men participating in an anti-poverty program at West Oakland's
Youth Opportunities Center threatened to dynamite the city's
police station when several officers and the deputy police chief visited the center to discuss police-community relations. One of the
young men shouted at the police: "We *tired* of talking! We want
some action! There's a new generation now. We ain't like the old
folks who took all this shit off the cops." Another demanded, "why
don't you just let us run our own damn community?" Across the
bay, the San Francisco NAACP Youth Council expressed the frustration of many African Americans when it announced that "we see
that the Negro today is plainly fed up. He's been beaten on the
head for being black and beaten on the head for being nonviolent.
He has exhausted nonviolent methods." The Youth Council concluded that "this is a time of bloodshed," and they proposed that
groups like the NAACP drop non-violence as their tool and integration as their aim and instead take up arms against an incorrigible
white power structure. "Today the cries are Black Power and Black
Nationalism," the Youth Council proclaimed. "The Negro is learning to think for himself and act for himself and to control his own
destiny. He is waking up. This is a revolution!" George Gilbert, a
reporter for the San Francisco *Chronicle*, discovered similar sentiments among the black youth of the Fillmore District. During a
brief interview at the police station with two young black men, Larry
Scott and Leon Beck, who had been arrested for disorderly conduct,
Gilbert learned of the depths of black frustration and rage. "You
know what happened in Watts and Chicago, man? Well that's
gonna happen here too. We can get guns,...." warned Scott. Beck
then stood up and shouted, "What do you mean we can get guns?

We've got guns, baby." Leon Beck, a high school graduate, complained of white employers' discriminatory hiring practices and the
fact that "there are no jobs for 'niggers.'" Scott berated the San
Francisco police department and charged that they constantly
harassed African Americans and terrorized black neighborhoods.
When asked what he wanted, Scott answered, "Power. That's the
only thing whitey understands. Power. And violence. Whitey will
see that too. All over his streets."[4]

That violence exploded most dramatically on the streets of San
Francisco in the fall of 1966. During the early afternoon of Tuesday,
September 27, sixteen year-old Matthew Johnson and several of his
friends were driving a stolen car through the predominantly black
neighborhood of Hunter's Point. Police Officer Alvin Johnson
stopped the teenagers, and when they panicked and fled on foot, he
chased them. Matthew Johnson ran across an empty lot, and when
he refused to stop, the policeman shot him in the back and killed
him. The young man lay in the lot for nearly an hour before medical officials took him to the morgue. Incensed, black residents of
Hunter's Point gathered at the intersection of Palou and Third
streets in the early evening, and black youths demanded a meeting
with Mayor Jack Shelley. By the time the mayor had arrived at the
Bayview Neighborhood Community Center to meet with black residents, an angry mob of three or four hundred black teenagers had
gathered outside. They shouted down the mayor as he tried to
address the crowd, and when he left hurriedly, they threw bricks and
firebombs at him and the police. The crowds then started breaking
windows and looting white- and Chinese-owned businesses, but
the police drove many of the rioters out of the area. Hunter's Point
was quickly sealed off by two hundred riot police, and the mayor
called the governor and requested that the national guard be sent
in to restore order. The riot lasted 128 hours, and the violence
petered out early on Saturday, October 1. In the end, property
damage estimates ran at about $100,000, and included five dam-
aged fire department vehicles, five damaged fire chief cars, and thirty-one damaged police vehicles. The police had made 146 arrests
and had logged in 5,000 man-hours of overtime. Forty-two black
people had been injured, ten from gunshot wounds, and two

policemen had been hurt. No one, other than Matthew Johnson, had been killed.[5]

During the riots, moderate, middle-class black leaders had been totally unable to check the anger of low-income ghetto residents. The unrest revealed the deterioration of the relationship between the traditional leadership of the African American communities and the growing numbers of desperate, frustrated, and jobless blacks. When Terry Francois, the only black member of the city's Board of Supervisors and a long-time resident and champion of the Bay Area's black neighborhoods, visited the riot scene to help calm tempers and end the violence, he was greeted with hostility and derision from the crowds. One angry black resident of Hunter's Point noted, "That cocksucker forget he's black, but when we put them fuckers on the run, they sure let him know at City Hall right away. Sheeit, man, who the fuck he think he's foolin'?" Fed-up with the non-violence and incrementalism espoused by the moderate black leaders such as Francois and the conservative black organizations such as the NAACP, the low-income residents of Hunter's Point put down their pickets and picked up stones, bricks, and Molotov cocktails. San Francisco's race war had entered a new and bloody stage.[6]

In the aftermath, city officials blamed the riots on high unemployment among San Francisco's blacks. Ignoring the crises in housing, education, and police-community relations, Mayor Shelley announced that African Americans "do not have the same economic and social opportunities that are taken for granted by their fellow citizens.... [H]ere in San Francisco, discrimination against the Negro and other minorities still persists, and it is a cancer on our city's economic life." He pledged that he would coordinate the city's resources to find jobs for minority workers, and he called on state and federal officials for assistance. Immediately after the riots, President Lyndon Johnson appointed Daniel M. Luevano, director of the Western Region of the Office of Economic Opportunity, to chair the San Francisco Task Force to investigate possible solutions to the jobs crisis in the Bay Area. When the task force reported their findings in June 1967, the members pointed to the lack of good jobs for low-income minority youths as the main cause of the riots. The task force strongly encouraged local, state, and federal agencies to create employment opportunities for the residents of the area, and they hinted that failure to do so might lead to further violence and civil unrest: "Direct contact with young men from the riot area indicated chronic unemployment and the existence of barriers to economic opportunities for minority youths and adults as continuing sources of irritation and resentment."[7]

By the time the task force had released its findings, however, the situation in the Bay Area had worsened.  One young black woman in Hunter's Point reported that police-community relations continued to deteriorate, and she recalled that "after the riot they had down to the community center...I was about...it was a week later goin' home from the store and I was I guess staring at this cop on Palou.... He told me, what I lookin' at nigger? and if I don't want to get a slap alongside the head to [move] on."  When asked why the police officer had been hostile, she responded, "man what you mean?...  I mean, I don't know...you think there's always some reason for things?  Sheeit, that's just the way it is.  My little baby girl knows better than that."  Small-scale riots erupted in Oakland and San Francisco in October 1966 and May 1967, respectively, and tensions between teenagers and police skyrocketed.  In Oakland, black youths laid siege to a ten-block area along East 14th Street, and they smashed windows, attacked cars, and threw gasoline bombs.  Sixty police officers finally restored order and arrested six adults and six youths.  Rumors that police officers had assaulted a black girl during the arrest of her brother and that they had tried to forcefully disband a crowd after a hit-and-run accident apparently touched off the riots.  In San Francisco the following spring, a fight between two black youths escalated into three days of rioting when police tried to intervene and were pelted with rocks and bottles by a large crowd of black teenagers who had gathered to watch the fight.  The violence spread into the city, and the rioters started fires in local schools and businesses, and interracial fights between teenagers broke out across San Francisco.[8]

Serious youth riots also plagued Richmond during the late 1960s.  In the spring of 1966, racial unrest paralyzed the city for two weeks.  In March, a fight involving two black teens, Charles Crowder and Ray Robinson, a white teen, Jerry Barnett, and a Latino teenager, Richard Marabuto, at Richmond Union High School sparked protests by parents and students over conditions at the school. Community workers at Richmond's Neighborhood House helped to cool tempers and keep black youths from taking to the streets, and Tony Scott, a Contra Costa County Junior College student and veteran of the civil rights projects in the South, encouraged a boycott of Richmond High and helped students and parents draw up a list of grievances for the principal. The students made eighteen demands, from hiring more counselors and "fairer" grading policies to showing newer black films and teaching black history, and Principal David Gray agreed to implement them. Although some white parents were enraged by the concessions and they demanded to know why the principal was "letting the Negroes take over the school," the situation improved and fortunately Gray did not have to take up a white parent's offer to "come down to the school with guns to keep things under control." Shortly after this agreement, however, black teenagers looted several downtown businesses and residents feared that more violence would erupt in the city. The Richmond police came out in force, and this time they were able to prevent further unrest.[9]

The peace was only temporary, however, and in the summer of 1968, black youths were back on the streets after another conflict with police. In the early evening of June 25, two officers stopped a car with four black teenagers under the suspicion that the car was stolen. The young men tried to escape by throwing "missiles" at the police, and the police shot one boy, who was taken to the hospital in critical condition. A large crowd of three or four hundred African Americans gathered at the scene, and police sealed off a 2.5 square-mile area of North Richmond. Gangs of black youths roamed through downtown breaking windows that night, and the next morning, fights broke out at JFK High School. At a meeting that afternoon, Bobby Seale, chairman of the Black Panther Party, "spoke and was well received.... Seale told [the] meeting that groups should act in small numbers, using guns, not rocks and bottles." Advocates of non-violence were apparently ignored by the crowd, and organized groups of black youths, some equipped with walkie-talkies, moved through downtown breaking windows and throwing fire-bombs. City leaders imposed a curfew and brought in help from San Francisco, neighboring counties, and the California

Highway Patrol. By the 27th, there were nearly 400 police officers in Richmond, and they were able to eventually restore order. In all, there were twenty cases of arson, ninety-five arrests, and five injuries reported.[10]

As violent outbursts between black youths and police increased during the 1960s, African American community organizers began to radicalize and move away from non-violence and integration and toward self-defense and black nationalism. Even young leaders who had been involved in civil rights demonstrations since the early 1960s began to lose heart with their former tactics and goals, and they questioned the wisdom of staging pickets and nonviolent sit-ins in the face of continued and unflinching white resistance. Jailed demonstrators paid high prices for their attempts to break through the Bay Area's color barrier, and fewer and fewer community leaders were willing to rot in jail as conditions on the outside failed to improve. The NAACP's approach of never-ending court battles and polite persuasion had long been out of favor with younger Bay Area black leaders, and even CORE's direct-action protests seemed passé as ghetto teens clashed with police on the streets.

Mark Comfort was one of the young black community organizers who decided in 1967 to change paths. A civil rights worker since the early 1960s, Comfort was instrumental in the Ad Hoc Committee to End Discrimination's protest against the *Oakland Tribune* in 1964. The Ad Hoc Committee charged that the paper's owner, the powerful Oakland politico William Knowland, discriminated against minorities and refused to hire qualified African Americans to work at the paper. A picket line went up in front of the *Tribune*'s offices, and the Oakland police department responded by harassing the protesters. Several of the Ad Hoc Committee's members were arrested during a protest on December 12, 1964, and Comfort distributed flyers throughout Oakland to request bail money for the jailed demonstrators. Several months later, Comfort himself was arrested for protesting against the paper, and the Citizens' Committee of Concern for Justice (CCCJ) organized a rally outside of the police department to protest his arrest. The CCCJ declared: "The truth is that there is no real difference between the Knowlands [of California] and the Wallaces of Alabama, or between the cops of

Selma and the cops of Oakland." Comfort's legal troubles dragged on until the next summer when he was sentenced to six months in the Alameda County Jail for his participation in the *Tribune* demonstrations. He received a bit of a respite, however, when United States Supreme Court Justice William O. Douglass granted Comfort a stay and released him from jail in July.[11]

In the summer of 1966, Comfort joined forces with the flamboyant black activist Curtis Lee Baker to bring the legendary community organizer Saul Alinsky to the Bay Area for a series of public speeches and to help low-income African Americans increase their power in Oakland. At a press conference announcing their plans, Comfort told reporters that organizing the poor was essential in avoiding a race rebellion in Oakland. He blasted Mayor John Reading and the Oakland City Council for ignoring the needs of the poverty population, and he argued that "you can't just take a group of people and toss them to one side and forget them." When Alinsky arrived at the San Francisco International Airport in May, he was met by Comfort and Baker, who were dressed entirely in black and sporting black berets. Alinsky announced to a throng of black community organizers and reporters that he had brought a "gift" of diapers to offer Reading and the city council, and he laced into the unresponsive white power structure of the East Bay. Baker, decked out in a black beret and cape, delivered the diapers to Mayor Reading at a council meeting the next day.[12]

Baker soon became well known among East Bay African Americans for his outlandish antics and spectacular wardrobe. Observers often spotted Baker draped in a cape, holding a giant staff, and wearing a beret jauntily cocked to one side of his head. He also used the ghettospeak of low-income black youth to reach out to an alienated segment of society in a way that they could understand and accept. Just as important, however, were the black nationalist speeches that he delivered at the West End Help Center in Oakland or throughout the East Bay. The son of black migrants from Louisiana, Baker embraced the self-defense doctrines of Malcolm X and campaigned among blacks for his efforts to build a base of self-government in Oakland. Baker preached race pride, political action, job development, and riot prevention to as many young ghetto blacks as would listen, and both his revolutionary rhetoric and style helped to create part of the militant subculture that the Black Panther Party would draw upon so effectively later in the decade.[13]

Increasingly concerned by the large numbers of unemployed black teenagers in Oakland, Mark Comfort repeatedly called for more job-creation programs for the East Bay. Oakland had the highest rate of unemployment among 16 to 21 year-old black men in the United States, and Comfort criticized the War on Poverty's Neighborhood Youth Corps and Job Corps programs as well as the Oakland Skills Center for providing black men with nearly useless training and for failing to place their graduates into decent full-time employment. Without also encouraging job growth in Oakland, the education and training programs that existed in the city were only temporarily keeping black youth off the streets. After accepting several weeks of pay, most graduates returned to the street corners to drink wine with their running partners and entered back into a life of petty crime to keep food in their bellies and their hours filled. Comfort argued that young black men were not fooled by white social servants' speeches about pulling themselves up by their own bootstraps, and they quickly became cynical and disaffected when Job Corps diplomas failed to take them out of the depressed ghetto economy.[14]

After his scrapes with the law, Comfort moved further away from his nonviolent roots and closer to the self-defense philosophy espoused by Malcolm X. In 1966, Comfort formed the Oakland Direct Action Committee (ODAC) and began an ambitious project to curb police brutality in Oakland. Warning that police brutality would "explode this city," Comfort berated the local police department and he proclaimed that "Oakland must stop hiring Ku Klux Klansmen and Mississippi hillbillies to do their killing. We want some action in Oakland for the people who are in need and threatened." Comfort and other members of ODAC began patrolling Oakland's black communities in the summer of 1966 to observe police activity and to make sure that African Americans were treated fairly. Some area ministers joined the frequent patrols, and ODAC members armed themselves with radios, cameras, and tape recorders to capture police in the act of harassing minority citizens. For a short time, ODAC representatives even followed police officers to the city jail to bail out black people who had been arrested, but Comfort had to abandon the practice because of its high cost. Then, in the spring of 1967, the mysterious death of a young black man at the hands of the Richmond police pushed Comfort forever away from the ideal of non-violence.[15]

Denzil Dowell, a 22 year-old black man with a history of confrontations with the police, was shot and killed by an officer of the Martinez Sheriff's Department on April 1. Conflicting testimony from black residents and white officers about the shooting sparked an uproar in Richmond's African American community, but officials turned a deaf ear to the Dowell family's request for a grand jury investigation. Stymied, George Dowell, Denzil's brother, appealed to Mark Comfort for help, and the Oakland community leader put the Dowell family in touch with a new militant organization that promised to end the police oppression of the ghetto—the Black Panther Party for Self-Defense. Comfort and the Panthers publicized the killing of Dowell throughout the East Bay, and they held a rally on April 29th in Richmond to protest Dowell's death and to spread their ideas of community self-defense. As police nervously looked on, fifteen armed Black Panthers demonstrated on the corner of Third and Chesley streets in North Richmond, brandishing their weapons and announcing to the astonished crowd that they were defending their constitutional rights to bear arms and speak freely against the ills that plagued their society. The Dowell murder quickly became a cause celebre among Bay Area African Americans, and the Panthers and Comfort catapulted to the top of the cops' enemies list.[16]

Comfort and the Panthers maintained a close alliance throughout the late 1960s, as Comfort moved further into militant black nationalist circles. The head of ODAC joined the BPP in its "invasion" of the California Assembly in the spring of 1967 to protest a proposed bill that would restrict the Panthers' ability to carry firearms openly in public. During a dramatic episode widely covered by the national press, the Panthers, decked out in their black berets and black leather jackets and carrying shotguns and pistols, marched into the assembly building and talked to reporters, unwittingly walked into the assembly's chambers as representatives were discussing legislation, and read an executive mandate from Huey P.

Newton on the capitol steps.  Police stood by waiting for the
Panthers to make a blunder, but the whole event went off without a
shot being fired.   Several Panthers were later arrested by
Sacramento police for carrying loaded weapons in their autos, and
Comfort had to serve four months of the sentence he received in
the *Tribune* case for violating the conditions of his parole.  In an
interview with the *Sun-Reporter*, an embittered Comfort urged other
blacks to abandon non-violence and prepare for the nation's collapse.[17]

Comfort himself adopted the habit of usually being armed, and
he and seven other Oakland black men were arrested in Tennessee
in the autumn of 1967 for carrying guns in a truck they were using
to transport donated food to African Americans in Lowndes County,
Alabama.  Comfort organized the cross-country relief effort as part
of his "Poor-to-Poor Project," where Oakland blacks sent food and
supplies to low-income blacks in the South.   Black leaders in
Oakland had heard of the problems that African Americans in
Alabama faced after they organized the Lowndes County Freedom
Organization (LCFO) with the assistance of Stokely Carmichael and
the Student Nonviolent Coordinating Committee in 1965.  Bobby
Seale and Huey Newton borrowed the LCFO's symbol of the black
panther for their revolutionary organization in 1966, and Comfort
and other black Oaklanders created assistance projects to help
their counterparts in Alabama weather the storm of white resistance and oppression.  By the late 1960s, even the Bay Area's food
assistance projects were laden with ideas of self-defense and the
ideology of black nationalism.[18]

Militant northern California African Americans would also add
their particular stamp on the most vivid and public display of the
frustration of low-income peoples in the United States—the Poor
People's Campaign of 1968.  Envisioned as another March on
Washington by Martin Luther King, Jr., before his death, the Poor
People's Campaign was managed by one of King's lieutenants from
the Southern Christian Leadership Conference (SCLC), Ralph
Abernathy, Jr.   The campaign culminated in the creation of
Resurrection City, a mish-mash camp of tents, cardboard boxes, and
shanties near the Capitol in Washington, D. C., and it quickly became
one of the worst debacles of the social  movements  of the 1960s.

Frequent rains turned the "city" into a swamp, and conditions for the inhabitants were appalling. News reports broadcast the misery of Resurrection City across the nation, as well as the militant attitudes of many of its residents. The Bay Area sent a contingent of 132 of the wretched of the earth led by Mark Comfort, and that number included several Black Panthers and other low-income people who had had their fill of life below the poverty line. Edith Hallberg, a black resident and welfare recipient from Berkeley, told reporters that she came to Washington "because I'm sick and tired of people being poor and people suffering. I want to end it at once." She warned that current welfare programs "are only minor reforms — we have to turn the whole society upside down."[19]

## THE ORIGINS OF THE BLACK PANTHER PARTY

In this season of discontent, two young ghetto blacks launched what would become the most important revolutionary nationalist group of the Black Power era. Bobby Seale and Huey Newton gathered in the back office of the North Oakland Neighborhood Anti-Poverty Center in October 1966, and they laid out the Ten Point Platform and Program of the Black Panther Party for Self-Defense. Focusing on employment, housing, education, and police-community relations, the two radicals drew upon their own experiences from living in Oakland's flatlands as well as upon the ideologies of other militant black thinkers and groups, including Malcolm X, Frantz Fanon, Elijah Muhammad and the Black Muslims, and Robert Williams, among others. The Panthers also developed their own brand of "Afro-Marxism" from the theories of Marx, Lenin, Mao Tse-Tung, and other Third World socialist and Communist leaders. Fed up with the "do-nothing" black intellectuals at Merritt College and around the Bay Area, however, Seale and Newton desired to create an organization that had practical goals and real programs that were relevant for the "brothers and sisters on the block." Moving beyond words and into action was important for these black revolutionaries, and Seale noted that:

> This is where the shit boils down to — to what the people want and not what some intellectual personally wants or some cultural

nationalists, like LeRoi Jones, want, or some jive-ass underground RAM motherfucker wants, or what some jive motherfucker in some college studying bullshit says, talking esoteric shit about the basic socio-economic structure, and the adverse conditions that we're subjected to so that no black man even understands. Huey was talking about some full employment, some decent housing, some education, about stopping those pigs from brutalizing us and murdering us.

After recruiting young Bobby Hutton from the ranks of Oakland's Neighborhood Youth Corps, Seale and Newton opened their first office, purchased their first guns, and started down the path to liberation. From their base in the Bay Area's black ghettoes, the Panthers spread their revolutionary message across the continent and around the world.[20]

Developing a broad vision of "self-defense," Seale and Newton argued that African Americans should not only protect themselves from police brutality and white mob violence, but they should also organize themselves to end their exploitation at the hands of racist capitalists. Building from Malcolm X's statement "that when the law fails to protect Negroes from whites' attack, then those Negroes should use arms if necessary, to defend themselves," the Panthers developed a view of community self-defense that incorporated physical safety and economic, social, and political strength. Newton, the party's main ideologue, claimed that "the conception that the Party was primarily a self-defense group against police brutality is a most narrow interpretation of the concept of self-defense by the oppressed masses." He pointed to the Ten Point Platform and Program as evidence that the Panthers had recognized that many low-income African Americans faced even larger problems in employment discrimination, poor housing, and segregated and inferior schools. The Panthers urged ghetto residents to rally together in common cause against the "capitalist oppressor" and wage a revolution that would overturn America's political economy and replace it with a more just system that protected community sovereignty and ended the exploitation of African American communities by outside forces. Eldridge Cleaver, the party's most important propagandist, explained that "our goal is political and economic self-determination for our people.... |O|*ur immediate aim is community control*—control of local schools, police forces, and all public agencies operating in our communities. The demand for community control builds a strong local base, and is the logical first step toward self-determination in the larger society."[21]

The Panthers' unique blend of black nationalist ideologies and socialist thought produced a new Afro-Marxism that fit the Bay Area radicals' needs and reflected their experiences and environment. Drawing inspiration from Karl Marx, Frantz Fanon, Ho Chi Minh, Che Guevara, Fidel Castro, Régis Debray, Lumumba, and Mao Tse-Tung, the Panthers' fused internationalist and localist perspectives and developed the theory of "revolutionary intercommunalism," which promised to connect a system of decentralized, independent communities through what Eldridge Cleaver termed an "embryonic sovereignty." The Panthers hoped to inspire oppressed peoples throughout the nation and the world to gain control of their communities and wrest power from the hands of corporate giants and exploitative political leaders. Tapping into the vast numbers of the "lumpenproletariat," or lower class, the Panthers hoped to create an army of the dispossessed and lead them in a revolution that would topple the "U.S.A. Monster" and destroy corporate capitalism. In an interview with Radio Havana, Bobby Seale told the Cubans that the Panthers hoped to "begin to work toward a socialist state...a system which will immediately put an end to racism in this country."[22]

The Panthers were unconventional "Marxists," however, and they used those parts of Communist doctrine that applied to their situation and that had particular resonance in the ghetto communities of northern California. Bobby Seale realized that the Panthers' interpretation of the role of the "lumpenproletariat" differed dramatically from the way that "strict doctrinaire Marxists" saw them. Marx had warned that capitalists would use the poor to undermine the strength of the working class and that, because of their proclivity toward crime, the lower class could never be organized into an effective unit for revolutionary change. Seale and the Panthers, however, saw the masses of low-income peoples as a source of revolutionary strength in their battle against the capitalist Establishment: "In other words, we didn't take the concept of the lumpenproletariat as strict as old doctrinaire Marxists, Leninists or Socialists do…. We looked at our lumpenproletariat in the context of where we were, the United States of America." Eldridge Cleaver also explained that Communist theory only made sense to black America if the Panthers shaped it to their needs and ends:

> When we say that we are Marxist-Leninists, we mean that we have studied and understood the classical principles of scientific socialism and that we have adapted these principles to our own situation for ourselves. However, we do not move with a closed mind to new ideas or information. At the same time, we know that we must rely upon our own brains in solving ideological problems as they relate to us. For too long Black people have relied upon the analyses and ideological perspectives of others. Our struggle has reached a point now where it would be absolutely suicidal for us to continue this posture of dependency. No other people in the world are in the same position as we are, and no other people in the world can get us out of it except ourselves.

Weaving this new tapestry of radical ideology, the Black Panthers hoped to create a system of thought that both explained the plight of low-income blacks in Bay Area ghettos and provided ways to organize them to end their oppression.[23]

The Panthers were also pragmatic, however, and they are most noted not for their Afro-Marxist ideology, but for the programs and tactics they used to try to spur a revolution from below. The party's main goals are contained in their Ten Point Platform and Program. The Panthers' program addressed the issues of employment, housing, education, and police brutality, and in Point 10, Newton and Seale proclaimed that, "we want land, bread, housing, education, clothing, justice and peace." Pressing for full employment, decent government housing for all people, and an educational system that recognized and met the needs and demands of minority students, the Panthers tried to address the problems that low-income blacks in the Bay Area had tried to overcome for years. Coming of age after the promise of industrial jobs had long since vanished, the young black leaders of the BPP channeled the frustration of their generation into an attack against the white Establishment.

Drawing support from the legions of unemployed black teens and underemployed young black men and women, the Panthers crystallized the mindset of their peers and gave voice to their complaints. Agitating for jobs, housing, and education, Newton and Seale tapped into the collective past of their "brothers and sisters on the block."

The Panthers are perhaps best known, however, for their conflicts with police. Bobby Seale noted that police brutality had been an issue that compelled him and Huey Newton to form the Black Panther Party in 1966. He remembered watching the national media's sensational coverage of civil rights demonstrations in the South, and he recalled seeing "policemen. White racist policemen. On horses. Each one of them mounted on a horse. Baseball bat like type billy clubs some of them had. Anyway, riding their horses they charged into all these peaceful demonstrators. The blood and the guts and the skulls being cracked...." Although the Panthers waited until Point 7 of their Ten Point Platform and Program to condemn local law enforcement, the BPP quickly directed its energies against the Oakland Police Department. Demanding "an immediate end to POLICE BRUTALITY and MURDER of black people," the Panthers used the issue of police brutality to attract the attention of the Bay Area's population and to show them that they could act against injustice. Frequent rumors of savage beatings of black residents and police cover-ups created an atmosphere conducive to the Panthers' attacks against the boys in blue. Newton and Seale's decision to publicly challenge Oakland police officers forever changed the direction of radical reform in the Bay Area and dictated the actions of the Black Panther Party throughout its short and tortured existence.[24]

The Panthers began their protest against police brutality with their now infamous armed patrols. Los Angeles's Community Alert Patrol had been organized after the Watts riots of August 1965, and Seale remembered hearing of black men, wearing armbands and armed with tape recorders and law books, who observed police in order to keep them from brutalizing black civilians. The Panthers drew upon this tactic and a similar one developed by Mark Comfort and the Oakland Direct Action Committee (ODAC), adding shotguns and pistols to the mix, and began following police cars around

Oakland. When patrolmen stopped black residents, Seale and Newton would stand nearby and inform the black men or women of their rights and glare menacingly at the officers. As with Comfort and the ODAC, the Panthers sometimes followed the police to the city jail to bail out black people who had been arrested on what the Panthers considered a "harassment" charge. The Panthers' actions, of course, sparked considerable interest both at police headquarters and throughout the black community.[25]

The BPP's police patrols were part of a history of demands for community control over the police in the Bay Area. Since the Second World War, African American activists had complained of frequent cases of police brutality against working- and lower-class blacks. Throughout the 1950s, calls for police review boards under civilian control continued unabated, and by the early 1960s, a climate of mistrust and hostility separated blacks and the white police officers who patrolled their neighborhoods. By 1966, the leaders of the Bay Area NAACP chapters had become more forceful in their demands for police review boards. Donald P. McCullum, chairman of the West Coast Region, lashed out at the Oakland Police Department, and he proclaimed that "the civilian review process restores confidence of the community in their Police Department. The Police are not the law unto themselves. Civilian review of the military and quasi-military in this country is as old as the Constitution. It inhibits the military junta and the development of the storm-trooper complex." Black community organizers working for the federal poverty program continued to put pressure on city hall for review boards in Oakland and San Francisco, and Huey Newton, Bobby Hutton, and Bobby Seale collected over five thousand signatures "on a petition that's calling for a community police review board." Although this gambit failed to move Oakland's city council, black activists, including Mark Comfort, Curtis Lee Baker, and the Black Panthers, launched other petition drives throughout the late 1960s. The Panthers even announced a plan to divide San Francisco into five separate zones (black, brown, Chinese, white, and ruling class) that would each have control over its own police department. Each area, in turn, would have fifteen precincts with a neighborhood representative on the police council. Members would be part time, and they would set policies for the officers and enforce discipline. Neighborhood councilmen would have had to have lived in the area they represented for at least six months, and officers would have to live in the areas they patrolled. Not surprisingly, the police department and city hall ignored the Panthers' plan; it did not, however, go unnoticed in San Francisco's black communities.[26]

The Panthers coupled their petition drives with a massive propaganda campaign against the police. Coining the term "pigs" for the police was only part of a larger verbal war that the BPP waged against law enforcement officials. The Panthers also covered the Bay Area ghettos with posters that pictured an armed Newton and Seale standing outside the BPP office and that read: "THE RACIST DOG POLICEMEN MUST WITHDRAW IMMEDIATELY FROM OUR COMMUNITIES, CEASE THEIR WANTON MURDER AND BRUTALITY AND TORTURE OF BLACK PEOPLE, OR FACE THE WRATH OF THE ARMED PEOPLE." Eldridge Cleaver, minister of information of the BPP, used the party's newspaper and the local black press to spread anti-police rhetoric, and in a November 1967 article, he wrote that "through murder, brutality, and the terror of their image, the police of America have kept black people intimidated, locked in a mortal fear, and paralyzed in their bid for freedom...." The Panthers also held frequent community rallies where they shouted down the walls of the establishment through loud-speakers and public address systems. On April 7, 1968, Bobby Seale addressed a large crowd in De Fremery Park in Oakland, three days after the assassination of Martin Luther King and one day after the death of Bobby Hutton in a shoot-out with police. Seale urged the audience to resist police oppression by "run[ning] in four and fives" rather than by rioting, which usually left many black people homeless or dead. Seale warned the crowd: "The pig department is the real power of the power structure. Let's learn a lesson today, brothers. It's no jive no mo'. Let's learn a lesson. Let's learn a lesson from brother Martin. Let's learn a lesson from what happened to our brother, Bobby Hutton, last night. And what's going to happen to many more brothers if we don't begin to organize." Through this propaganda, the Panthers' hoped to organize the thousands of Bay Area African Americans into a strong political body who could fight against the power of the Establishment and end the centuries-old exploitation of blacks in America.[27]

Violence and controversy flared up again in the fall of 1968 on the campus of San Francisco State College. On November 6, a two-day student strike began after the college fired George Murray, an English instructor and member of the Black Panther Party. Murray's dismissal inflamed African American students, and the militant Black Students' Union organized the strike. San Francisco's TAC Squad was called in to restore order, and as had happened so many times in the past, the police unit clashed with student demonstrators. African American leaders had sharply criticized the TAC Squad during the summer of 1968, and Cliffron R. Jeffers of the NAACP wrote to Attorney General Ramsey Clark to protest that the elite unit was systematically violating the civil liberties of blacks in San Francisco. In September, Rev. Donald M. Cowan, of Good Samaritan Mission on Potrero Avenue, testified at a public meeting in the Hall of Justice that officers of the TAC Squad had maced him twice during recent anti-war protests, and other speakers claimed to have seen the police needlessly beat nonviolent demonstrators. The *Sun-Reporter* concluded that "the tactical squad is just seven months old but it holds records for savagery among some elements of the population which could make the once-feared Nazi storm troopers look like amateurs." The confrontation at San Francisco State sparked a five-month strike at the college, which ended in April 1969. One leader of the San Francisco State Black Students' Union later admitted that the organization had been influenced by the ideas and militancy of the Black Panther Party.[28]

The culmination of the Black Panther Party's efforts to organize Bay Area black communities around the issue of police brutality came with the Free Huey Movement. On October 28, 1967, Newton was stopped by Oakland Patrolman John F. Frey for a minor traffic violation. The events that followed are unclear, but as Frey attempted to arrest Newton, both he and the minister of defense went down in an exchange of gunfire. Frey was killed and his partner, Herbert C. Heanes, was wounded, and Newton was able to make it to a local hospital where he was treated and arrested. The death of Frey garnered national media attention, and soon the Panthers were on the front pages of major newspapers across the country. Newton became an instant hero for Bay Area radicals, black and white, and meetings and protests were regularly orchestrated by the BPP outside the Alameda County Courthouse. In February 1968, the Panthers organized a large Free Huey Rally in the Oakland Auditorium, and many Black Power luminaries, including Stokely Carmichael, H. Rap Brown, and James Foreman, attended the meeting and expressed their support for Newton. Most of the speakers called for revolutionary violence against the racist white power structure, and Brown told the audience: "the only thing that is going to free you is gunpowder." Over six thousand people attended the rally, and the speakers were frequently interrupted by enthusiastic applause from the crowd. The following year, about two thousand people joined a birthday celebration and rally for Newton at the Berkeley Community Theater, and the Panthers' collected several thousand dollars for the Newton Defense Fund. Several months later, over eight thousand demonstrators gathered outside the Federal Building in San Francisco to demand Newton's freedom. There was a lot of posturing and energy at the rally, and the protesters chanted Black Power songs and slogans. Support from low-income blacks in the Bay Area began to solidify behind Newton's cause, and many long-time residents felt that this was just another case of Oakland's police officers stepping over the line. This time, however, it had cost one of them his life.[29]

As Newton's celebrity status grew, more Bay Area African Americans came forward to voice their support for the Black Panther Party. Reports of official police harassment of the Panthers increased, and black citizens denounced the deaths of party members at the hands of the police. In April 1968, the *Sun-Reporter* ran an editorial that urged citizens to "protect the Panthers" and claimed that the series of conflicts between the BPP and law enforcement officials "suggest[s] a studied, methodical strategy on the part of the police establishment, without legal authority, to harass, intimidate, physically attack and even murder proclaimed members of the Black Panther Party." At a public rally in support of the Panthers, Dr. Carlton Goodlett, publisher of the *Sun-Reporter*, claimed that black Americans would "engage in guerrilla warfare...in the steel and concrete merciless canyons of America's great cities" if police continued to attack the Panthers. Ruth

Hagood, a resident of Oakland, promised the "wrath of black mothers" if the police hurt more men and children. She proclaimed that: "The Black Panthers are the true Americans because they are the ones that are trying to bring the American Dream to reality that every man, woman, and child in this country has ample food, [and] ample housing...." After Bobby Hutton's death, thousands of mourners turned out for the funeral, and the Panthers received positive coverage in the local black press. Even the *Sun-Reporter's* advice columnist, Aunt Sarah, caught the revolutionary fever, and in 1969, she gave the following response to a person who wanted to know how to free Huey:

> I alone cannot free Huey. But he can be freed if concerned people organize a strong protest movement against the government, which in it's [sic] blood-drenched history, has always isolated, emasculated, and tortured leaders like Huey, Marcus Garvey, John Brown as well as Indians, Chicanos, etc. The movement should force the government to disgorge its fascist judiciary, legislative and executive powers. In short, people should have [the] right to control their own destinies, which Huey so eloquently preached to black people. Yes, all political prisoners should be freed everywhere — by revolutionary methods.

In the late 1960s, the Black Panthers had become the embodiment of black rage in the Bay Area. More than two decades of racial strife since the Second World War had come home to roost.[30]

## FROM COMMUNITY ACTION PROGRAM TO COMMUNITY SURVIVAL PROGRAM

In 1969, Bobby Seale unveiled a new series of party programs that addressed the employment, housing, education, and social service needs of the Bay Area's low-income communities. Seale and others tried to change the Panthers' image as foes of the police and add more substance to the party's efforts to liberate oppressed communities. The party's Community Survival Programs ranged from the famous Free Breakfast for Children Program to Free Food and Free Shoes programs, Free Sickle Cell Anemia Tests, and legal aid projects. Drawing from his experiences as an employee of Oakland's Community Action Programs (CAPs) of the War on Poverty, Seale designed the Panthers' Community Survival Programs in part from the models provided by federal liberalism earlier in the decade. Although the BPP used the programs for ends that were much different than the ones proposed by federal planners in Washington, many of the basic organizational principles and tactics that were at the heart of the Great Society poverty programs resurfaced in a new form in the Panthers' Survival Programs.

Many of the federal anti-poverty programs in black ghettos in the East Bay had been dominated by African American radicals and activists who hoped to organize low-income black communities into a powerful political force. Oakland's Mayor John Reading tried desperately to rout the radicals out of the city's Community Action Programs, and the Oakland Economic Development Council fired at least one organizer when it learned that he was a member of the Black Panther Party. Militants, however, still controlled much of the ground-level operations of the East Bay's poverty programs, and they infused their ideologies into the services they dispensed to the poor and the training they gave to unemployed teenage blacks. Seale's supervisor at one of the poverty programs, an older black Communist named Mr. Low, helped to change the young radical's views on community organization and Black Power. Growing frustrated with the "do-nothing" black intellectuals at Merritt College, Seale dropped out of the social circles at the college and began to invest more of his time and energy with the disaffected young blacks at the street level. There, he developed further his ideas about community organization and he learned how to attract low-income youths into the program and teach them some of the values of hard work, self-respect, and Black Power. Seale later credited the poverty program with helping him and Huey Newton to craft the basic framework of the Black Panther Party:

> Other factors that helped lead to us creating the Black Panther Party was The Neighborhood Services where we worked. A community group of people, black people and about five or six white people—about 30 some odd people—...[were] on this board which was an advisory board, that gave advice and recommended

how War on Poverty moneys and funds should be spent. And that whole advisory board actually came out of the Title II War on Poverty moneys that stated that you had to have some community participation.

Unlike some other radical community organizers in the Bay Area, including most notably Mark Comfort and Wilfred Ussery, Seale gained much of the organizational knowledge and experience that he would use in the late 1960s and 1970s from his days as a foot soldier in Lyndon Johnson's War on Poverty, rather than from participation in the civil rights demonstrations in the South or in the Bay Area during the early 1960s. It was a relatively short leap from the kinds of Community Action Programs sponsored by the OEO, including literacy courses, employment counseling, job training, home economics, health services, consumer education, and Head Start, to the Black Panther Party's Community Survival Programs, which included Free Breakfasts for Children, People's Medical Care Centers, Sickle-Cell Anemia Tests, Free Food, Clothing, and Shoes programs, the Pocket Lawyer of Legal First Aid, and the Liberation Schools. Drawing from the organizational experience he gained as an anti-poverty agent, Seale designed many of the Panthers' Survival Programs in ways that paralleled the Great Society's Community Action Programs.[31]

Of all of the Panthers' Community Survival Programs, Free Breakfast for Children attracted the most attention. The BPP leaders convinced, and perhaps sometimes coerced, local store owners to donate food and supplies to the party for their daily breakfast programs, which they usually operated out of the basements of local churches. Low-income children received oranges, hot chocolate, eggs, and meat to get them to school with a full stomach, and the program was a tremendous public-relations success for the party in the Bay Area. About one hundred fifty children were being fed at the St. Augustine Episcopal Church in Oakland by March 1969, and more than two hundred participated in the Free Breakfast Program at the Sacred Heart Church in San Francisco. The children thought the Panthers were "very nice" and "groovy" for helping them with the breakfasts, and many youngsters noted that they had not eaten as well before the programs started. The program allowed the Panthers some moral high ground upon which to stand, and one California policeman even asked: "How can anyone be against feeding kids?" Many former party members explain that they were convinced to join the Black Panthers after coming into contact with the breakfast program, and they argue that the Community Survival Programs were one of the positive legacies of community empowerment left by the BPP. Deborah Bremond, who was active in the Berkeley chapter in the early 1970s, noted that "we provided...a role model in the community.... We showed them how to organize effectively and get the things that they needed. It was a way to show the people that they could be empowered." Free Breakfast for Children was indeed popular among low-income residents of the Bay Area, and it would remain the most successful Community Survival Program that the Panthers ever launched.[32]

African Americans throughout the Bay Area responded positively to the party's Community Survival Programs, and the Panthers were able to broaden their base of support in the late 1960s and early 1970s because of the public relations successes they gained with their socialistic programs. Other community organizations began to form allegiances with the Black Panther Party, and in the East Bay, one female activist for the People Pledged for Community Progress noted that she "thought they did good work. We felt they were intelligent young men—were so proud of them—with a well-thought-out program which they laid out to the city council. They were nice kids." In San Francisco, the Western Addition Community Organization, led by Rev. A. Cecil Williams, Hannibal Williams, Inez Andry, and Mary Rogers, announced in 1968 that it would work with the Black Panthers on the issues relating to self-defense, and they promised to send representatives to school board meetings and establish a Western Addition switchboard for the community. The popularity of the Panthers' Community Survival Programs also worried the party's opponents, and in May 1969, FBI Director J. Edgar Hoover wrote that the Free Breakfast for Children Program was "the best and most influential activity going for the BPP and as such is potentially the greatest threat to efforts by authorities to neutralize the BPP and destroy what it stands for."[33]

Perhaps because of its success, there is a tenacious myth in Panther folklore that the BPP's Free Breakfast for Children Program ired the federal government's school lunch and school breakfast programs. For example, in his autobiography, David Hilliard, the BPP's chief of staff for most of the late 1960s and early 1970s, claims that "the federal government itself took over programs we initiated like the free Breakfast for Children program...." There were, however, precedents for the Panthers' breakfast program in the federal projects of the early and mid-1960s. In 1965, President Lyndon Johnson named the week of October 10-15 "National School Lunch Week," and he encouraged more local charities to distribute school lunches to needy children across the country. The United States Department of Agriculture (USDA) and the Office of Economic Opportunity (OEO) offered assistance in organizing these school lunch programs. The following year, Elijah Turner, of the Ad Hoc Committee for Quality Education, and Agnes Woods, of Oakland's anti-poverty program, led protests outside of the business of the president of the Oakland Board of Education to denounce the inadequacy of the poverty program's school lunch program. Turner and Woods argued that the program should be expanded so that more people could have access to the lunches. By 1967, the federal government had also begun its own pilot school breakfast program under the Child Nutrition Act. Congress sought to use the breakfasts to supplement the School Lunch Act programs that served about 19 million of the estimated 51 million schoolchildren in the nation. About 200,000 children received free breakfasts by 1967, at an annual cost of $2 million, but federal planners hoped to expand the program by another 650,000 children the following year. By 1969, schoolchildren in San Francisco could receive free milk in the morning and free lunch if their parents requested it, although the East Bay did not offer any breakfast programs. It is likely that with the exposure these programs received in the Bay Area, Seale and the Panthers developed their own version of a free breakfast program to help supplement the diets of low-income children in northern California. While the Panthers' actions might have spurred the expansion of the programs, the evidence clearly shows that federal planners had already developed school lunch and breakfast programs long before the Panthers were serving their breakfasts in church basements in the Bay Area. In fact, it seems more likely that the Panthers used the poverty programs of the mid-1960s as models for their Community Survival Programs, rather than the other way around.[34]

Despite their similarity in form, however, the ideologies behind the Community Action Programs and the Community Survival Programs could hardly have been more different.  The intent of the Panthers' programs was to liberate the poor rather than reform them, and the basic drive behind the Survival Programs was socialism, not liberalism.  The Panthers infused their programs with the tenets of their Afro-Marxist ideology, and they used them to spread their doctrine throughout the Bay Area black ghettos.  By providing low-income African Americans with services they needed to survive, the Panthers hoped to win their support and lead them down the path to revolution.  In a 1969 interview, Bobby Seale noted that the basic purpose behind the Panthers' programs was to educate the black masses about the evils of capitalism and the virtues of a socialistic solution to their problems.  "It's a socialistic program," Seale said of the Free Breakfast for Children Program.  "Once the people see a socialistic program is valuable to them, they won't throw it away.   By practicing socialism they learn it better." Reaching out to the African American lumpenproletariat, the Black Panthers sought to create a Communist revolution and topple the capitalist system in the United States.   "If we can understand Breakfast for Children," wrote Eldridge Cleaver from exile in 1969, "can we not also understand Lunch for Children, and Dinner for Children, and Clothing for Children, and Education for Children, and Medical Care for Children?  And if we can understand that, why can't we understand not only a People's Park, but People's Housing, and People's Transportation, and People's Industry, and People's Banks?  And why can't we understand a People's Government?" Much as the Panthers had appropriated Marxism for their own uses, the black militants created their version of community action programs to instruct African Americans to embrace Black Power instead of federal liberalism.   For Bobby Seale and others, the Community Survival Programs were simply the means to a revolutionary end; they were the spark that would rally blacks in the Bay Area together to form any army that would topple the white power structure.  At the front of this great phalanx, the Black Panthers hoped to lead oppressed African Americans in a glorious People's Movement.[35]

By the late 1960s, the social crises created by the Second World War had borne full fruit in the San Francisco Bay Area. The problems that African Americans faced in employment, housing, education, and police-community relations laid the foundations for the black radicalism of the Sixties. The migrants who had done so much to upset the delicate balance struck between long-time black and white residents of the Bay Area passed on an even greater threat to established ways of life in their sons and daughters. The second generation of black newcomers challenged not only the policies of segregation and discrimination that had characterized Bay Area society for more than a century, but they also threatened the basic assumptions and principles of the social and economic organization of northern California's major cities. The racial unrest of the late 1960s was produced by the decades-old conflicts over fair employment, decent housing, segregated schools, and police brutality. The greatest challenge to this history of discord came in the form of the Black Panther Party, and its young radical leaders voiced the rage of thousands of alienated low-income African Americans. The Panthers' police patrols and Community Survival Programs drew from a tradition of militant reform in the urban West and tapped into the nation's recent concern over the legions of its poor and dispossessed citizens. At the end of the decade, the Bay Area was engulfed in a revolution.

# Notes

1.   United States Department of Commerce, *The Eighteenth Decennial Census of the United States, Census of the Population*: 1960, Vol. 1, Part 6 (Washington, D. C.: United States Government Printing Office, 1961), 58, 475; United States Department of Commerce, 1970 *Census of Population*, Part

6, Section 1 (Washington, D. C.: United States Government Printing Office, 1973), 86, 127.

2.   Transcript, Bobby Seale Oral History Interview, 4 May 1989, by Ronald Jemal Stephens and Clyde Robertson, n.p., in possession of the author; Bobby Seale, *Seize the Time: The History of the Black Panther Party and Huey P. Newton* (New York: Random House, 1968), Chp. 1; Seale, *A Lonely Rage: The Autobiography of Bobby Seale* (New York: Times Books, 1978), 18–19 passim; The Church League of America, *The Black Panthers in Action* (Wheaton, IL: The Church League of America, 1969), 11; Huey P. Newton, *Revolutionary Suicide* (New York: Harcourt, Brace, Jovanovich, Inc., 1973), 16–96 passim; Gene Marine, *The Black Panthers* (New York: New American Library, 1969), 12–13; W. J. Rorabaugh, *Berkeley at War: The 1960s* (New York: Oxford University Press, 1989), 77–78; Hugh Pearson, *The Shadow of the Panther: Huey Newton and the Price of Black Power in America* (Reading, MA: Addison-Wesley Publishing Company, 1994), 17, 45–47, 97, 107–13; Gene Marine, *The Black Panthers*(New York: American Library, 1969), 137; Quotation from Hilliard is in David Hilliard and Lewis Cole, *This Side of Glory: The Autobiography of David Hilliard and the Story of the Black Panther Party* (Boston: Little, Brown and Company, 1993), 27, 22–69.

3.   Tom Roland, "Oakland: Crisis Next Door," *The Campus Core-Lator: Magazine of the Berkeley Campus Chapter of the Congress of Racial Equality* (January 1965), 26, Carton 3, Social Protest Collection, Bancroft Library, University of California, Berkeley [Hereafter cited as Social Protest Collection]; Warren Hinckle, "Metropoly: The Story of Oakland, California," *Ramparts* 4 (February 1966), 50; M. C. Stallings, "Second Watts in Oakland?" *Sun-Reporter*, 30 April 1966, 7.

4.   The black men at the Youth Opportunities Center are quoted in David Wellman, "Putting on the Youth Opportunity Center," in *Soul*, ed. Lee Rainwater (Chicago: Aldine Publishing Company, 1970), 108, 113; San Francisco NAACP Youth Council, "Black Revolution Supported by NAACP Youth Council," *Sun-Reporter*, 13 August 1966, 7; George Gilbert, "Two Young Men Who Hate Whitey: Fillmore's 'Warm-Up,'" San Francisco *Chronicle*, 19 July 1966, 5.

5.   For general accounts of the riots, see Thomas C. Fleming, "Violence Hits the Streets," *Sun-Reporter*, 1 October 1966, 2; John Laurence Brown, "Hell in Hunter's Point," *Sun-Reporter*, 1 October 1966, 3; Memo, Fred M. Vinson, Jr., to Ramsey Clark, 28 September 1966, Personal Papers of Ramsey Clark, Box 75, Lyndon Baines Johnson Presidential Library, Austin,

Texas [Hereafter cited as LBJL]; and Arthur E. Hippler, *Hunter's Point: A Black Ghetto* (New York: Basic Books, 1974), Chp. 10. The property damage estimates are from Memo, Tom McTiernan to Attorney General, 29 September 1966, Personal Papers of Ramsey Clark, Box 75, LBJL.

6.    Hippler, *Hunter's Point*, 206.

7.    Press Release by Mayor John F. Shelley, 29 September 1966, attached to Memo, T. J. Kent, Jr., to Mayor's Advisory Committee on Proposed City Demonstration Program, Office Files of Fred Bohen, Box 7, LBJL; Memo, Daniel M. Luevano to Joe Califano, 30 June 1967, Ex LG/A-Z, WHCF, Box 11, LBJL; for the creation of the task force see, Telegram, Joseph A. Califano, Jr. to Honorable John F. Shelley, 29 September 1966, Ex LG/San Francisco, WHCF, Box 11 LBJL; and Dick Meister, "President Orders S.F. Job Study," San Francisco *Chronicle*, 30 September 1966, clipping attached to Luevano to Califano memo. See also, Edward Howden, "Observations on Recent San Francisco Disturbance and the Community's Response" (Sacramento: California Fair Employment Practice Commission, 1966).

8.    Woman quoted in Hippler, *Hunter's Point*, 59; Thomas C. Fleming, "Wild Rioting by Oakland Youths," *Sun-Reporter*, 22 October 1966, 2; Thomas C. Fleming, "Youths Rampage on S.F. Streets," *Sun-Reporter*, 20 May 1967, 2, 38.

9.    Robert Wenkert, John Magney, and Ann Neel, *Two Weeks of Racial Crisis in Richmond, California* (Berkeley: Survey Research Center, University of California, 1967), Chapter IV and V, quotations from 145–46.

10.    Memo, "Richmond, California," 27 June 1968, Personal Papers of Ramsey Clark, Box 73, LBJL; Summary of Daily Log, 26–27 June 1968, Box 73, Personal Papers of Ramsey Clark, LBJL.

11.    Quotation is from Flyer, 5 May 1965, Box 1, Newell Hart Papers, Bancroft Library, University of California, Berkeley [Hereafter cited as Hart Papers]. See also, Ad Hoc Committee to End Discrimination, "Don't Buy the *Oakland Tribune*," 18 December 1964, Box 1, Hart Papers; "Oakland Rights Demonstrator Is Sentenced," San Francisco *Chronicle*, 10 June 1966, 2; "Mark Comfort Free on Stay," San Francisco *Chronicle*, 23 July 1966, 4.

12.    "Additional $8.2 Million for Oakland Jobs Project," San Francisco *Chronicle*, 30 April 1966, 2; "Alinsky Takes Aim at Oakland Critics," San Francisco *Chronicle*, 3 May 1966, 20; "Council is Given Alinsky's 'Gift,'" San Francisco *Chronicle*, 4 May 1966, 2.

13.    For Curtis Lee Baker's story, see, Marion Fay, "Baker and the West End Help Center," *Sun-Reporter*, 25 November 1967, 9–10; and Amory

Bradford, *Oakland's Not for Burning* (New York: David McKay Company, Inc., 1968), 15–17 passim.

14.     "Conditions in the Oakland Ghetto: Mark Comfort interviewed by Elsa Knight Thompson," cassette E2BB1309, Pacifica Radio Archive, North Hollywood, California, 1967.  For a similar critique of the East Bay anti-poverty programs, see Wellman, "Putting on the Youth Opportunity Center," 93–115.

15.     Quotation from "Police Brutality: Statements on Police Community Relations by the California Advisory Commission of the U.S. Civil Rights Commission," *Flatlands*, 5 June to 18 June 1966, 1, 4; "Conditions in the Oakland Ghetto"; "Oakland Groups to Watch Police," *Sun-Reporter*, 3 September 1966, 2.

16.     Seale, *Seize the Time*, 134–49; Marine, *The Black Panthers*, 57 passim. The first issue of the Black Panther Party's newspaper, *The Black Panther*, was devoted to the Dowell case and the North Richmond rally.  It is reprinted in Philip S. Foner, ed., *The Black Panthers Speak* (Philadelphia: J. B. Lippincott Company, 1970), 9–12.

17.     The Sacramento invasion has been well covered in much of the literature on the BPP.  A good source is Seale, *Seize the Time*, 155–176.  For Comfort's role in the invasion, see "Conditions in the Oakland Ghetto"; and Thomas C. Fleming, "Panthers Formed Out of Despair," *Sun-Reporter*, 13 May 1967, 3.

18.     "Mark Comfort Arrested in Tenn. for Carrying Guns of Food Mission," *Sun-Reporter*, 2 September 1967, 2.  For a history of the Lowndes County Freedom Organization, see Stokely Carmichael and Charles V. Hamilton, *Black Power: The Politics of Liberation* (New York: Random House, 1967); and Clayborne Carson, *In Struggle: SNCC and the Black Awakening of the 1960s* (Cambridge: Harvard University Press, 1981).  For the influence of the LCFO on the Black Panther Party, see Rorabaugh, *Berkeley at War*, 78.

19.     Hallberg quoted in Marion Fay, "Resurrection City — A Challenge to the American Dream," *Sun-Reporter*, 29 June 1968, 2–3.  See also Marion Fay, "Western Caravan Joins Poor People's Campaign," *Sun-Reporter*, 25 May 1968, 3; Memo, George W. Culberson for Roger W. Wilkins to Ramsey Clark, 21 May 1968, Box 73, Personal Papers of Ramsey Clark, LBJL; and the series of memos from the Community Relations Service to the attorney general in the folder "Poor People's Campaign - CRS - Daily Log" in Box 73, Personal Papers of Ramsey Clark, LBJL.

20.    Seale, *Seize the Time*, 63–64; the Ten Point Platform and Program is in the Appendix.

21.    Malcolm X with Alex Haley, *The Autobiography of Malcolm* X (New York: Ballantine Books, 1964), 366; Seale Interview; Huey P. Newton, *To Die for the People* (New York: Vintage Books, 1972), 20, 172; Cleaver is quoted in, "Why Peace & Freedom Should Nominate Eldridge Cleaver for President," n.d., Carton 12, Social Protest Collection.

22.    The transcript of the Seale interview is included as Exhibit 341 in United States Senate, Permanent Subcommittee on Investigations, Committee on Government Operations, *Riots, Civil and Criminal Disorders*, Part 19: June 18, 24, 25, 1969 (Washington, D. C.: United States Government Printing Office, 1969), 3735–56.

23.    Seale Interview; Eldridge Cleaver, *On the Ideology of the Black Panther Party*, Part I (San Francisco: Ministry of Information, Black Panther Party, 1969 [?]), 1. For more on Panther ideology, see, "Exclusive: Angela Answers 13 Questions," special supplement to *Muhammad Speaks*, Winter 1970, Carton 3, Social Protest Collection; John T. McCartney, *Black Power Ideologies: An Essay in African American Political Thought* (Philadelphia: Temple University Press, 1992); and William L. Van Deburg, *New Day in Babylon: The Black Power Movement and American Culture, 1965–1975* (Chicago: The University of Chicago Press, 1992).

24.    Seale Interview.

25.    *Ibid.*; Seale, *Seize the Time*, 85–98.

26.    "Statement by Donald P. McCullum, Chairman West Coast Region, NAACP on Alameda County Grand Jury report calling for resistance to formation of a Police Review Board in Oakland," 25 August 1966, Carton 9, NAACP West Coast Region Papers, Bancroft Library, University of California, Berkeley; Seale Interview; "Panthers Mount Campaign for Community Police Control," *Sun-Reporter*, 30 August 1969, 6; Ministry of Information Bulletin No. 9, 6 January 1968, Carton 18, Social Protest Collection.

27.    Seale explains the origins and use of the term "pigs" in *Seize the Time*, 404–411; The poster is located in Afro-American Posters, circa 1960–1969, Bancroft Library, University of California, Berkeley; Eldridge Cleaver, "Huey Must Be Set Free," *Sun-Reporter*, 11 November 1967, 13, 16; "Bobby Seale in Oakland," cassette BB5462, Pacifica Radio Archive, North Hollywood, California, 1968.

28.    United States Senate, *Riots, Civil and Criminal Disorders*, 3774–75;
Joyce Powell, "TAC SQUAD CHARGES: Student Strike at SF State Closes
Campus," *Sun-Reporter*, 16 November 1968, 2; "Call for Investigation: TAC
Squad Blasted by NAACP Leader," *Sun-Reporter*, 31 August 1968, 2; Thomas
Fleming, "Attacks on Tac Squad Continue," *Sun-Reporter*, 7 September 1968,
2; "Dr. Goodlett Arrested: Black Community Stands behind Black Student
Union," *Sun-Reporter*, 7 December 1968, 1, 2, 3, 12, 23; William Barlow and
Peter Shapiro, *An End to Silence: The San Francisco State College Student Movement
in the '60s* (New York: Pegasus, 1971); Kay Boyle, *The Long Walk at San
Francisco State and Other Essays* (New York: Grove Press, Inc., 1969); Dikran
Karagueuzian, *Blow It Up! The Black Student Revolt at San Francisco State College
and the Emergence of Dr. Hayakawa* (Boston: Gambit, Inc., 1971); DeVere
Pentony, Robert Smith, and Richard Axen, *Unfinished Rebellions* (San
Francisco: Jossey-Bass, Inc., 1971); Robert Smith, Richard Axen, and
DeVere Pentony, *By Any Means Necessary: The Revolutionary Struggle at San
Francisco State* (San Francisco: Jossey-Bass, Inc., 1970); and John
Summerskill, *President Seven* (New York: The World Publishing Co., 1971).

29.    Accounts of Newton's "shoot-out" with Frey are standard fare for
most books on the Panthers.  The most interesting ones are in Newton,
*Revolutionary Suicide*, Part Two passim; and Pearson, *Shadow of the Panther*,
145–47 passim.  A helpful newspaper summary of the events, with photos
of Newton, Frey, and Haines, is Thomas C. Fleming, "Black Panther Shot by
Police: Charged with Murder," *Sun-Reporter*, 4 November 1967, 2.  Marion
Fay, "Vanguards of Black Militancy Speak at Huey Newton Benefit Rally,"
*Sun-Reporter*, 24 February 1968, 2; International Historic Films, *Black
Panthers: Huey Newton*, 53 min., 1968, videocassette; "Birthday Celebration
for Huey," *Sun-Reporter*, 22 February 1969, 10; "8000 at Newton Rally," *Sun-
Reporter*, 10 May 1969, 1, 2.

30.    For a typical partisan account of the police actions against the
BPP, see Terry Canon, *All Power to the People: The Story of the Black Panther Party*
(San Francisco: Peoples Press, 1970).  "Protect the Panthers," *Sun-Reporter*,
20 April 1968, 12; "Black Panther Community Support Rally," cassette
BB5461.01, Pacifica Radio Archive, North Hollywood, California, 1968;
Thomas C. Fleming, "Thousands at Funeral for Panther Martyr," *Sun-
Reporter*, 20 April 1968, 3, 9; IHF, *Black Panthers: Huey Newton*, contains footage
of the funeral procession and the services; "Aunt Sarah," advice column,
*Sun-Reporter*, 8 November 1969, 16; "Angry Bay Area Response," *Sun-
Reporter*, 13 December 1969, 3.

31.    Mayor Reading's testimony is in United States Senate, Subcommittee on Employment, Manpower, and Poverty, Committee on Labor and Public Welfare, *Examination of the War on Poverty*, May 10–11, 1967, Part 11 (Washington, D. C.: United States Government Printing Office, 1967), 3478–79; Seale, *A Lonely Rage*, 139–52 passim; Seale Interview; Seale, *Seize the Time*, 35–44. A convenient summary of the kinds of programs sponsored by the OEO can be found in the OEO's *Community Action Program Guide*, Vol. I: *Instructions for Applicants* (Washington, D. C.: Office of Economic Opportunity, 1965), 7. Information on the BPP's Community Survival Programs is in Foner, ed., *The Black Panthers Speak*, Chp. 9.

32.    Father Earl Neil of St. Augustine's worked closely with the Panthers throughout the late 1960s. See, Ministry of Information Bulletin, No. 9. "Panthers Serve Free Breakfast to Black School Children," *Sun-Reporter*, 1 March 1969, 11; "Panthers Offer Free Breakfast," editorial, *Sun-Reporter*, 15 March 1969, 9; the policeman is quoted in Peter Goldman, *Report from Black America* (New York: Simon and Schuster, 1969), 73; Deborah Bremond, Interview by Charles E. Jones, 17 June 1992, transcript in possession of the author, 1–2; Terry Cotton, Interview by Charles E. Jones, 13 March 1993, transcript in possession of the author, 1; Emory Douglas, Interview by Charles E. Jones, 15 June 1992, transcript in possession of the author, 4–5. For photos of the Community Survival Programs, see Ruth-Marion Baruch and Pirkle Jones, *The Vanguard: A Photographic Essay on the Black Panthers* (Boston: Beacon Press, 1970), esp. 10, 113–117; and Mario Van Peebles, Ula Y. Taylor, and J. Tarika Lewis, *Panther: A Pictorial History of the Black Panthers and the Story behind the Film* (New York: New Market Press, 1995), esp. 99–110. A piece of Panther propaganda promoting the Free Breakfast Program is included as Exhibit 388 in United States Senate, *Riots, Civil and Criminal Disorders*, 3872–74. Hugh Pearson has recently argued that the Panthers often forced local black merchants to contribute goods to the survival programs, especially the Breakfast for Children Program. Pearson claims that the Panthers threatened store owners with physical violence or other reprisals if they did not comply with the militants' demands. See, *Shadow of the Panther*, 240–41.

33.    Activist quoted in Gretchen Lemke-Santangelo, *Abiding Courage: African American Migrant Women and the East Bay Community* (Chapel Hill: University of North Carolina Press, 1996), 176; Anne Ross, "WACO Resolves to Work with Black Panthers," *Sun-Reporter*, 6 July 1968, 3; Hoover quoted in Helen L. Stewart, "Buffering: The Leadership Style of Huey P. Newton, Co-

founder of the Black Panther Party" (Ph.D. diss., Brandeis University, 1980), 79.

34.     Hilliard, *This Side of Glory*, 14.  For scholars who promote this interpretation, see Jennifer B. Smith, *An International History of the Black Panther Party* (New York: Garland, 1999), 51; and Stewart, "Buffering: The Leadership Style of Huey P. Newton," 78–79.  For evidence of federal programs, see "Central Kitchens Will Offer More School Lunches," *Sun-Reporter*, 2 October 1965, 2; "Free Lunch Picketing in Oakland," San Francisco *Chronicle*, 23 July 1966, 3; Staff paper, "Food Assistance," n.d., Personal Papers of Bertrand M. Harding, Box 59, LBJL; and the letters from Benjamin W. Lashkoff to Perman Clay, 30 June 1969, George Murphy to Jerome S. Adlerman, 3 July 1969, and Howard P. Davis to Senator Jacob K. Javits, n.d., included as an exhibit in United States Senate, *Riots, Civil and Criminal Disorders*, 3883–84.

35.     Seale's interview from the Students for a Democratic Society's paper, *The Movement*, is excerpted in The Church League of America, *The Black Panthers in Action*, 15; Eldridge Cleaver, "On Meeting the Needs of the People," *The Black Panther*, 16 August 1969, quoted in Foner, ed., *The Black Panthers Speak*, 167.  See also, Huey P. Newton, *The Genius of Huey P. Newton, Minister of Defense, Black Panther Party* (San Francisco: Ministry of Information, Black Panther Party, n.d.), 28.

# LIBERATION

For decades, the San Francisco Bay Area, and the nation, would reel from the aftershocks of the Black Revolution. As the country's urban crisis worsened during the 1970s and 1980s, social scientists and community activists continued to wrestle with the perplexing legacies left behind by the Age of Aquarius. Many scholars have attempted to solve the riddle of persistent urban poverty, and their answers range from the absence of individual responsibility, the failure of the welfare state, the persistence of racism, and the structural changes in the American economy after the 1960s. Perhaps the most promising scholarly efforts, however, are those that probe the history of America's urban collapse and trace the long decline of our nation's cities. One noted critic has recently argued that "it is only through the complex and interwoven histories of race, residence, and work in the postwar era that the state of today's cities and their impoverished residents can be fully understood and confronted." An examination into the history of African American communities in the San Francisco Bay Area illuminates how and why black poverty became a fixture of urban life in northern California, and an understanding of the origins of the Black Panther Party reveals the limitations and nature of black responses to the urban crisis.[1]

## THE LIMITS OF RADICAL REFORM

The Black Panther Party owed its meteoric rise and rapid fall to its own militancy. The Panthers' rhetoric and actions attracted the attention of the media, African American citizens, and the law enforcement establishment. While their sensational news coverage brought the BPP support and donations from the white left as well as many members of Bay Area black communities, the Panthers also invited the scrutiny of local, state, and federal police forces with their apocalyptic denunciations of white capitalist America. Although Andrew Young of the Southern Christian Leadership Conference was essentially correct when he noted that the Panthers had no support "until they became the victims of the persecution campaign of the FBI," the party's sensational conflicts with law enforcement officials cost the Panthers dearly, and they easily lost more in blood and treasure than they gained by being the lead story on the evening news. Frequent arrests and violent shoot-outs with police drained the Panthers' war chest and their membership rolls, and the instability created by the shadow of death that hung over the party's headquarters derailed the Panthers' efforts to solidify their position in black communities across the United States. After assessing the toll of the Panthers' conflicts with law enforcement officials, one scholar noted that "the immediate impact of the domestic war against the Black Panther Party was nothing short of internal chaos."[2]

In the San Francisco Bay Area, black community-police relations had been on a downward spiral since the Second World War, and they continued to deteriorate during the late 1960s. Although the Panthers did occupy much of the police establishment's attention during the final days of the decade, white police officers still found time to brutalize other African American citizens. In July 1968, for example, two white officers of the Oakland Police Department beat George Woods after they had taken him to the police station in handcuffs. Alarmed, a black police officer intervened and stopped the beating. Although Police Chief Thomas J. Cahill insisted that the incident was an isolated case and he promised a thorough investigation, one witness noted that "the tenseness of the situation might have exploded into an incident where police officers would have been shooting their fellow officers." In San Francisco the following year, Mr. and Mrs. Wayland Fuller, a prominent middle-class black couple who owned a drugstore on Third Street, accused officers from the city's TAC Squad of beating them and their daughter, Wayzel, following a minor traffic accident outside of their home. Officer James G. Aligo later admitted spraying Mace into Wayzel Fuller's face when he was trying to force her into the paddy wagon. Local black leaders condemned the episode, and the leading black newspaper warned that such events could spark riots in the city: "The 37.4 per cent of the population of San Francisco which is racial minority feel insecure in their homes and in their persons when confronted by the San Francisco police department. The Fuller incident has resulted in conversation. Beware of the possibility of fire next time!" It is not surprising, then, that members of the Black Panther Party and officers of Bay Area police departments attacked each other with such vigor from the time the Panthers first started their armed patrols of Oakland in 1966.[3]

The national law enforcement campaign against the Black Panther Party was perhaps even more alarming than the conflicts in the Bay Area. Although the figures are difficult to verify, several scholars have reported that in 1969 alone, at least ten Black Panthers died in confrontations with the police and more than three hundred were arrested. The police tactic of using frequent arrests to deplete the Panthers' financial resources was very successful, and in one two-year period, the national office paid out more than $200,000 in bail bond premiums to secure the release of party members from jails across the country. The Federal Bureau of Investigation (FBI) coordinated many of the police actions against the Black Panther Party as part of its massive counterintelligence program (COINTELPRO). J. Edgar Hoover was particularly disturbed by the Panthers, and he sought to use his agents to harass, intimidate, and ultimately destroy the BPP. The FBI exploited the tensions between the Black Panthers and other militant black nationalist groups, especially Ron Karenga's Los Angeles-based United Slaves (US), and they provoked confrontations between Black Power leaders that sometimes erupted into violence. By the summer of 1969, the Black Panther Party was "the target of 233 out of 296 total counterintelligence operations directed at African American political groups," and the FBI continued to press forward in the hope that it could undermine the stability of the BPP.[4]

Although the party faced serious opposition from established law enforcement agencies throughout its tumultuous history, the main causes for its collapse came from within its own institutional culture. Despite their militant rhetoric and claims that they would recreate society and ensure equality, the Panthers' approach contained serious flaws that circumscribed their abilities to bring about revolutionary change. Bounded by sexism and hindered by their violent imagery, the Panthers failed to transcend their humble origins. The Black Panther Party was the product of years of racial conflict in the San Francisco Bay Area and it drew upon decades of black protest to shape its message and build a limited base of support among African Americans. The Panthers ultimately failed, however, to win their war against racism, and they have left a mixed legacy for future generations of black activists. Two of the most troubling of these factors were the sexism that pervaded the party and the Panthers' use of violent rhetoric and violent action in their struggle for self-determination.

Instead of uniting them, sex split the Panthers apart. Sexism plagued the relationships between men and women, black and white, in many of the organizations of the Civil Rights Movement, the Black Power Movement, and the New Left, and the Black Panther Party was no exception. Stokely Carmichael's infamous quip that "the only position for women in the Movement is prone," was parroted by Chaka Walls, a Panther from the Illinois chapter: "the way women contribute [to the revolution] is getting laid." Many male advocates of Black Power sought to destroy the image of the emasculated black man and counter the widely held idea that black matriarchs dominated black families and black communities. Reasserting the superiority of husbands and fathers, young black male radicals often focused on gender relationships when confronting the issue of perceived black family instability and the "tangle of pathology" that supposedly plagued low-income African American communities. In July 1967, for example, the National Conference on Black Power issued a set of resolutions on "Black Women and the Home," and the largely male delegates advocated "that intensified efforts and programs be evolved to stabilize the Black family Unit by emphasizing emotional security, protection, |and| love and respect for each family member." The conference attendees also announced that the major role for African American women would be as schoolteachers for future revolutionary generations: "That as sisters, mothers, teachers, and nation builders, Black women be committed to learning, understanding and perpetuating our Black Heritage." The Black Revolution thus began with the reactionary mandate that African American women play supporting roles in the upcoming drama.[5]

For many Black Panthers, the revolution they sought was about much more than destroying the American capitalist superstructure; it was about recreating themselves as black individuals and as a black people. Likewise, for many of the "young warriors" drawn into the party, the struggle was about redefining themselves as *black men*. Influenced by the mania surrounding the 1965 *Moynihan Report*, many Black Power adherents concluded that the path to black male power was blocked, in part, by African American females who succeeded in a society predicated upon the impotence of black men. Huey Newton reflected that the black man "feels that he is something less than a man.... Often his wife...is the breadwinner. He is, therefore, viewed as quite worthless by his wife and children. He is ineffectual both in and out of the home. He cannot provide for, or protect his family.... Society will not acknowledge him as a man." The quest to regain black manhood was an essential driving force behind the Black Power Movement, and it brought a flood of young black men into the Black Panther Party offices. "We shall have our manhood," declared Eldridge Cleaver. "We shall have it or the earth will be leveled by our attempts to gain it." Panther symbolism and speech appealed to what one female critic of the Black Power Movement has called "Black Macho," and the BPP's revolutionary imagery, including guns, uniforms, "Power to the People" signs, and even the great black panther, was created by black men largely for other black men.[6]

Revolution allowed African American men to assert their masculinity. Killing the white oppressor, according to Eldridge Cleaver, was a way for them "to achieve their manhood," and "to experience themselves as men." The young ghetto toughs who joined the ranks of the Panther drills and marched in formation with "Free Huey!" flags near the Alameda County Courthouse were showing their own strength and prowess, much like the police officers who stood clasping nightsticks opposite them. These shows of strength occasionally erupted into violence, as Panthers and police traded blows and gunshots on the cold stone streets of Oakland, Chicago, and New York. Although Newton later claimed that "the Party acted as it did because we *were* men," the BPP undoubtedly attracted much enthusiasm from young urban black males because it allowed them to play the roles of liberating soldier and defender of the community. By standing up to face white oppression and bearing arms to resist it, these righteous black warriors were, in their own eyes at least, reclaiming a fundamental part of their self-esteem, indeed a part of their soul. In short, "manhood was essential to revolution...."[7]

While in one sense this self-affirmation of the urban black male perhaps had a positive effect on the self-esteem of the revolutionary youth, the cult of "Black Macho" rested ultimately upon the subordination of black women. According to the party line, the sexualized racism of the oppressor's capitalist system had masculinized black women and stripped them of their identity. In part, the BPP's own sexualized propaganda reflected a desire to restore femininity to black women. The images of such idealized revolutionary sisters as Kathleen Cleaver fostered, perhaps unwittingly on the part of the women involved, the supersexual ideal of black women in the party, and made a striking contrast to other women civil rights leaders like Fannie Lou Hamer or Ella Baker. Kathleen Cleaver was for many Panthers the epitome of revolutionary womanhood. Ironically, her own image was one of a dedicated radical with a very soft feminine side. Her large, but well-kept, afro and her striking physical beauty only reinforced the sexual nature of black women and created a super-feminine counterpart to the super-masculine revolutionary warrior role filled by black men. The feminine glamour embodied in such women Panthers as Cleaver, Elaine Brown, Assata Shakur, and Gwen Fountaine gave them some modicum of power, but it was a power based upon sexual exploitation by and of women and not upon the ideals of revolutionary equality.[8]

The sexual separation of revolutionary imagery was echoed in the BPP's sexual division of labor. Although some women, such as Elaine Brown and Kathleen Cleaver, rose to positions of power and authority in the Black Panther Party, most female Panthers continued to work in traditionally feminine sex-typed employment, such as cooking and cleaning up at Panther meetings, doing secretarial chores, and running the BPP's Liberation School and many of its Community Survival Programs. Although they had long been responsible for operating the Survival Programs and overseeing the day-to-day operations of the BPP, it was not until the early 1970s, after the Panthers had passed their zenith and begun to decline, that women assumed real positions of authority in the party. Even prominent women like Kathleen Cleaver frequently faced the obstacle of male chauvinism, and she later recalled that during party meetings "*if* I *suggested* [an idea], the suggestion might be rejected; if they were suggested by a man the suggestion would be implemented. It seemed throughout the history of my working with the Party, I always had to struggle with this.... The suggestion itself was never viewed objectively. The fact that the suggestion came from a woman gave it some lesser value." Women's roles were seen in a surprisingly traditional light by the male members of the revolutionary organization, and the quest for black male identity did not always lead to a similar quest for black female identity. "Black Macho allowed for only the most primitive notion of women," said radical critic Michele Wallace, "women as possessions, women as the spoils of war, leaving black women with no resale value." Unfortunately, the male Panthers were not carving out a very large role in the new black community for their revolutionary sisters.[9]

The only productive role for women in the party, at least so far as many male Panthers were concerned, was a reproductive one. Female Panthers were to use sex as a weapon, both to bear more revolutionaries and to seduce and destroy the enemy. Communal family structures encouraged Panther women to get pregnant quickly and often to replace those brave revolutionary soldiers (men) killed in the course of the struggle. Both Elaine Brown and Assata Shakur, in good radical fashion, bore revolutionary babies, ironically both of them daughters, although each certainly felt great affection toward their children and their children's fathers.

Similarly, women were to use their "pussy power" to destroy white men, who were irresistibly attracted to them, by manipulating their own sexual attractiveness and the oppressors' insatiable lust for black flesh.  Women's roles were thus circumscribed by the sexist attitudes and stereotypes held by the male leadership of the Black Panther Party.  These destructive sexist notions undermined the Panthers' goals and meant that they would have to fight the great revolution for international liberation with one hand behind their back.  "Perhaps the single most important reason the Black Movement did not work," concluded Wallace, "was that black men did not realize they could not wage struggle without the full involvement of women."[10]

Not only were they denied equal participation in the party, but black women also suffered considerable emotional and physical abuse at the hands of their revolutionary brothers.  Women faced continual discriminatory treatment and attitudes.  They did different jobs, participated differently in protests, and, according to Elaine Brown, the BPP even indoctrinated its new recruits according to gender, separating and training men and women differently. The male Panther leadership ignored the discontent of the women members, and when harassment increased in the early 1970s, many women, including Regina Davis, Ericka Huggins, Norma Armour, Phyllis Jackson, and even Elaine Brown, left the party.  The "macho cult" that dominated the upper echelons of the party structure disillusioned many women activists and further soured male-female relationships.  Physical abuse at the hands of male Panthers destroyed what little peace was left between the sexes, and although "nobody said it,...it was understood that the Panther was a man."  Despite the insistence of such leaders as Newton and Seale that the Panthers were not sexist and that they were indeed in touch with women's rights and concerns, the Black Panther Party has left a sorry legacy of male chauvinism and callous and brutal treatment of black women.  The panther's roar was the voice of a man.[11]

The Panthers' roar was also the voice of rage.  The party leaders' militant rhetoric was fueled by the years of frustration and anger that African Americans had felt since the end of the Second World War.  Black residents of the Bay Area were understandably enraged by the decades of inequality, discrimination, segregation, and brutality that characterized their dealings with many of their white counterparts. During the late 1960s, many radical black leaders from Stokely Carmichael to H. Rap Brown voiced this rage, but no one was more effective at expressing the anxiety and energy of the younger generation than the Black Panthers. Few African American militants had been bold enough to display loaded guns in public, and the Panthers even used their weapons to patrol police in black neighborhoods in the East Bay. The party's internal culture was as infested with this revolutionary zeal as was their public persona. Panthers who were killed while defending the black community from the "racist, pig oppressors" were lionized by their fellow revolutionaries, and the party created its own Valhalla of slain black warriors that included fallen comrades Bobby Hutton, John Huggins, Alprentice "Bunchy" Carter, Fred Hampton, Mark Clark, and others. Ultimately, this violent militancy was not an effective means to achieve the goals the Panthers stated in their Ten Point Platform and Program.[12]

The Panthers' violent image was reinforced by their brutal rhetoric, especially that which spewed forth from the mouth of Eldridge Cleaver. Punctuated with constant obscenities, Cleaver's verbal style often annoyed party leaders and others who felt that such violent language only alienated older blacks in the community. Bobby Seale's mother told her son, "well, I like everything that Eldridge is saying. And he's right. He's telling them the truth. But I wish he wouldn't cuss so much.... I respect him. I understand why he cusses those low-down politicians out. Still, I do wish he'd stop cussin' just a little bit." Cleaver's speech could be a barrier against effective communication with the black community, and it could get him into trouble with high-ranking government officials. Cleaver had a long ongoing verbal war with California Governor Ronald Reagan, and once the minister of information threatened to beat the governor "to death with a marshmallow." On two occasions in October 1968, Cleaver challenged Reagan to a duel and insulted the governor's bravery and manhood. "I think you are a cowardly, craven-hearted wretch," Cleaver announced to a startled crowd. "You are not a man. You are a punk.... Walk, chicken, with your ass picked clean." While this type of speech might attract media attention and fan the flames of radical energy, in the end it was self-defeating because it detracted from the humanitarian message the Panthers were trying to send via their Community Survival Programs and their alliances with such groups as the Peace and Freedom Party, the Student Nonviolent Coordinating Committee, the Young Lords, and the Young Patriots.[13]

The revolutionary art that adorned issues of the party's newspaper, *The Black Panther*, also promoted the Panthers' violent image. Emory Douglas, the party's minister of culture and the main artist for *The Black Panther*, caricatured the figure of "U.S. Imperialism" in numerous drawings as a giant pig or rat often toting a machine gun, or being pursued and attacked by black revolutionary warriors empowered by the fury of firearms. In many such drawings, the corrupt power of capitalist wealth is turned against itself with the liberating force of captured guns. "So, here is where we began to create our revolutionary art," explained Douglas. "We draw pictures of our brothers with stoner guns with one bullet going through forty pigs taking out their intestines along the way...." Such propaganda was to inspire black youth by filling them with pride and by weakening the Establishment in their eyes through degrading and insulting portrayals of the bestial nature of capitalist goons. The liberating power of the gun, when properly used, promised to free black America from the yoke of exploitation and ensure the safety and security of the black community. The effectiveness of such tactics was limited, however, and the Panthers' decision to employ paramilitary and violent imagery in their newspaper and other forms of propaganda was a poor one. The radical community organizer Saul Alinsky cajoled the Panthers for their apocalyptic rhetoric, and he noted that "they haven't got the numbers and they know nothing about revolutionary tactics. What kind of revolutionary is it who shouts that all power comes out of the muzzle of a gun when he knows damn well the other side's got all the guns?" Acknowledging the brashness of carrying loaded firearms in public, Bobby Seale later admitted that the Panthers' use of guns was possibly counterproductive. "We knew that if we went out there and dealt with the issues straight up, particularly police brutality, which was a hot issue then, very very hot,...that we could attract the attention of young brothers and sisters, that's what we believed," he explained. "And a lot of people were skeptical. And I can't blame them when I look back on it."[14]

Although the Panthers could credit their militant image with bringing them unparalleled media coverage and public attention, the violent legacy that the party created was a large factor in its demise. Not only did the Panthers bring down upon their heads the wrath of local and federal law enforcement agencies, but they also alienated a substantial segment of the black population with their apocalyptic pronouncements and their frequent armed clashes with the police. Most African Americans remained dedicated to the nonviolent beliefs espoused by Martin Luther King, Jr., and relatively few subscribed to the view that race relations had reached the point where only a shoot-out would solve their problems. After the Panthers' "gunslinger invasion" of the California Assembly in the spring of 1967, the *Sun-Reporter* warned that "this truly astonishing caper probably did more harm than good for the Negro's cause in general and civil rights in particular.... [A]cross the country in ghetto after ghetto, black young-turk militants are chuckling with glee over the exploit and may be emboldened to try something similar, regardless of consequences. There's the rub...." The consequences of this behavior were indeed severe. Not only did their "cult of violence" send many Panthers to the morgue, but it also redefined the debate over race in America and fed white fears of armed black men eager to destroy the nation. More than two decades of racial struggle reached a momentary climax with the radicalism of the Black Panther Party in the late 1960s. The controversy surrounding the Panthers would not bring a meaningful or a peaceful resolution to African Americans' search for civil liberties or racial equality in the Bay Area or the nation. Indeed, after the tumultuous final days of the 1960s, African Americans would be faced with many of the same old problems and a host of new ones. The race war that began in the Bay Area during the Second World War is unfortunately far from over.[15]

## POPULAR SUPPORT FOR THE BLACK PANTHER PARTY

Even if male and female Panthers had equally joined together in a chorus of denunciation against the evils of capitalist America, they could not have toppled Wall Street. A small band of armed revolutionaries constantly harried by police and the FBI, the Panthers captured national attention more because of their style than because they actually threatened "the internal security of the country." Americans have never done very well in supporting radical, much less revolutionary, movements, and despite romantic expressions to the contrary, the Sixties proved the rule rather than the exception. Now and again, disgruntled groups and idealistic visionaries take up radical doctrines and join social movements, but once initial needs are met or substantial problems arise, then much of the radical support fades back into the woodwork. With the Panthers, there is also a substantial question of how much support they won in the first place. Despite the turmoil of the 1960s, black America was not radicalizing as fast as were many of the point-man civil rights groups. While organizations like the Student Nonviolent Coordinating Committee (SNCC) and the Congress of Racial Equality (CORE) were ejecting their white membership and embracing the doctrine of black separatism and other organizations like the Black Panther Party were advocating international socialist revolution, most African Americans were dearly holding on to the principles of nonviolent action and integration. They remained true to the dream of Martin Luther King, Jr., even in the nightmarish final days of the decade.

A series of *Newsweek*-Gallup polls from 1963-1969 shows that black public opinion remained surprisingly steady throughout the period. Some of the old-guard civil rights organizations, such as the National Association for the Advancement of Colored People (NAACP), were beginning to lose support among the nation's black population, but no other groups were clearly replacing the void they left. Regional and age differences did mark these results from the survey, as the NAACP did best among older, poor southern blacks, but most African Americans still viewed these groups favorably. Importantly, however, Martin Luther King, Jr., scored remarkably well on all three of the surveys, and his name actually gained support after his assassination in 1968. There were no appreciable regional, age, or income level differences among those black Americans who favored King, and by 1969, over nine out of ten rated him as "pretty good" or "excellent." Many civil rights activists and Black Power advocates may have radicalized late in the decade, but the results from the *Newsweek* polls suggest that the majority of the black population, while frustrated, remained true to the original goals of the Civil Rights Movement.[16]

At the very least, most African Americans did not support the leading militant Black Power organizations to the degree that media airplay of such figures as Stokely Carmichael, Eldridge Cleaver, or H. Rap Brown might suggest. The public's response to Carmichael solidified between 1966 and 1969, but the number of those *dis*approving of his tactics and person actually increased in greater proportion than did the number of those supporting SNCC's radical leader. Nearly half of the respondents thought that Carmichael was "only fair" or "poor" in 1969, and less than one-third rated him as high as King. His supporters were nearly evenly divided between the North and the South, although he scored appreciably better among younger respondents than among older blacks. Even with this latter group, however, northern respondents split evenly between favoring and opposing Carmichael, and southern blacks were slightly more skeptical of the Black Power prophet. SNCC, Carmichael's now radical organization, scored a little better than its troubled leader, but those African Americans surveyed by the Gallup Organization did not rate it as highly as either the NAACP or CORE in any of the polls, and many respondents remained undecided about the student-led group. It received roughly the same support or opposition in both the North and South, and age and class differences were not strongly reflected in the results. The Black Power generation was still struggling outside the mainstream of both black and white America at the end of the decade, and considering the demise of many Black Power organizations in the early 1970s, the chances that any of these groups had for radicalizing a majority of African Americans seem remarkably slim.[17]

Even the great radical figure Malcolm X did not fare well with black America in 1969. Over one-third of those polled were unsure about his impact on race relations in the United States, and more than half of those who did offer an opinion gave an unfavorable assessment. One in five blacks gave the former minister from the Nation of Islam a "poor" rating, and fourteen percent more said that he was "only fair." Malcolm X received the most support from northern youth, capturing high marks from more than half of the under-30 population. This approval from young northern blacks was markedly better than the response given for Malcolm X's old teacher-turned-nemesis Elijah Muhammad, leader of the Black Muslims, but in terms of overall performance, both generated similar responses from the black public at large. Racial separatism and militant self-defense were not selling well in black America.[18]

The Black Panther Party, the "heirs of Malcolm X" and liberators of the black ghetto, fared little better in black public opinion. Their greatest support came from middle-income young northern blacks, but even among this group feelings were mixed. In 1969, about one in three northern blacks under 30 stated that the party was "excellent" or "pretty good." An equal amount of the same group, however, gave the BPP negative marks, and the final third were unsure about the effect the party would have on racism in America. Of the total sample polled, only five percent gave the Panthers full support, and more than one in five thought the BPP was undermining the black struggle. The Black Panther Party fared somewhat better in a survey of black high-school students conducted by social scientists in 1970, and more than half of the young African Americans reported that the Panthers were successful in "developing black pride." The supporters of the Black Panther Party were more likely than their classmates to support black separatism and "guerilla warfare," and less likely to have faith in non-violence, white Americans, and their own chances for personal success. Although the students split their support almost evenly between the BPP and the NAACP, the survey coordinators concluded that "the widespread support which the Panthers received is but the surface manifestation of widespread and perhaps explosive alienation among black youth in...cities in which the Panthers have gained...support." In the *Newsweek* survey, by contrast, more than one-half of the African American population were "not sure" about their attitudes toward the party, which was hardly auspicious news for the Panther leadership. The BPP did only marginally better than the black separatist Nation of Islam, although more African Americans actually disapproved of the Black Muslims than they did the Black Panther Party. Although the Panthers had "picked up the gun" and shot back at the "pigs," this brazen, if courageous, act had not endeared them to the black majority. Few African Americans, indeed, had strayed far from the path begun with *Brown v. Board of Education* in 1954, and most still followed the spiritual lead of Martin Luther King, Jr.[19]

In 1969, African Americans still preferred nonviolence as the main tactic to gain equality. Few blacks agreed that they would have to resort to violence to achieve civil rights, and this attitude had changed little since early in the decade despite the mounting tensions in the middle and late 1960s. The assassinations of Malcolm X and Martin Luther King, Jr., had not turned blacks away from their peaceful demonstrations or hardened them to callously accept violence as the solution to their problems. In fact, most blacks felt that they had "more to lose" by striking against white oppression with violence rather than with love. Contrary to the hopes of many Panthers, the poorest blacks in both the North and South most adamantly opposed violent means, with seven out of ten affirming their commitment to the policies of nonviolent protest. The poorest blacks from both regions also stated that they would not join a riot or loot local businesses during times of civil disorder, in nearly equal proportions as they had rejected violent tactics. Unlike the young activists in SNCC, the BPP, and CORE, most African Americans apparently did not radicalize in the late 1960s, and they did not support those groups who pushed beyond what they felt was best for themselves or their community.[20]

Support for black protest also faded throughout the decade as fewer blacks agreed that they would participate in demonstrations and boycotts, or that they were willing to go to jail. A majority still conceded that they would "stop buying at a store" that discriminated against blacks, but the tide of protest was ebbing. Younger blacks still remained the most enthusiastic about protest, but the poor were less inclined to strike against the system than were the middle class. Furthermore, all groups, northern and southern, young and old, poor and middle class, thought that arming themselves was foolish and self-destructive. Only about a quarter of African Americans were willing to endorse owning guns, a remarkable statement in favor of King's philosophy and against the revolutionary ideology of the Black Panther Party. The clarion call for revolutionary action issued by the Panthers went largely unheed by the mass of black America. The young radicals' attempts to rebuild the black community and save it from the oppression of vile capitalist control did not meet the needs or concerns of the majority of black people. Although the Panthers were sincere in their commitment to recreating American society for the benefit of all peoples, their actions and their words did not strike a chord in the minds of those they sought to liberate.[21]

## LEGACIES

By the 1990s, the Black Panthers had returned to the public spotlight, and it seems that this particular cat might indeed have nine lives. A spate of books, a major motion picture, a scholarly conference in Atlanta, newspaper articles and letters to the editor, the release of ex-Panther Geronimo Pratt from prison, and even a Black Panther Party Legacy bus tour of the party's former stomping grounds in West Oakland have rekindled interest in these African American radicals and spurred conversations about their impact upon American society and American history. The Panthers have continued to amaze observers since the early days of their armed invasion of the California Assembly to protest a gun-control bill and their notorious shoot-outs with police SWAT teams that would leave city streets littered with spent ammunition casings, broken glass, and sometimes even corpses. The story of the Black Panther Party is one filled with hope and promise as well as fear and weakness; it is part triumph and part tragedy, and its telling is fraught with complexities and paradoxes. In the end, the great black cat that reared its head out of the ghettos of the San Francisco Bay Area in the 1960s remains as elusive as ever, yet its great paw print has made an indelible impression upon the sands of our past.

Calling for full employment, decent housing, non-racist public education, and an end to police brutality against African Americans, the Panthers opened their first office on the corner of 56th and Grove streets in the heart of Oakland's black community. For the next several years, the Panthers established chapters across the country, from San Francisco to Chicago to New York, and as their membership approached its zenith of around 5,000 young revolutionaries, they fell further into furious and deadly combat with federal and state law enforcement officials. High-profile shoot-outs between police and the Panthers in 1967 and 1968 sent leaders Huey P. Newton and Eldridge Cleaver to jail and numerous other Panthers to the morgue. The conflicts between the knights in blue and the revolutionaries in black quickly drained the party's treasury, and it diverted attention away from the Panthers' Community Survival Programs, like the Free Breakfast for Children Program, and focused the nation's eyes on the violent aspects of the Black Panther Party. By the mid-1970s, the party's energies had dissipated, and chapters around the nation fell into decline or shut down altogether. In the early 1980s, the last of the Panthers' projects, the Oakland Community School, closed its doors and the party faded into memory. The leading organization of the Black Power Movement burned brilliantly for several years in the late 1960s and early 1970s, yet the Black Panther Party has left a mixed legacy for a nation still divided by the ghosts of the Civil Rights Movement and the Vietnam War.[22]

The Panthers have become a symbol for the social and political revolutions that occurred three decades ago. For the defenders of the 1960s, the Panthers represent all that was good from an age of grass-roots activism. A. A. Elmore, a retired insurance agent who recently participated in the Black Panther Legacy bus tour, noted that "Things have changed a great deal for the better since the 1960s, and it was groups like the Panthers who helped change them." The Black Panthers sacrificed themselves for the good of the whole community. They created survival programs, including the Free Breakfast for Children Programs and the Free Health Clinics, and they stood up to an oppressive police state that had beaten civil rights demonstrators in Birmingham and murdered anti-war demonstrators at Kent State. Several scholars have suggested that the Panthers' Community Survival Programs were so popular and successful that they spurred the federal government to institute such programs at the national level. Particularly praiseworthy were the party's campaign against sickle-cell anemia, which first brought that issue to the nation's attention, and the Panthers' breakfast for schoolchildren program, which is often improperly credited with spurring the Department of Education into establishing the breakfast and lunch programs in America's public schools. Furthermore, the party's champions argue, the Panthers helped to foster a sense of black pride and African American cohesiveness that is one of the most important legacies of the Black Power Movement.[23]

The critics of the Black Panther Party, on the other hand, see the Panthers as a symbol of the excesses of the 1960s, and they paint the black revolutionaries as glorified ghetto hoodlums. Some writers point to the party's ties to the drug trade in Oakland and its affiliations with underworld crime figures in the 1970s and 1980s. Others stand in horror at the Panthers' eagerness to confront the police and shoot at the largely white ranks of the defenders of the public. Two of the party's staunchest critics, David Horowitz and Peter Collier, have written books denouncing the Panthers and tying them to the murder of several police officers, a black prostitute, and a bookkeeper for the radical Berkeley magazine, *Ramparts*. Another critic, the son of the judge who presided over the infamous Panther 21 case in New York, recently denounced the Panthers' "legacy of crime and terror," and he insinuated that the party tried to bomb his home to stop the conviction of Panthers indicted in a conspiracy to blow up several buildings in downtown New York City. Finally, Hugh Pearson, a black journalist who penned a criminal exposé entitled *The Shadow of the Panther*, denounced the party's defenders and lambasted their attempts to praise the Panthers for their Free Breakfast for Children Program: "Given the way the group's romantics are fond of trotting out that accomplishment as a major legacy," Pearson wrote, "one would think that no African American had ever thought of feeding people for free before the Panthers. What do they think African American churches had been doing for so many years?"[24]

The truth about the Black Panther Party lies somewhere in between these two extremes. The Panthers both strengthened and weakened the Black Power Movement, and their actions sometimes propelled and sometimes hindered African American progress toward the goal of equality and self-determination. In cultural, political, economic, and social terms, the party affected the course of recent American history and shaped the destiny of African American communities across the nation.

One of the most enduring legacies of the Black Panthers was their contribution to African American culture. Among historians, the Black Panthers are most often applauded for creating a new image of black men and women during the 1960s and 1970s. The familiar old stereotypes of Uncle Tom, Mammy, Sambo, and Jezebel were supplanted by images of proud black warriors and righteous revolutionary women who were both fiercely independent and dedicated to the needs of the community. The Black Panthers did in political terms what Muhammad Ali did in the boxing ring, what James Brown and Aretha Franklin did on Motown records, and what Richard Roundtree did on the big screen as Shaft. Eldridge Cleaver, Angela Davis, Huey Newton, Kathleen Cleaver, and Bobby Seale created a new revolutionary style that incorporated afros, African American dress, and ghetto language, and they offered young urban blacks a counter to the staid formality of Martin Luther King, Jr., and other traditional civil rights leaders. The Panthers' image was built upon race pride, defiance of white authority, and black nationalism; ideas of Black Power that pressed beyond the boundaries of a campaign against segregation and toward a movement for full equality and self determination. The Panthers' challenge to traditionalism was wildly popular among the younger generation of African Americans, who were the most willing to adopt the new style offered by the Black Power revolutionaries. A colleague recently told me of a trip he took to San Francisco in the late 1960s, where he met two young black boys playing with toy guns. He asked the kids if they were playing cops and robbers or cowboys and Indians, and one of the boys enthusiastically replied, "No, we're playing pigs and Panthers!" The new images of black men and women permeated most levels of popular culture and African American life, and the new black aesthetic that the Panthers helped to create redefined the cultural landscape of African America.[25]

The images produced by the Black Panthers were not wholly positive, however. The tendency of Panther leaders to appear in public with shotguns and bandoleers of shells casually strung across their shoulders tainted everything that the party did with the hint of brutality and violence. Indeed, the Panthers did much to reinforce old white fears of uncontrolled, rampaging armed black men, and often the Panthers derailed any chance of civilized conversation by appearing with a small arsenal in tow. The Panthers' use of the gun as a symbol of black masculinity and black liberation perhaps also contributed to the prevalence of violence in contemporary urban black culture and fanned the flames of the gangsta image that has left Huey Newton, Bobby Hutton, Tupac Shakur, and the Notorious B.I.G. dead in its wake. Even more troubling is the overt male chauvinism that is also a large component of the Panthers' revolutionary image. The absurd and insulting notion of "making babies for the revolution" coupled with the resistance to black female leadership eroded the bonds of trust and respect that were necessary to bind together black men and women during the height of the Black Revolution. The vilification of black womanhood and the creation of a super-virile black masculinity not only undercut the potency of the movement in the 1960s and 1970s, but it has left an enduring legacy of mistrust and misunderstanding between black men and women that still clouds such recent events as the Million Man March and the Clarence Thomas-Anita Hill hearings. Many of the cultural images created by the Black Panthers stand in testament of how not to run a revolution.

Politically speaking, the Black Panthers had a major effect upon both local and national events. In the early 1970s when the Panthers began to reassess their approach to community reform in Oakland, the party forged a coalition with other African American groups to register black voters and place black candidates on the ballot for local and national office. Building a movement similar to the Freedom Summer drive in the rural South during 1964, the Panthers went door-to-door to contact prospective black voters and enlist their support for a progressive slate of candidates who promised reform for the inner cities. The Black Panther Party was part of the resurgence of African American political power in America's urban cores from Oakland to Detroit to Atlanta to Washington; D. C. Some Panther leaders even ran for office in a sincere attempt to combat the system from within and take power from city hall and return it to neighborhood centers, street corners, and community meeting places across the black community. Bobby Seale and Elaine Brown lost by very narrow margins when they ran unsuccessfully for mayor and city council, respectively, but their energies spurred interest in politics throughout East Bay African American communities. Several years later, the Panthers helped elect the city's first black mayor, Lionel Wilson, and they were a firm base of support for the area's black congressman, Ron Dellums.[26]

On the national scene, however, the Panthers' effect on political affairs was less positive. Although one scholar has argued that the Panthers formed a "positive radical flank effect" during the 1960s and 1970s, which forced established white political leaders to deal with more moderate groups such as the National Association for the Advancement of Colored People (NAACP) or the Southern Christian Leadership Conference (SCLC), the ultimate result of the radicalism of groups like the Black Panther Party was to undermine support for the liberal government of Lyndon Johnson, derail social reform programs like the War on Poverty, and usher in an age of conservative dominance in the White House that began with Richard Nixon in 1968. White suburban voters in the North and West were alarmed by the pronouncements of Black Power figures like Huey Newton and H. Rap Brown, and they quickly tired of the rhetoric of revolution. As Watts, Newark, Detroit, and New York burned, whites flinched away from America's racial crisis and demanded a return to "law and order." Although the Panthers pressed for solutions to the crises facing urban African Americans in the late 1960s, their radicalism swept away the foundations of the limited reforms the liberals were willing to offer. The age of experimentation in the War on Poverty with innovative ideas like the Community Action Program was replaced by the numbing compromise of inadequate transfer payment programs like Aid to Families with Dependent Children (AFDC). Ironically, the champions of community action in the ghetto sabotaged the federal programs that might have helped restore some measure of self-determination to inner-city African American communities. The legacy of black radicalism instead pushed politicians' energies away from a War on Poverty and toward a War on Welfare.[27]

Finally, the Black Panthers forever changed the meaning of black nationalism. Huey Newton and Bobby Seale were influenced by the ideas and actions of earlier black nationalists, from Marcus Garvey to Malcolm X, and the Black Panther Party's early years reflect this tradition of self-sufficiency and self-defense. The Panthers exerted considerable energies to create or strengthen

African American institutions and organizations that would support the freedom struggle of black Americans. Eventually, the party also embraced a black *inter*nationalism, which connected the struggles of colored peoples in North American with their compatriots in Latin America, Africa, and Asia. The Black Panther Party fostered the growth of pan-Africanism and interest in the Third World, and the party's newspaper included a sizable international news section that kept its readers informed of conditions and major events around the world. The Panthers never fully solved the riddle, however, of how to create a viable national or international movement that would pose a significant challenge to the powers they were trying so desperately to overthrow. Tangling with the complex causes of poverty ultimately proved more daunting than trading shots with the police, and the Panthers were unable to translate their desires for a unified black movement into a workable reality. Not enough African Americans cast their lot with the black nationalists, and in the end, the Panthers failed to spark the revolution that they hoped would bring all power to the people.[28]

The two young black men who met in the back room of an Oakland anti-poverty center in the fall of 1966 hoped to unleash a revolution that would wash away centuries of oppression and bring freedom to their people. Although their efforts failed, their history, and the histories of those people who stood for and against them, can still tell us much about our past, something about the present, and perhaps even give us a sense of direction for the future. We need not, and we should not, look to the Black Panther Party for heroes and saints, for we will probably find none. Part of what the Panthers did was motivated by altruism and racial pride; part of it was tainted by lawlessness, super machismo, and violence. The Panthers remind us that the Civil Rights Era was not one of undisputed triumph, and that we still face considerable challenges in our nation's persistent urban crisis. Indeed, for African Americans, there is still a long way to go on the road to freedom.

# Notes

1.   The quotation is from Thomas J. Sugrue, *The Origins of the Urban Crisis: Race and Inequality in Postwar Detroit* (Princeton: Princeton University Press, 1996), 5.   For representative arguments that explain the causes of the urban crisis in terms of a failure of individual responsibility, the corruption of the welfare state, the persistence of racism in the United States, and severe structural changes in America's economy, see, respectively, Lawrence M. Mead, *Beyond Entitlement: The Social Obligations of Citizenship* (New York: Free Press, 1986); Charles Murray, *Losing Ground: American Social Policy, 1950–1980* (New York: Basic Books, 1984); Jill Quadagno, *The Color of Welfare: How Racism Undermined the War on Poverty* (New York: Oxford University Press, 1994); and William Julius Wilson, *The Truly Disadvantaged: The Inner City, the Underclass, and Public Policy* (Chicago: University of Chicago Press, 1987); and Wilson, *When Work Disappears: The World of the New Urban Poor* (New York: Alfred A. Knopf, 1996).   For historical treatments of the development of the urban crisis, see Sugrue, *The Origins of the Urban Crisis*, and Michael B. Katz, ed., *The "Underclass" Debate: Views from History* (Princeton: Princeton University Press, 1993).

2.   Young quoted in Kenneth O'Reilly, *"Racial Matters": The FBI's Secret File on Black America, 1960–1972* (New York: Free Press, 1989), 302; Second quotation from Winston A. Grady-Willis, "The Black Panther Party: State Repression and Political Prisoners," in *The Black Panther Party Reconsidered*, ed. Charles E. Jones (Baltimore: Black Classic Press, 1998), 375; Gene Marine, *The Black Panthers* (New York: New American Library, 1969), esp. Chps. 11–14.

3.   "Cop Halts Brutality," *Sun-Reporter*, 6 July 1968, 1; Thomas Fleming, "Fuller Incident: Citizens Protest Police Brutality," *Sun-Reporter*, 15 February 1969, 2, 24; Editorial, *Sun-Reporter*, 15 February 1969, 10; "Fuller Incident: Cop Who Used Mace Is Identified," *Sun-Reporter*, 22 February 1969, 3; Charles E. Jones, "The Political Repression of the Black Panther Party, 1966–1971: The Case of the Oakland Bay Area," *Journal of Black Studies* (June 1988): 415–21.

4.   Philip S. Foner, ed., *The Black Panthers Speak* (Philadelphia: J. B. Lippincott Company, 1970), xxvi, 257–58; Manning Marable, *Race, Reform, and Rebellion: The Second Reconstruction in Black America, 1945–1990*, 2nd. ed.

(Jackson: University Press of Mississippi, 1991), 111–12; O'Reilly, *"Racial Matters"*, 297, 305–09; Grady-Willis, "The Black Panther Party: State Repression and Political Prisoners," 366; Earl Anthony, *Spitting in the Wind: The True Story Behind the Violent Legacy of the Black Panther Party* (Malibu, CA: Roundtable Publishing, Inc., 1990), 38–45 passim; Michael Newton, *Bitter Grain: The Story of the Black Panther Party* (Los Angeles: Holloway House Publishing Co., 1980), 96–97. See also, Ward Churchill and Jim Vander Wall, *Agents of Repression: The FBI's Secret War Against the Black Panther Party and the American Indian Movement* (Boston: South End Press, 1988); Commission of Inquiry into the Black Panthers and the Police, *Search and Destroy: A Report* (New York: Metropolitan Applied Research Center, 1973); and Paul Chevigny, *Cops and Rebels: A Study of Provocation* (New York: Pantheon Books, 1972).

5.    Carmichael and Walls are quoted in David Caute, *The Year of the Barricades: A Journey through 1968* (New York: Harper & Row, 1988), 268–69; The National Conference on Black Power, "Resolutions," 20–23 July 1967, Reel 6, Subgroup A, Series II, File 69, The Papers of the Congress of Racial Equality, Addendum: 1944–1968, Microfilm, Sanford, NC: Microfilming Corporation of America, 1980. For other analyses of black women and the left during the 1960s, see, Paula Giddings, *When and Where I Enter: The Impact of Black Women on Race and Sex in America* (New York: William Morrow and Company, Inc., 1984), 315–35; Sara Evans, *Personal Politics: The Roots of Women's Liberation in the Civil Rights Movement and the New Left* (New York: Vintage Books, 1979); and Cynthia Griggs Fleming, "Black Women Activists and the Student Nonviolent Coordinating Committee: The Case of Ruby Doris Robinson," in *"We Specialize in the Wholly Impossible": A Reader in Black Women's History*, ed. Darlene Clark Hine, Wilma King, and Linda Reed (New York: Carlson Publishing, Inc., 1995), 561–77. For discussions of the images of black women in American culture, see, Patricia Morton, *Disfigured Images: The Historical Assault on Afro-American Women* (Westport, CT: Praeger, 1991); Patricia Hill Collins, *Black Feminist Thought: Knowledge, Consciousness, and the Politics of Empowerment* (Boston: Unwin Hyman, 1990), esp. Chp. 4; and Kenneth Goings, *Mammy and Uncle Mose: Black Collectibles and American Stereotyping* (Bloomington: Indiana University Press, 1994).

6.    Newton quoted in Tracye Matthews, "'No One Ever Asks, What a Man's Place in the Revolution Is': Gender and the Politics of the Black Panther Party 1966–1971," in *The Black Panther Party Reconsidered*, 276; Eldridge Cleaver, *Soul on Ice* (New York: Dell Publishing Company, Inc.,

1968), 66; Michele Wallace, *Black Macho and the Myth of the Superwoman* (New York: The Dial Press, 1978). The social scientists Richard Majors and Janet M. Billson argue that black men were symbolically castrated or bereft of their manhood because they were denied access to economic opportunity. This fundamental inequality stripped black men of their "pride," which the two scholars conclude is an essential component of male identity: "Pride is of colossal importance to black males. They engage in an unyielding drive toward the pursuit of pride. Pride, dignity, and respect hold such a high premium for black men that many are willing to risk anything for it, even their lives." See Majors and Billson, *Cool Pose: The Dilemmas of Black Manhood in America* (New York: Simon and Schuster, 1992), 39.

7.    Eldridge Cleaver, *Post-Prison Writings and Speeches* (New York: Random House, 1967), 20; Huey P. Newton, *Revolutionary Suicide* (New York: Harcourt Brace Jovanovich, Inc., 1973), 133; Wallace, *Black Macho*, 13. For provocative, and problematic, psychological and anthropological analyses of young black men in the late 1960s, see, Lee Rainwater, ed., *Soul* (Chicago: Aldine Publishing Company, 1970); and Christina Milner and Richard Milner, *Black Players: The Secret World of Black Pimps* (Boston: Little, Brown and Co., 1972).

8.    For photographic evidence of women in the BPP, see International Historic Films, *Black Panthers: Huey Newton*, 53 min., 1968, videocassette; Ruth-Marion Baruch and Pirkle Jones, *The Vanguard: A Photographic essay on the Black Panthers* (Boston: Beacon Press, 1970), 28, 58, 105, 120, 122; and the photographic inserts in David Hilliard and Lewis Cole, *This Side of Glory: The Autobiography of David Hilliard and the Story of the Black Panther Party* (Boston: Little, Brown and Company, 1993); and Elaine Brown, *A Taste of Power: A Black Woman's Story* (New York: Pantheon Books, 1992).

9.    Cleaver quoted in Giddings, *When and Where I Enter*, 317; Wallace, *Black Macho*, 68. Several recent studies outline the importance of female activism in the BPP, but they highlight the period after 1972 as the time when women rose to prominence in the party. See, Matthews, "'No One Ever Asks, What a Man's Role in the Revolution Is'"; Angela D. LeBlanc-Ernest, "'The Most Qualified Person to Handle the Job': Black Panther Party Women, 1966–1982," in *The Black Panther Party Reconsidered*; and Karl Knapper, "Women and the Black Panther Party," *Socialist Review* 26 (Winter-Spring 1996): 25–67.

10.    See, Brown, *A Taste of Power*, 136–37, 189–90; Assata Shakur, *Assata: An Autobiography* (London: Zed Books Ltd., 1987); Giddings, *When and Where*

I *Enter*, 318–19; and Wallace, *Black Macho*, 165–67, where she claims that there were basically two paths for women in the Black Power Movement, "Do-it-for-your-man" or "Have-a-baby." Panther women often resisted these sexist attitudes, however, and Brown states that a "clique" of women dissatisfied with their treatment in the BPP organized and vowed: "We would not be rewarding *any* Brother with our bodies, in the bedroom or in the kitchen," pg. 191–92. Quotation from Wallace, *Black Macho*, 81.

11.     Brown, A *Taste of Power*, 135, 225, 367–71, 441–444; Shakur, *Assata*, 223 passim; Regina Jennings, "Why I Joined the Party: An Africana Womanist Reflection," in *The Black Panther Party Reconsidered*, 262–64. For the different roles men and women played in the BPP's protests, see the "Free Huey" demonstration outside the Alameda County Courthouse in the documentary, IHF, *Black Panthers: Huey Newton*.

12.     For examples of this propaganda, see Afro-American Posters, circa 1960–1969, Bancroft Library, University of California, Berkeley; and IHF, *Black Panthers: Huey Newton*.

13.     Bobby Seale, *Seize the Time: The Story of the Black Panther Party and Huey P. Newton* (New York: Random House, 1968), 258–59; Cleaver, *Post-Prison Writings and Speeches*, 111–12, 133.

14.     Emory Douglas, "Revolutionary Art/Black Liberation," in *The Black Panthers Speak*, 16–18. Also see Douglas's drawings in *The Black Panthers Speak*, 155, 186, 221, 240. Alinsky quoted in Hugh Pearson, *The Shadow of the Panther: Huey Newton and the Price of Black Power in America* (Reading, MA: Addison-Wesley Publishing Co., 1994), 210; Transcript, Bobby Seale Oral History Interview, 4 May 1989, by Ronald Jemal Stephens and Clyde Robertson, n.p., in possession of the author.

15.     "Panthers a Bit Too Audacious," *Sun-Reporter*, 6 May 1967, 7; Christopher Lasch, *The Agony of the American Left* (New York: Alfred A. Knopf, 1969), 152–54 passim; Pearson, *Shadow of the Panther*, 128–29, 339–40; Allen J. Matusow, *The Unraveling of America: A History of Liberalism in the 1960s* (New York: Harper and Row, 1984), esp. Chp. 12.

16.     The results of the surveys are collected in the appendices of Peter Goldman, *Report from Black America* (New York: Simon and Schuster, 1969), 213–70. They are the most complete recording of African American public opinion in the late 1960s of which I am aware.

17.     *Ibid.*, 234–35, 237–38. In all three surveys, black America remained uncertain about SNCC. In 1963, a whopping 78% of those polled were "not sure" about the group, and the following studies obtained slight-

ly improved, but no less striking results, 42% for 1966 and 48% for 1969. While it is not entirely clear that this was necessarily negative for SNCC, it was certainly not the kind of unshakable support for which the student leaders were searching. The best history of the "radicalization" of SNCC, and indeed one of the best institutional histories of a Civil Rights/Black Power organization, is Clayborne Carson, *In Struggle: SNCC and the Black Awakening of the 1960s* (Cambridge: Harvard University Press, 1981).

18.   *Ibid.*, 236–37.

19.   *Ibid.*, 239–40; Daniel U. Levine, Norman S. Fiddmont, Robert S. Stephenson, Charles Wilkinson, "Differences Between Black Youth Who Support the Black Panthers and the NAACP," *The Journal of Negro Education* XLII (Winter 1973): 19–32. In the final question of the 1969 *Newsweek* survey, blacks were asked if they favored separate community control of institutions such as schools, businesses, and the like, or if they still desired integration as the goal of the Civil Rights Movement. While in the North more pushed for community control than their brethren in the South, blacks in both areas overwhelmingly supported the policy of integration. Of the total response, 13% favored community control, 78% favored integration, and another 10% were unsure. Even the most consistently militant group, northern youth under 30, supported integration by a margin of nearly two to one (59% to 30%). See, *Ibid.*, 270.

20.   *Ibid.*, 246–49. In the three polls, black Americans were asked if they could win their rights with nonviolent tactics, and the majority responded that they could. In 1963, 63% favored nonviolence, and this trend continued in 1966 (59%) and 1969 (63%). Only about one in five thought they would have to resort to violent means, 22% in 1963, 21% in 1966, and 21% in 1969. Most African Americans also felt that violence would only hurt the movement for equality, 67% stating this in 1966 and 65% in 1969 (the question was not asked in 1963).

21.   *Ibid.*, 242, 249–50.

22.   The best sources for the decline of the Black Panther Party are, Brown, *A Taste of Power*; Hilliard and Cole, *This Side of Glory*; Pearson, *Shadow of the Panther*; and Jones, ed., *The Black Panther Party Reconsidered.*

23.   Elmore quoted in Don Terry, "Soul on Wheels: A Bus Tour of Black Panther Turf," *New York Times*, 10 November 1997, A14. See also, Michael A. Fletcher, "The Allure of the Black Panthers," *Washington Post National Weekly Edition*, 23 December 1996 to 5 January 1997, 34.

24.     Peter Collier and David Horowitz, *Destructive Generation: Second Thoughts About the Sixties* (New York: Summit Books, 1989); John M. Murtagh, Jr., and Hugh Pearson, letters to the editor, *New York Times*, 14 November 1997, A34.

25.     See, William L. Van Deburg, *New Day in Babylon: The Black Power Movement and American Culture, 1965–1975* (Chicago: University of Chicago Press, 1992); Van Deburg, *Black Camelot: African American Culture Heroes in Their Times, 1960–1980* (Chicago: University of Chicago Press, 1997); and Helen L. Stewart, "Buffering: The Leadership Style of Huey P. Newton" (Ph.D. diss., Brandeis University, 1980), esp. 124.

26.     For the Panthers electoral efforts in Oakland, see the materials in Carton 18, Social Protest Collection, Bancroft Library, University of California, Berkeley.

27.     The quotation is from Herbert H. Haines, *Black Radicals and the Civil Rights Mainstream, 1954–1970* (Knoxville: University of Tennessee Press, 1988), esp. 56–57. For the collapse of the liberal consensus, see, Matusow, *The Unraveling of America*; Gareth Davies, *From Opportunity to Entitlement: The Transformation and Decline of Great Society Liberalism* (Lawrence: University Press of Kansas, 1996); and Lasch, *The Agony of the American Left*.

28.     For an international perspective on the Black Panther Party, see, Jennifer B. Smith, *An International History of the Black Panther Party* (New York: Garland Publishing, 1999).

# APPENDIX

THE TEN-POINT PLATFORM AND PROGRAM
Black Panther Party
October 1966

**What We Want**
**What We Believe**

*We want freedom. We want power to determine the destiny of our Black Community.*

We believe that black people will not be free until we are able to determine our destiny.

*We want full employment for our people.*

We believe that the federal government is responsible and obligated to give every man employment or a guaranteed income. We believe that if the white American businessmen will not give full employment, then the means of production should be taken from the businessmen and placed in the community so that the people of the community can organize and employ all of its people and give a high standard of living.

*We want an end to the robbery by the white man of our Black Community.*

We believe that this racist government has robbed us and now we are demanding the overdue debt of forty acres and two mules. Forty acres and two mules was promised 100 years ago as restitution for slave labor and mass murder of black people. We will accept the payment in currency which will be distributed to our many communities. The Germans are now aiding the Jews in Israel for the genocide of the Jewish people. The Germans murdered six million Jews. The American racist has taken part in the slaughter of over fifty million black people; therefore, we feel that this is a modest demand that we make.

*We want decent housing, fit for shelter of human beings.*

We believe that if the white landlords will not give decent housing to our black community, then the housing and the land should be made into cooperatives so that our community, with government aid, can build and make decent housing for its people.

*We want education for our people that exposes the true nature of this decadent American society. We want education that teaches us our true history and our role in present-day society.*

We believe in an educational system that will give to our people a knowledge of self. If a man does not have knowledge of himself and his position in society and the world, then he has little chance to relate to anything else.

*We want all black men to be exempted from military service.*

We believe that black people should not be forced to fight in the military service to defend a racist government that does not protect us. We will not fight and kill other people of color in the world who, like black people, are being victimized by the white racist government of America. We will protect ourselves from the force and violence of the racist police and the racist military, by whatever means necessary.

*We want an immediate end to* POLICE BRUTALITY *and* MURDER *of black people.*

We believe we can end police brutality in our black community by organizing black self-defense groups that are dedicated to defending our black community from racist police oppression and brutality. The Second Amendment to the Constitution of the United States gives a right to bear arms. We therefore believe that all black people should arm themselves for self-defense.

*We want freedom for all black men held in federal, state, county and city prisons and jails.*

We believe that all black people should be released from the many jails and prisons because that have not received a fair and impartial trial.

*We want all black people when brought to trial to be tried in court by a jury of their peer group or people from their black communities, as defined by the Constitution of the United States.*

We believe that the courts should follow the United States Constitution so that black people will receive fair trials. The 14th Amendment of the U.S. Constitution gives a man a right to be tried by his peer group. A peer is a person from a similar economic, social, religious, geographical, environmental, historical, and racial background. To do this the court will be forced to select a jury from the black community from which the black defendant came. We have been, and are being tried by all-white juries that have no understanding of the "average reasoning" man of the black community.

*We want land, bread, housing, education, clothing, justice and peace. And as our major political objective, a United Nations-supervised plebiscite to be held throughout the black colony in which only black colonial subjects will be allowed to participate, for the purpose of determining the will of black people as to their national destiny.*

When, in the course of human events, it becomes necessary for one people to dissolve the political bands which have connected them with another, and to assume, among the powers of the earth, the separate and equal station to which the laws of nature and nature's God entitle them, a decent respect of the opinions of mankind requires that they should declare the causes which impel them to the separation.

We hold these truths to be self-evident, that all men are created equal; that they are endowed by their Creator with certain unalienable rights; that among these are life, liberty, and the pursuit of happiness. That, to secure these rights, governments are instituted among men, deriving their just powers from the consent of the governed; that, whenever any form of government becomes destructive of these ends, it is the right of the people to alter or abolish it, and to institute a new government, laying its foundation on such principles, and organizing its powers in such form, as to them shall seem most likely to effect their safety and happiness. Prudence, indeed, will dictate that governments long established should not be changed for light and transient causes; and, accordingly, all experience hath shown, that mankind are more disposed to suffer, while evils are sufferable, than to right themselves by abolishing the forms to which they are accustomed. But, when a long train of abuses and usurpations, pursuing invariably the same object, evinces a design to reduce them under absolute despotism, it is their right, it is their duty, to throw off such government, and to provide new guards for their future security.

# BIBLIOGRAPHY

**ARCHIVAL MATERIALS:**

Bancroft Library, University of California, Berkeley:
 Afro-American Posters, circa 1960-1969.
 California Federation for Civic Unity Records, 1945-1956.
 Newell Hart Ephemera, 1961-1969, Papers.
 Tarea Hall Pittman Papers.
 William Byron Rumford Papers.
 Social Protest Collection.
 Taylor Memorial Methodist Church. *Yesterday-Today, Tomorrow and Forever: Through Faith with Work.* Oakland: Taylor Memorial Methodist Church, 1954.
 West Coast Region, NAACP Papers.

Labor Archives and Research Center, San Francisco State University:
 Andersen, George R., Herbert Resner, and Thurgood Marshall, "Brief for Respondent," S.F. No. 17,015, 1944, In the Supreme Court of the State of California, Joseph James v. Marinship Corporation, Local Union No. 6 of International Brotherhood of Boilermakers, Iron Shipbuilders and Helpers of America....
 International Ladies Garment Workers Union, San Francisco Joint Board Records, 1931-1969.
 Papers of the American Federation of Musicians, Ephemera Collection.
 Papers of the International Longshoremen's and Warehousemen's Union, Ephemera Collection.
 Papers of the National Union of Marine Cooks and Stewards, Ephemera Collection.

Papers of the Service Employees International Union,
        Hospital and Insitutional Workers's Union, Local 250.
San Francisco Labor Council Records, 1902-1976.
Unpublished paper, Richard Grant, "The Case of Audley
        Cole: Racial Policy in the AFL and the CIO."

Lyndon Baines Johnson Presidential Library, Austin, Texas:
        Administrative History of the Office of Economic
        Opportunity.
        Aides' Office Files:
                Cecil Bellinger.
                Fred Bohen.
                Joseph Califano.
                Douglass Cater.
                James C. Gaither.
                Charles Horsky.
                Harry McPherson.
                Bill Moyers.
                Matthew Nimetz.
                Fred Panzer.
                John E. Robson and Stanford G. Ross.
        Confidential Files:
                Agency Reports, Office of Economic Opportunity.
                Ex FG 11-11.
                Ex FG 11-15.
                WE 9.
        White House Central Files (WHCF):
                Ex FG 11-15.
                Ex HU 2.
                Ex HU 2/ST 2-12.
                Ex LG/A-Z.
                Ex LG/San Francisco.
                Ex WE 9.
                Gen WE 9.
                FA 4.
                FG 690.
        Personal Papers of Ramsey Clark.
        Personal Papers of Bertrand M. Harding.

National Archives, College Park, Maryland: Record Group 381. Office of Economic Opportunity. Inspection Division. Inspection Reports, 1964-1967.

The Papers of the Congress of Racial Equality, 1941-1967. Microfilm. Sanford, NC: Microfilming Corporation of America, 1980.

The Papers of the Congress of Racial Equality, Addendum: 1944-1968. Microfilm. Sanford, NC: Microfilming Corporation of America, 1980.

## ORAL HISTORIES AND INTERVIEWS:

Alley, Edward. Interview by Jesse J. Warr. 19 September 1978. Transcript. San Francisco African American Historical and Cultural Society, Research Library and Archives.

Amerson, A. Wayne. "Northern California and Its Challenges to a Negro in the Mid-1900s." An oral history conducted by Joyce A. Henderson. Earl Warren Oral History Project. Regional Oral History Office. The Bancroft Library. University of California, Berkeley, 1974.

Anderson, Glenn M. Transcript of Oral History Interview. 12 November 1970 and 31 January 1971, by James A. Oesterle. John F. Kennedy Presidential Library, Boston, Massachusetts.

Baker, Donald M. Transcript of Oral History Interview. 24 February 1969, by Stephen Goodell. Lyndon Baines Johnson Presidential Library, Austin, Texas.

Baker, John A. Transcript of Oral History Interview. 21 April 1981, by Michael L. Gillette. Lyndon Baines Johnson Presidential Library, Austin, Texas.

Banks, James G. Transcript of Oral History Interview. 14 December 1966, by William McHugh. John F. Kennedy Presidential Library, Boston, Massachusetts.

Bradley, Don L. Transcript of Oral History Interview. 6 June 1966, by Ronald J. Grele. John F. Kennedy Presidential Library, Boston, Massachusetts.

Brandeis University Conference on Poverty and Urban Policy. 16-
          17 June 1973. Transcript. John F. Kennedy Presidential
          Library, Boston, Massachusetts.

Bremond, Deborah. Interview by Charles E. Jones. 17 June 1992.
          Transcript in possession of the author.

Brooks, Alma Thomas. Interview by Jesse J. Warr. 17 October
          1978. Transcript. San Francisco African American
          Historical and Cultural Society, Research Library and
          Archives.

Brooks, Willie. Interview by Jesse J. Warr. 19 June 1978.
          Transcript. San Francisco African American Historical and
          Cultural Society, Research Library and Archives.

Calbert, Sadie. Interview by Jesse J. Warr. 11 July 1978.
          Transcript. San Francisco African American Historical and
          Cultural Society, Research Library and Archives.

Cavanagh, Jerome P. Transcript of Oral History Interview. 22
          March 1971, by Joe B. Frantz. Lyndon Baines Johnson
          Presidential Library, Austin, Texas.

Cerrell, Joseph R. Transcript of Oral History Interview. 12 June
          1969, by Dennis O'Brien. John F. Kennedy Presidential
          Library, Boston, Massachusetts.

Clarke, Alan. "Recollections of Point San Pablo and San Francisco
          Bay." An oral history conducted in 1985 and 1986 by
          Judith K. Dunning. Regional Oral History Office. The
          Bancroft Library. University of California, Berkeley, 1990.

Cole, Josephine E. Interview by Jesse J. Warr. 8 May 1978.
          Transcript. San Francisco African American Historical and
          Cultural Society, Research Library and Archives.

Conway, Jack T. Transcript of Oral History Interview. 13 August
          1980, by Michael L. Gillette. Lyndon Baines Johnson
          Presidential Library, Austin, Texas.

Conway, Jack T. Transcript of Oral History Interview. 10 April 1972
          and 11 April 1972, by Larry J. Hackman. John F. Kennedy
          Presidential Library, Boston, Massachusetts.

Cotton, Terry. Interview by Charles E. Jones. 13 March 1993.
          Transcript in possession of the author.

Dickson, Melvin. Interview by Charles E. Jones. 9 June 1992.
          Transcript in possession of the author.

Douglas, Emory. Interview by Charles E. Jones. 15 June 1992. Transcript in possession of the author.

Eaton, Eddie. "In Search of the California Dream: From Houston, Texas to Richmond, California, 1943." An oral history conducted in 1986 by Judith K. Dunning. Regional Oral History Office. The Bancroft Library. University of California, Berkeley, 1990.

Goldfarb, Roland. Transcript of Oral History Interview. 24 October 1980, by Michael L. Gillette. Lyndon Baines Johnson Presidential Library, Austin, Texas.

Green, Edith. Transcript of Oral History Interview. 23 August 1985, by Janet Kerr-Tener. Lyndon Baines Johnson Presidential Library, Austin, Texas.

Hackett, David L. Transcript of Oral History Interview. 22 July 1970 and 21 October 1970, by John W. Douglas. John F. Kennedy Presidential Library, Boston, Massachusetts.

Harding, Bertrand M. Transcript of Oral History Interview. 20 November 1968, by Stephen Goodell. Lyndon Baines Johnson Presidential Library, Austin, Texas.

Horowitz, Harold W. Transcript of Oral History Interview. 23 February 1983, by Michael L. Gillette. Lyndon Baines Johnson Presidential Library, Austin, Texas.

Houghteling, Joseph C. Transcript of Oral History Interview. 19 June 1969, by Dennis J. O'Brien. John F. Kennedy Presidential Library, Boston, Massachusetts.

Howard, Jack. Transcript of Oral History Interview. 20 October 1980, by Michael L. Gillette. Lyndon Baines Johnson Presidential Library, Austin, Texas.

Hughes, Richard and Betty. Transcript of Oral History Interview. 6 August 1969, by Joe B. Frantz. Lyndon Baines Johnson Presidential Library, Austin, Texas.

Jordan, Barbara. Transcript of Oral History Interview. 28 March 1984, by Roland C. Hayes. Lyndon Baines Johnson Presidential Library, Austin, Texas.

Kelly, Jr., William P. Transcript of Oral History Interview. 11 April 1969, by Stephen Goodell. Lyndon Baines Johnson Presidential Library, Austin, Texas.

Kent, Roger.  Transcript of Oral History Interview.  19 November 1970, by Ann M. Campbell.  John F. Kennedy Presidential Library, Boston, Massachusetts.

Kramer, Herbert.  Transcript of Oral History Interview.  10 March 1969, by Stephen Goodell.  Lyndon Baines Johnson Presidential Library, Austin, Texas.

Lampman, Robert.  Transcript of Oral History Interview.  24 May 1983, by Michael L. Gillette.  Lyndon Baines Johnson Presidential Library, Austin, Texas.

Levine, Robert A.  Transcript of Oral History Interview.  26 February 1969, by Stephen Goodell.  Lyndon Baines Johnson Presidential Library, Austin, Texas.

Markman, Sherwin J.  Transcript of Oral History Interview.  21 May 1969, by Dorothy Pierce McSweeny.  Lyndon Baines Johnson Presidential Library, Austin, Texas.

Marshall, Toronto Cannaday.  Interview by Jesse J. Warr.  5 October 1978.  Transcript.  San Francisco African American Historical and Cultural Society, Research Library and Archives.

May, Bernice Hubbard.  "A Native Daughter's Leadership in Public Affairs."  An oral history conducted in 1974 by Gabrielle Morris.  2 vols.  Women in Politics Oral History Project.  Regional Oral History Office.  The Bancroft Library.  University of California, Berkeley, 1976.

McGuire, Marie C.  Transcript of Oral History Interview.  3 April 1967, by William McHugh.  John F. Kennedy Presidential Library, Boston, Massachusetts.

Merrick, Samuel V. Transcript of Oral History Interview.  28 September 1981, by Michael L. Gillette.  Lyndon Baines Johnson Presidential Library, Austin, Texas.

Metz, Clifford.  "A City in Transition: Richmond during World War II."  An oral history conducted in 1986 by Judith K. Dunning.  Regional Oral History Office.  The Bancroft Library.  University of California, Berkeley, 1992.

Moss, John E.  Transcript of Oral History Interview.  13 April 1965, by Philip M. Stern.  John F. Kennedy Presidential Library, Boston, Massachusetts.

Nystrom, Stanley. "A Family's Roots in Richmond: Recollections of a Lifetime Resident." An oral history conducted in 1985 by Judith K. Dunning. Regional Oral History Office. The Bancroft Library. University of California, Berkeley, 1990.

Osborne, Johyne Beverly. Interview by Jesse J. Warr. 18 August 1978. Transcript. San Francisco African American Historical and Cultural Society, Research Library and Archives.

Perrin, C. Robert. Transcript of Oral History Interview. 10 March 1969, by Stephen Goodell. Lyndon Baines Johnson Presidential Library, Austin, Texas.

Phillips, William G. Transcript of Oral History Interview. 16 April 1980, by Michael L. Gillette. Lyndon Baines Johnson Presidential Library, Austin, Texas.

Powers, Robert B. "Law Enforcement, Race Relations: 1930-1960." An oral history conducted by Amelia R. Fry. Earl Warren Oral History Project. Regional Oral History Office. The Bancroft Library. University of California, Berkeley, 1971.

Pratt, Geronimo ji-jaga and Mumia Abu-Jamal. "The Black Panthers: Interviews with Geronimo ji-jaga Pratt and Mumia Abu-Jamal." Interview by Heike Kleffner (October 1992). *Race & Class* 35 (July-September 1993): 9-26.

Rees, Thomas M. Transcript of Oral History Interview. 5 March 1969, by Dennis J. O'Brien. John F. Kennedy Presidential Library, Boston, Massachusetts.

Rumford, William Byron. "Legislator for Fair Employment, Fair Housing, and Public Health." An oral history conducted by Joyce A. Henderson, Amelia Fry, and Edward France. Earl Warren Oral History Project. Regional Oral History Office. The Bancroft Library. University of California, Berkeley, 1973.

Sanders, Jr., Harold Barefoot. Transcript of Oral History Interview. N.D., by Joe B. Frantz. Lyndon Baines Johnson Presidential Library, Austin, Texas.

Scott, Lora Toombs. Interview by Jesse J. Warr. 23 August 1978. Transcript. San Francisco African American Historical and Cultural Society, Research Library and Archives.

Seale, Bobby. Interview by Ronald Jemal Stephens and Clyde
        Robertson. 1989. Transcript in possession of the author.
Singletary, Otis A. Transcript of Oral History Interview. 12
        November 1970, by Joe B. Frantz. Lyndon Baines Johnson
        Presidential Library, Austin, Texas.
Slayton, William L. Transcript of Oral History Interview. 3
        February 1967, by William M. McHugh. John F. Kennedy
        Presidential Library, Boston, Massachusetts.
Sugarman Jule M. Transcript of Oral History Interview. 14 March
        1969, by Stephen Goodell. Lyndon Baines Johnson
        Presidential Library, Austin, Texas.
Sundquist, James L. Transcript of Oral History Interview. 7 April
        1969, by Stephen Goodell. Lyndon Baines Johnson
        Presidential Library, Austin, Texas.
Swig, Benjamin H. Transcript of Oral History Interview. 18
        November 1970, by Ann M. Campbell. John F. Kennedy
        Presidential Library, Boston, Massachusetts.
Tolmach, Eric. Transcript of Oral History Interview. 5 March 1969,
        19 March 1969, and 16 April 1969, by Stephen Goodell.
        Lyndon Baines Johnson Presidential Library, Austin,
        Texas.
Voorhis, H. Jerry. Transcript of Oral History Interview. 15 May
        1969, by David McComb. Lyndon Baines Johnson
        Presidential Library, Austin, Texas.
Weeks, Christopher. Transcript of Oral History Interview. 10
        December 1980, by Michael L. Gillette. Lyndon Baines
        Johnson Presidential Library, Austin, Texas.
Williams, Archie F. "The Joy of Flying: Olympic Gold, Air Force
        Colonel, and Teacher." An oral history conducted in 1992
        by Gabrielle Morris. Regional Oral History Office. The
        Bancroft Library. University of California, Berkeley, 1993.
Williams, Harry and Marguerite. "Reflections of a Longtime Black
        Family in Richmond." An oral history conducted in 1985
        by Judith K. Dunning. Regional Oral History Office. The
        Bancroft Library. University of California, Berkeley, 1990.
Yarmolinsky, Adam. Transcript of Oral History Interview. 11
        November 1964, 28 November 1964, and 5 December

1964, by Daniel Ellsberg. John F. Kennedy Presidential
Library, Boston, Massachusetts.

Yorty, Samuel. Transcript of Oral History Interview. 7 February
1970, by Joe B. Frantz. Lyndon Baines Johnson
Presidential Library, Austin, Texas.

Ziffren, Paul. Transcript of Oral History Interview. 11 November
1970, by Ann M. Campbell. John F. Kennedy Presidential
Library, Boston, Massachusetts.

## AUDIO-VISUAL MATERIALS:

"Black Panther Community Support Rally." Cassette BB5461.01.
Pacifica Radio Archive, North Hollywood, California, 1968.

"Black Panthers and the High School Coalition." Cassette BB1723.
Pacifica Radio Archive, North Hollywood, California, 1969.

"Bobby Seale in Oakland." Cassette BB5462. Pacifica Radio
Archive, North Hollywood, California, 1968.

"Conditions in the Oakland Ghetto: Mark Comfort Interviewed by
Elsa Knight Thompson." Cassette BB1309. Pacifica Radio
Archive, North Hollywood, California, 1967.

"Five Black High School Students: A Black Caucus." Cassette
BB3116. Pacifica Radio Archive, North Hollywood,
California, 1968.

International Historic Films. *Black Panthers: Huey Newton*. 53 min.
1968. Videocassette.

"The Legacy of the Black Panther Party." Cassette BB3116.
Pacifica Radio Archive, North Hollywood, California, 1989.

"Mighty Oaks? Thomas Bell Interviewed by Elsa Knight
Thompson." Cassette BB0320. Pacifica Radio Archive,
North Hollywood, California, 1962.

"The Oakland General Strike of 1946." Cassette AZ0049. Pacifica
Radio Archive, North Hollywood, California, 1976.

"Tune in on Contra West: Downtown Redevelopment in
Richmond." Cassette BB1430. Pacifica Radio Archive,
North Hollywood, California, 1966.

"Voices of Poverty." Cassette BB1337. Pacifica Radio Archive,
North Hollywood, California, 1966.

## NEWSPAPERS AND PERIODICALS:

*Crisis.*
*Flatlands.*
*Ramparts.*
San Francisco *Chronicle.*
San Francisco *Sun-Reporter.*

## PARTICIPANT NARRATIVES AND AUTOBIOGRAPHIES:

Angelou, Maya. *I Know Why the Caged Bird Sings.* New York: Bantam, 1970.

Anthony, Earl. *Picking up the Gun: A Report on the Black Panthers.* New York: Dial Press, 1970.

_____. *Spitting in the Wind: The True Story Behind the Violent Legacy of the Black Panther Party.* Malibu, CA: Roundtable Publishing, Inc., 1990.

Boyle, Kay. *The Long Walk at San Francisco State and Other Essays.* New York: Grove Press, Inc., 1967.

Brown, Elaine. *A Taste of Power: A Black Woman's Story.* New York: Pantheon Books, 1992.

Brown, H. Rap. *Die Nigger Die!* New York: The Dial Press, 1969.

Carmichael, Stokely, and Charles V. Hamilton. *Black Power: The Politics of Liberation.* New York: Random House, 1967.

Cleaver, Eldridge. *On the Ideology of the Black Panther Party.* Part I. San Francisco: Ministry of Information, Black Panther Party, 1969 [?].

_____. *Post-Prison Writings and Speeches.* New York: Random House, 1967.

_____. *Soul on Ice.* New York: Dell Publishing Co., Inc., 1968.

Davis, Angela. *Angela Davis: An Autobiography.* New York: Random House, 1974.

Foner, Philip S., ed. *The Black Panthers Speak.* Philadelphia: J. B. Lippincott Co., 1970.

Heath, G. Louis, ed. *The Black Panther Leaders Speak.* Metuchen, NJ: The Scarecrow Press, Inc., 1976.

Hilliard, David and Lewis Cole. *This Side of Glory: The Autobiography of David Hilliard and the Story of the Black Panther Party.* Boston: Little, Brown and Company, 1993.

Jackson, George. *Soledad Brother: The Prison Letters of George Jackson.* New York: Coward-McCann, 1970; reprint, Chicago: Lawrence Hill Books, 1994.

_____. *Blood in My Eye.* New York: Random House, 1972; reprint, Baltimore: Black Classic Press, 1990.

Johnson, Lyndon B. *The Vantage Point: Perspectives on the Presidency.* New York: Holt, Rinehart and Wilson, 1971.

Malcolm X with Alex Haley. *The Autobiography of Malcolm X.* New York: Ballantine Books, 1964.

Mankiller, Wilma and Michael Wallis. *Mankiller: A Chief and Her People.* New York: St. Martin's Press, 1993.

Newton, Huey P. *The Genius of Huey P. Newton, Minister of Defense, Black Panther Party.* San Francisco: Ministry of Information, Black Panther Party, n.d.

_____. *Revolutionary Suicide.* New York: Harcourt Brace Jovanovich, Inc., 1973.

_____. *To Die for the People.* New York: Vintage Books, 1972.

Newton, Michael. *Bitter Grain: The Story of the Black Panther Party.* Los Angeles: Holloway House Publishing Co., 1980.

Seale, Bobby. *Seize the Time: The Story of the Black Panther Party and Huey P. Newton.* New York: Random House, 1968.

_____. *A Lonely Rage: The Autobiography of Bobby Seale.* New York: Times Books, 1978.

Shakur, Assata. *Assata: An Autobiography.* London: Zed Books Ltd., 1987.

Summerskill, John. *President Seven.* New York: The World Publishing Co., 1971.

Thompson, Willie. *Enemy of the Poor: A Report of the Struggle of the War on Poverty in San Francisco.* n.p., n.d.

Williams, Robert F. *Negroes with Guns.* New York: Marzani & Munsell, 1962.

## GOVERNMENT DOCUMENTS AND REPORTS:

Advisory Commission on Intergovernmental Relations.
　　　　*Intergovernmental Relations in the Poverty Program: A Commission
　　　　Report*. Washington, D. C.: United States Government
　　　　Printing Office, 1966.
Becker, Natalie and Marjorie Myhill. *Power and Participation in the
　　　　San Francisco Community Action Program, 1964-1967*.
　　　　Berkeley: Institute of Urban and Regional Development,
　　　　1967.
Bernardi, Gene. *Evaluation Analysis of the Council of Social Planning's
　　　　Neighborhood Organization Program*. Oakland: Department of
　　　　Human Resources, 1966.
　　　　_____. *Income Needs in West Oakland: A Preliminary Report*.
　　　　Oakland: Oakland Economic Development Council, 1967.
　　　　_____. *Oakland's Poverty Population, 1965*. Oakland: n.p., 1967.
City of Berkeley. "The First Fifty Years of the Community Welfare
　　　　Commission." Berkeley: n.p., 1959.
Council of Social Planning—Berkeley Area. *Community Action under
　　　　"Economic Opportunity Act of 1964"*. Berkeley: n.p., 1965.
Howden, Edward. "Observations on Recent San Francisco
　　　　Disturbance and the Community's Response."
　　　　Sacramento: California Fair Employment Practice
　　　　Commission, 1966.
Marascuilo, Leonard A. "Attitudes Toward de facto Segregation in
　　　　a Northern City." Berkeley: University of California, 1964-
　　　　1965.
Nawy, Harold, and Martin Thimel. *The East Bay Community Action
　　　　Program; Part Two: Strategy or Stratagem*. Berkeley: University
　　　　of California, 1966 [?].
Nicholls, II, William L. *Poverty and Poverty Programs in Oakland*.
　　　　Berkeley: n.p., 1966.
　　　　_____. *Tables on Employment and Unemployment from the 701
　　　　Household Survey of Oakland*. Oakland: Survey Research
　　　　Center, 1968.

Nicholls, II, William L., Esther S. Hochstim, and Sheila Babbie. *The Castlemont Survey: A Handbook of Survey Results.* Berkeley: Survey Research Center, June 1966.

Oakland Economic Development Council, Inc. *The Press and the O.E.D.C.I., 1969-1971: How the Press Reported Oakland's Controversial Anti-Poverty Program which Governor Reagan Vetoed Because It Gave too Much Power to the City's Poor.* Oakland: OEDCI, 1971.

Office of Economic Opportunity. *Community Action Program Guide, Vol. I: Instructions for Applicants.* Washington, D. C.: Office of Economic Opportunity, 1965.

Record, Wilson. *Minority Groups and Intergroup Relations in the San Francisco Bay Area.* Berkeley: Institute of Governmental Studies, 1963.

United States Department of Commerce. *Fifteenth Census of the United States: 1930; Population.* Volume III. Parts 1 and 2. Washington, D. C.: United States Government Printing Office, 1932.

_____. *Sixteenth Census of the United States: 1940; Population.* Volume II. Parts 1, 3, and 5. Washington, D. C.: United States Government Printing Office, 1943.

_____. *A Report of the Seventeenth Decennial Census of the United States, Census of Population: 1950.* Volume II. Parts 2, 5, and 33. Washington, D. C.: United States Government Printing Office, 1952.

_____. *The Eighteenth Decennial Census of the United States, Census of the Population: 1960.* Volume I. Parts 2, 6, and 35. Washington, D. C.: United States Government Printing Office, 1961.

_____. *1970 Census of Population.* Volume I. Parts 2, 6, and 35. Washington, D. C.: United States Government Printing Office, 1973.

United States Senate. Permanent Subcommittee on Investigations, Committee on Government Operations. *Riots, Civil and Criminal Disorders.* Part 19: June 18, 24, 25, 1969. Washington, D. C.: United States Government Printing Office, 1969.

United States Senate. Subcommittee on Employment, Manpower, and Poverty. *Examination of the War on Poverty.* Part 11: May 10-11, 1967. Washington, D. C.: United States Government Printing Office, 1967.

Wenkert, Robert, John Magney, and Ann Neel. *Two Weeks of Racial Crisis in Richmond, California.* Berkeley: University of California, 1967.

## SECONDARY BOOKS AND ARTICLES:

Allen, Robert L. *The Port Chicago Mutiny.* New York: Warner Books, 1989.

Anderson, Karen Tucker. "Last Hired, First Fired: Black Women Workers during World War II." *Journal of American History* 69 (June 1982): 82-97.

Anderson, Martin. *The Federal Bulldozer: A Critical Analysis of Urban Renewal, 1949-1962.* Cambridge: The MIT Press, 1964.

Archibald, Katherine. *Wartime Shipyard: A Study in Social Disunity.* Berkeley: University of California Press, 1947.

Barlow, William and Peter Shapiro. *An End to Silence: The San Francisco State College Student Movement in the '60s.* New York: Pegasus, 1971.

Baruch, Ruth-Marion and Pirkle Jones. *The Vanguard: A Photographic Essay on the Black Panthers.* Boston: Beacon Press, 1970.

Bazaar, Mona, ed. *The Trial of Huey Newton.* Oakland: Mona Bazaar, 1968.

Bernstein, Irving. *Guns or Butter: The Presidency of Lyndon Johnson.* New York: Oxford University Press, 1996.

*The Black Revolution: An Ebony Special Issue.* Chicago: Johnson Publishing Co., Inc., 1970.

Bradford, Amory. *Oakland's Not for Burning.* New York: David McKay Company, Inc., 1968.

Brauer, Carl M. "Kennedy, Johnson, and the War on Poverty." *Journal of American History* 69 (June 1982): 98-119.

Broussard, Albert S. *Black San Francisco: The Struggle for Racial Equality in the West, 1900-1954.* Lawrence: University Press of Kansas, 1993.

Brown, Hubert Owen. "The Impact of War Worker Migration on the Public School System of Richmond, California, from 1940-1945." Ph.D. Diss. Stanford University, 1973.

Califano, Joseph S. *The Triumph and Tragedy of Lyndon Johnson: The White House Years.* New York: Simon and Schuster, 1991.

Cannon, Terry. *All Power to the People: The Story of the Black Panther Party.* San Francisco: Peoples Press, 1970.

Carson, Clayborne. *In Struggle: SNCC and the Black Awakening of the 1960s.* Cambridge, MA: Harvard University Press, 1981.

Caute, David. *The Year of the Barricades: A Journey Through 1968.* New York: Harper and Row, 1988.

Chafe, William H. *The Unfinished Journey: America Since World War II.* 2nd ed. New York: Oxford University Press, 1991.

Chevigny, Paul. *Cops and Rebels: A Study in Provocation.* New York: Pantheon Books, 1972.

Chow, Willard T. *The Reemergence of an Inner City: The Pivot of Chinese Settlement in the East Bay Region of the San Francisco Bay Area.* San Francisco: R&E Research Associates, 1977.

Church League of America. *The Black Panthers in Action.* Wheaton, IL: Church League of America, 1969.

Churchill, Ward and Jim Vander Wall. *Agents of Repression: The FBI's Secret War Against the Black Panther Party and the American Indian Movement.* Boston: South End Press, 1988.

Cohen, William. *At Freedom's Edge: Black Mobility and the Southern White Quest for Racial Control, 1861-1915.* Baton Rouge: Louisiana State University Press, 1991.

Collier, Peter and David Horowitz. *Destructive Generation: Second Thoughts About the Sixties.* New York: Summit Books, 1989.

Collins, Patricia Hill. *Black Feminist Thought: Knowledge, Consciousness, and the Politics of Empowerment.* Boston: Unwin Hyman, 1990.

Commission of Inquiry into the Black Panthers and the Police. *Search and Destroy: A Report.* New York: Metropolitan Applied Research Center, 1973.

Crouchett, Lawrence P., Lonnie G. Bunch, III, and Martha Kendall Winnacker. *Visions toward Tomorrow: The History of the East Bay Afro-American Community, 1852-1977.* Oakland: Northern

California Center for Afro-American History and Life, 1989.

Daniels, Douglas Henry. *Pioneer Urbanites: A Social and Cultural History of Black San Francisco*. Philadelphia: Temple University Press, 1980.

Davies, Gareth. *From Opportunity to Entitlement: The Transformation and Decline of Great Society Liberalism*. Lawrence: University Press of Kansas, 1996.

Davis, Angela. *Women, Race, & Class*. New York: Random House, 1981.

Eddington, Neil Arthur. "The Urban Plantation: An Ethnography of an Oral Tradition." Ph.D. Diss. University of California, Berkeley, 1967.

Evans, Sara. *Personal Politics: The Roots of Women's Liberation in the Civil Rights Movement and the New Left*. New York: Vintage Books, 1979.

Fanon, Frantz. *The Wretched of the Earth*. Translated by Constance Farrington. New York: Grove Press, Inc., 1963.

France, Edward Everett. "Some Aspects of the Migration of the Negro to the San Francisco Bay Area since 1940." Ph.D. Diss. University of California, Berkeley, 1962.

Fraser, Steve and Gary Gerstle. *The Rise and Fall of the New Deal Order, 1930-1980*. Princeton: Princeton University Press, 1989.

Fure-Slocum, Eric. "Emerging Urban Redevelopment Policies: Post-World War II Contests in San Francisco and Los Angeles." M.A. Thesis. San Francisco State University, 1990.

Giddings, Paula. *When and Where I Enter: The Impact of Black Women on Race and Sex in America*. New York: William Morrow and Company, 1984.

Gitlin, Todd. *The Sixties: Years of Hope, Days of Rage*. New York: Bantam, 1987.

Goings, Kenneth. *Mammy and Uncle Mose: Black Collectibles and American Stereotyping*. Bloomington: Indiana University Press, 1994.

Goldman, Peter. *Report from Black America*. New York: Simon and Schuster, 1969.

Gottlieb, Peter. *Making Their Own Way: Southern Blacks' Migration to Pittsburgh, 1916-1930*. Urbana: University of Illinois Press, 1987.

Graham, Hugh Davis. *The Civil Rights Era: Origins of National Policy*. New York: Oxford University Press, 1991.

Groneman, Carol and Mary Beth Norton, eds. *"To Toil the Livelong Day": America's Women at Work, 1780-1980*. Ithaca, NY: Cornell University Press, 1987.

Grossman, James. *Land of Hope: Chicago, Black Southerners, and the Great Migration*. Chicago: University of Chicago Press, 1989.

Haines, Herbert H. *Black Radicals and the Civil Rights Mainstream, 1954-1970*. Knoxville: University of Tennessee Press, 1988.

Hamilton, Kenneth M. *Black Towns and Profit: Promotion and Development in the Trans-Appalachian West, 1877-1915*. Urbana: University of Illinois Press, 1991.

Harrington, Michael. *The Other America*. New York: Penguin Books, 1963.

Haskins, James. *Profiles in Black Power*. Garden City, NY: Doubleday & Company, Inc., 1972.

Hernton, Calvin C. *Sex and Racism in America*. New York: Grove Weidenfeld, 1965.

Hine, Darlene Clark, Wilma King, and Linda Reed, eds. *"We Specialize in the Wholly Impossible": A Reader in Black Women's History*. New York: Carlson Publishing, Inc., 1995.

Hippler, Arthur E. *Hunter's Point: A Black Ghetto*. New York: Basic Books, 1974.

Hirsch, Arnold R. *Making the Second Ghetto: Race and Housing in Chicago, 1940-1960*. New York: Cambridge University Press, 1983.

Honey, Michael K. *Southern Labor and Black Civil Rights: Organizing Memphis Workers*. Urbana: University of Illinois Press, 1993.

Hopkins, Charles W. "The Deradicalization of the Black Panther Party, 1967-1973." Ph.D. Diss. University of North Carolina, Chapel Hill, 1978.

hooks, bell. *Ain't I A Woman: black women and feminism*. Boston: South End Press, 1981.

Horne, Gerald. *Fire This Time: The Watts Uprising and the 1960s.*
       Charlottesville: University Press of Virginia, 1995.

Howe, Irving, ed. *Beyond the New Left.* New York: Vintage Books,
       1979.

Johnson, Charles S. *The Negro War Worker in San Francisco.* n.p.,
       1944.

Johnson, Marilynn S. *The Second Gold Rush: Oakland and the East Bay
       during World War II.* Berkeley: University of California
       Press, 1993.

Jones, Charles E., ed. *The Black Panther Party Reconsidered.*
       Baltimore: Black Classic Press, 1998.

_____. "The Political Repression of the Black Panther Party,
       1966-1971." *Journal of Black Studies* (June 1988): 415-21.

Jones, Jacqueline. *The Dispossessed: America's Underclasses from the Civil
       War to the Present.* New York: Basic Books, 1992.

*The Journal of Urban History* 21 (March and May 1995).

Karagueuzian, Dikran. *Blow It Up! The Black Student Revolt at San
       Francisco State College and the Emergence of Dr. Hayakawa.*
       Boston: Gambit, Inc., 1971.

Katz, Michael B. *The Undeserving Poor: From the War on Poverty to the
       War on Welfare.* New York: Pantheon, 1989.

_____, ed. *The "Underclass" Debate: Views from History.* Princeton:
       Princeton University Press, 1993.

Kearns, Doris. *Lyndon Johnson and the American Dream.* New York:
       Harper and Row, 1976.

Kelley, Robin D. G. *Hammer and Hoe: Alabama Communists During the
       Great Depression.* Chapel Hill: University of North Carolina
       Press, 1990.

_____. *Race Rebels: Culture, Politics, and the Black Working Class.*
       New York: Free Press, 1994.

*The Kerner Report.* Report of the National Advisory Commission on
       Civil Disorder, March 1968. 20th Anniversary Edition.
       New York: Pantheon Books, 1988.

Knapper, Karl. "Women and the Black Panther Party." *Socialist
       Review* 26 (Winter-Spring 1996): 25-67.

Kramer Ralph. *Participation of the Poor: Comparative Community Case
       Studies in the War on Poverty.* Englewood Cliffs, NJ: Prentice-
       Hall, Inc., 1969.

Kusmer, Kenneth. *A Ghetto Takes Shape: Black Cleveland, 1870-1930*. Urbana: University of Illinois Press, 1976.

Lasch, Christopher. *The Agony of the American Left*. New York: Alfred A. Knopf, 1969.

Lemann, Nicholas. *The Promised Land: The Great Black Migration and How It Changed America*. New York: Alfred A. Knopf, 1991.

Lemke-Santangelo, Gretchen. *Abiding Courage: African American Migrant Women and the East Bay Community*. Chapel Hill: University of North Carolina Press, 1996.

Leonard, Kevin A. "Years of Hope, Days of Fear: The Impact of World War II on Race Relations in Los Angeles." Ph.D. Diss. University of California, Davis, 1992.

Levine, Daniel U., Norman S. Fiddmont, Robert S. Stephenson, Charles Wilkinson. "Differences Between Black Youth Who Support the Black Panthers and the NAACP." *The Journal of Negro Education* XLII (Winter 1973): 19-32.

Levine, Robert A. *The Poor Ye Need Not Have With You: Lessons from the War on Poverty*. Cambridge: The MIT Press, 1970.

Levitan, Sar A. *The Great Society's Poor Law: A New Approach to Poverty*. Baltimore: Johns Hopkins University Press, 1969.

Lichtman, Sheila Tropp. "Women at Work, 1941-1945: Wartime Employment in the San Francisco Bay Area." Ph.D. Diss. University of California, Davis, 1981.

Major, Reginald. *A Panther Is a Black Cat*. New York: William Morrow & Company, Inc., 1971.

Majors, Richard and Janet Mancini Billson. *Cool Pose: The Dilemmas of Black Manhood in America*. New York: Simon and Schuster, 1992.

Marable, Manning. *Race, Reform, and Rebellion: The Second Reconstruction in Black America, 1945-1990*. 2nd ed. Jackson: University Press of Mississippi, 1991.

Marine, Gene. *The Black Panthers*. New York: New American Library, 1969.

Marks, Carole. *Farewell—We're Good and Gone: The Great Black Migration*. Bloomington: Indiana University Press, 1989.

Marris, Peter and Martin Rein. *Dilemmas of Social Reform: Poverty and Community Action in the United States*. 2nd. ed. Chicago: Aldine Publishing Co., 1973.

Matusow, Allen J. *The Unraveling of America: American Liberalism During the 1960s.* New York: Harper and Row, 1984.

McCartney, John T. *Black Power Ideologies: An Essay in African American Political Thought.* Philadelphia: Temple University Press, 1992.

Mead, Lawrence. *Beyond Entitlement: The Social Obligations of Citizenship.* New York: Free Press, 1986.

Meier, August and Elliott Rudwick. *CORE: A Study of the Civil Rights Movement, 1942-1968.* Urbana: University of Illinois Press, 1973.

Miller, James. *"Democracy Is in the Streets": From Port Huron to the Siege of Chicago.* New York: Simon and Schuster, 1987.

Milner, Christina and Richard. *Black Players: The Secret World of Black Pimps.* Boston: Little, Brown and Co., 1972.

Moore, Shirley Ann. "The Black Community in Richmond, California, 1910-1963." Ph.D. Diss. University of California, Berkeley, 1989.

Morton, Patricia. *Disfigured Images: The Historical Assault on Afro-American Women.* Westport, CT: Praeger, 1991.

Moss, Larry E. *Black Political Ascendancy in Urban Centers and Black Control of the Local Police Function: An Exploratory Analysis.* San Francisco: R&E Research Associates, 1977.

Moynihan, Daniel P. *Maximum Feasible Misunderstanding: Community Action in the War on Poverty.* New York: Free Press, 1969.

_____, ed. *On Fighting Poverty: Perspectives from the Social Sciences.* New York: Basic Books, 1969.

Murray, Charles. *Losing Ground: American Social Policy, 1950-1980.* New York: Basic Books, 1984.

Nash, Gerald D. *The American West Transformed: The Impact of the Second World War.* Bloomington: Indiana University Press, 1985.

Ohlin, Lloyd and Richard Cloward. *Delinquency and Opportunity: A Theory of Delinquent Gangs.* New York: Free Press, 1960.

O'Reilly, Kenneth. *"Racial Matters": The FBI's Secret File on Black America, 1960-1972.* New York: Free Press, 1989.

Osofsky, Gilbert. *Harlem: The Making of a Ghetto; Negro New York, 1890-1930.* New York: Harper and Row, 1966.

Painter, Nell I. *Exodusters: Black Migration to Kansas after Reconstruction.* New York: Alfred A. Knopf, 1986.

Patterson, James T. *America's Struggle Against Poverty, 1900-1985.* Cambridge: Harvard University Press, 1981.

Pearson, Hugh. *The Shadow of the Panther: Huey Newton and the Price of Black Power in America.* Reading, MA: Addison-Wesley Publishing Company, 1994.

Pentony, DeVere, Robert Smith, and Richard Axen. *Unfinished Rebellions.* San Francisco: Josey-Bass, Inc., 1971.

Piven, Frances Fox and Richard Cloward. *Poor People's Movements: Why They Succeed, How They Fail.* New York: Vintage, 1977.

_____. *Regulating the Poor: The Functions of Public Welfare.* New York: Vintage, 1971.

Quadagno, Jill. *The Color of Welfare: How Racism Undermined the War on Poverty.* New York: Oxford University Press, 1994.

Rainwater, Lee., ed. *Soul.* Chicago: Aldine Publishing Company, 1970).

Richardson, James. *Willie Brown: A Biography.* Berkeley: University of California Press, 1996.

Rorabaugh, W. J. *Berkeley at War: The 1960s.* New York: Oxford University Press, 1991.

Sale, Kirkpatrick. SDS. New York: Random House, 1973.

Sheehy, Gail. *Panthermania.* New York: Harper and Row, 1971.

Silverman, Max. "Urban Redevelopment and Community Response: African Americans in San Francisco's Western Addition." M.A. Thesis. San Francisco State University, 1994.

Skolnick, Jerome H. *The Politics of Protest.* New York: Ballantine Books, 1968.

Smith, Brian Henry. "The Role of the Poor in the Poverty Program: The Origin and Development of 'Maximum Feasible Participation.'" M.A. Thesis. Columbia University, 1966.

Smith, J. Alfred. *Thus Far by Faith: a Study of Historical Backgrounds and the First Fifty Years of the Allen Temple Baptist Church.* Oakland: Color Art Press, 1973.

Smith, Jennifer B. *An International History of the Black Panther Party.* New York: Garland Publishing, 1999.

Smith, Robert, Richard Axen, and DeVere Pentony. *By Any Means Necessary: The Revolutionary Struggle at San Francisco State.* San Francisco: Jossey-Bass, Inc., 1970.

Spear, Allan H. *Black Chicago: The Making of a Negro Ghetto, 1890-1920.* Chicago: University of Chicago Press, 1967.

Stewart, Helen L. "Buffering: The Leadership Style of Huey P. Newton, Co-founder of the Black Panther Party." Ph.D. Diss. Brandeis University, 1980.

Sugrue, Thomas J. *The Origins of the Urban Crisis: Race and Inequality in Postwar Detroit.* Princeton: Princeton University Press, 1996.

Sundquist, James L., ed. *On Fighting Poverty: Perspectives from Experience.* New York: Basic Books, 1969.

Tate, Will D. *The New Black Urban Elites.* San Francisco: R&E Research Associates, 1976.

Taylor, Quintard. *The Forging of a Black Community: Seattle's Central District from 1870 through the Civil Rights Era.* Seattle: University of Washington Press, 1994.

_____. *In Search of the Racial Frontier: African Americans in the American West, 1528-1990.* New York: W. W. Norton and Company, 1998.

Trotter, Jr., Joe William. *Black Milwaukee: The Making of a Black Industrial Proletariat.* Urbana: University of Illinois Press, 1985.

_____, ed. *The Great Migration in Historical Perspective: New Dimensions of Race, Class, and Gender.* Bloomington: Indiana University Press, 1991.

Van Deburg, William L. *Black Camelot: African American Culture Heroes in Their Times, 1960-1980.* Chicago: University of Chicago Press, 1997.

_____. *New Day in Bablyon: The Black Power Movement and American Culture, 1965-1975.* Chicago: University of Chicago Press, 1992.

Van Peebles, Mario, Ula Y. Taylor, and J. Tarika Lewis. *Panther: A Pictorial History of the Black Panthers and the Story behind the Film.* New York: New Market Press, 1995.

Vincent, Theodore. *Black Power and the Garvey Movement.* Berkeley: Ramparts Press, 1970.

Wallace, Michele. *Black Macho and the Myth of the Superwoman.* New York: The Dial Press, 1978.

Watkins, Ben. *We Also Serve: 10 Per Cent of a Nation Working and Fighting for Victory.* San Francisco: The Tilghman Press, n.d.

Williamson, Joel. *The Crucible of Race: Black-White Relations in the American South since Emancipation.* New York: Oxford University Press, 1984.

Wilson, William Julius. *The Truly Disadvantaged: The Inner City, the Underclass, and Public Policy.* Chicago: University of Chicago Press, 1987.

_____. *When Work Disappears: The World of the New Urban Poor.* New York: Alfred A. Knopf, 1996.

# Index